THE VILLAGE SHOP FOR LONELY HEARTS

ALISON SHERLOCK

Boldwood

First published in Great Britain in 2020 by Boldwood Books Ltd.

Cover Design by Alice Moore Design

Cover photography: Shutterstock

A CIP catalogue record for this book is available from the British Library.

Paperback ISBN 978-1-83889-980-6

Hardback ISBN 978-1-80426-223-8

Large Print ISBN 978-1-83889-976-9

Ebook ISBN 978-1-83889-974-5

Kindle ISBN 978-1-83889-975-2

Audio CD ISBN 978-1-83889-981-3

MP3 CD ISBN 978-1-83889-978-3

Digital audio download ISBN 978-1-83889-973-8

Boldwood Books Ltd
23 Bowerdean Street
London SW6 3TN
www.boldwoodbooks.com

This book is dedicated to Gill Collins, with grateful thanks for being the most wonderful sister I could have wished for and who still holds my hand and lets me scream in her ear on the Gringotts Ride even though I'm old enough to know better. With much love x

1

Amber Green stood in the pouring rain and sighed. The things you do for family, she thought.

As the taxi drove away, she drained the last of the coffee that she had picked up at Heathrow Airport even though it was now stone cold. She was past caring. She just needed the caffeine.

A rough overnight flight from JFK trying to find a comfortable position in a cramped economy seat hadn't allowed her any sleep. The passenger in the next seat had hogged most of her personal space as well so she had been bunched up in the corner next to the cold window for most of the night.

To add insult to injury, the airline had sent her luggage to the Caribbean by mistake, so presumably it was now enjoying a cocktail on a sunny beach instead of the drizzly and damp English village she was now standing in. She wished she could join it.

The jet lag had kicked in, she was exhausted and she really didn't want to be in Cranbridge. And yet, here she was. Still being bossed around at the age of thirty and trying to please everyone but herself.

'You will go, won't you?' her mother had said on the phone only a fortnight ago. 'Cathy is my oldest friend as well as your godmother.'

'Who I haven't seen for about ten years,' Amber had reminded her.

'That doesn't matter,' her mum had told her, as usual dismissing her daughter's point of view. 'You know that we talk almost every day. Breaks my heart not to see my best friend any more. She's like a sister to me. She's had such a rubbish time, what with being widowed and then getting so poorly. I just thought that you could pop in to cheer her up before coming on to see us.'

'Pop in!' Amber had laughed with incredulity. 'Mum, I'm in New York! You've just moved to New Zealand. England is the wrong way round the world.'

'Oh, that doesn't matter,' her mum had replied. 'People catch flights to England every day from New York.'

'That wasn't what I meant,' Amber had said, rolling her eyes down the phone line. 'Look, I haven't got time for this. I need to find a job.'

'Maybe you could find one in Cranbridge. It's got quite a few shops, including Cathy's, of course. Cranbridge Stores has been in the village forever. It's ever so sweet.'

Amber didn't want to upset her mum, but Cathy's local village shop wasn't sounding much like Saks Fifth Avenue in New York.

But you don't work at Saks any more, Amber had to remind herself. With the retail sector struggling so much everywhere, even the luxury shops in Manhattan weren't immune to the economic downturn. So she had found herself included in the wave of recent redundancies at the famous department store.

She still felt numb from the shock that after two years of working in New York, she'd been let go. With no other jobs to go to, her work visa had run out, so she could no longer live and work in the United States. Thanks to the financial crisis spreading worldwide, none of the big shops back home in England were taking on window dressers either. With nobody recruiting, her career and life had crashed to a sudden halt.

Having to leave the United States was bad enough, but even worse, her parents didn't live in England any more. As far back as Amber could remember, her parents had been looking for their next big adventure. Amber had spent her entire childhood trailing around as they moved from home to home, north to south of the country and back again whilst they tried their hand at running a restaurant, a bed and breakfast, owning a bookshop and even a brief sojourn into the world of gin distilleries.

However, this time they had really outdone themselves and had emigrated to New Zealand a couple of months ago to become sheep farmers, despite never having kept sheep or even run a farm before! There was no other close family in England and her parents had never stayed anywhere long enough for her to make any real friends during her childhood. As an only child, it had been a lonely start to her life, which had carried on into adulthood.

She felt completely adrift at the unexpected turn of events in her life that summer. Window dressing and design had been her lifeline during the lonelier moments of her life. It had been something to lean on when things had become really tough. And now she didn't even have that to comfort her.

When her mum had originally suggested that she join them to live in New Zealand, Amber had laughed at the limited career options for her on a sheep farm.

Take a look at where you've ended up instead, she thought, standing in the drizzle that autumnal morning.

'You'll love Cranbridge,' her mum had told her. 'You used to play in the river when you were little.'

'I don't even remember it,' Amber had replied.

'I always loved going back to see Cathy there,' her mum had said. 'I grew up there, you know. The people are lovely. It's such a beautiful vibrant village. It'll be a nice little holiday for you after working so hard.'

Amber stared across the river which split the village into two halves. Vibrant wasn't quite what came to mind. Deserted, definitely. She didn't know which village her mum had been describing but it certainly wasn't Cranbridge that Monday morning.

The only thing she had to concede was that it was rather beautiful as a setting, with its sandy coloured brick cottages lining the river banks and the green rolling hills surrounding the village peeping through from between each house. Instead of a main street, there was a wide shallow river running down the middle of the village, with three ancient pedestrian stone bridges connecting either side over the clear, bubbling water.

Next to where she stood was a pub, a faded sign showing The Black Swan. Or rather, that was what she guessed it was supposed to say as it was missing a couple of letters and the sign actually read The B ack Sw n. It could be quite pretty if you ignored the rotten windows and air of shabbiness about the place. In fact, she realised as she looked around once more that the whole village appeared to have an air of neglect about it. It was hardly the idyll that her mother had tempted her with as a short stay holiday destination.

On the opposite side of the river, there were four detached buildings which ran along the grassy bank and wide path. Amber could just about make out the words on a faint road sign proclaiming it to be Riverside Lane. All four of the detached buildings were shops. They each had the same pretty coloured stone with wobbly chimney pots and slate roofs. However, they were all as equally run-down as the pub; each one appeared more dilapidated than the last. Roof tiles were missing. Window frames appeared rotten. Two of the shops were completely boarded up.

At the very end of Riverside Lane, almost hidden by the large willow trees that flanked the river, was a water mill, although the huge wheel looked as if it hadn't turned in many years. It added to the sense that the village had long since closed down.

But whereas the run-down nature of the shops and businesses was a surprise, what was most shocking was the fact that there were no people. Amber blinked and looked around the village once more, but, no, there wasn't a person in sight. Yes, it was drizzling. It was also Monday morning, but where was everyone?

Used to the crowded, chaotic streets of New York whatever the time of day, all she could hear was birdsong and the river bubbling up against the narrow bridges as it slowly meandered through the village. The peace unnerved her. She was used to being on her own. In a big city, wasn't everyone? But this was more than a little strange.

Finally, she looked across the narrow bridge in front of her at Cranbridge Stores, the first shop on the corner of Riverside Lane, facing out towards the river.

It was a detached brick building in the same honey-coloured brick as the rest of the village. On the upper floor were three sash windows, above which the roof narrowed to a point. On the ground floor, the main shop had a large front door in the middle, flanked by two huge bay windows on either side. Outside the shop was a large wooden veranda that ran the entire width of the shop, covered by a wonky roof in the same dark oak. It looked shabby with its faded sign adding to the air of neglect.

Amber screwed up her eyes and tried to connect the ramshackle shop with her godmother. She had last seen Cathy Kennedy at her twenty-first birthday party in London. She was a warm, attractive woman who always gave out the most enormous bear hugs.

Amber could just about remember Cathy's husband, the infamous Todd Kennedy, laughing with her dad about something. Todd had been a man who didn't appear to take anything seriously, as begat a man who had been a rock guitarist for most of his adult life.

Then there were two sons, Josh and Pete, but she couldn't remember them at all, having not seen them since she was ten years old or so.

But that all seemed a long time ago now. She wondered why a famous musician with a dazzling personality had ended up bringing his family to such a quiet village.

Aware that the drizzle was beginning to frizz up her long dark blonde hair, Amber took a step forward towards the bridge and found something crunching underneath her Converse trainers. She looked down to see a carpet of acorns that had fallen from the oak tree beside her.

It was autumn already. That back-to-school feeling after the long summer holidays. The nausea washed over her as she glanced down at the jeans and leather jacket which she had travelled in. She instantly felt frumpy. Weird. A loner.

The school bullies' taunts went around and around inside her head – *Oh my God, look at her shoes! Have you seen her earrings? Her hair is awful! She's got no friends. Just spends all her time alone, drawing.*

She automatically tucked a long lock of blonde hair behind her ear and then wondered whether it made her ear stick out and drew it back in front of her face. Since leaving school well over a decade ago, she had told herself that the bullies hadn't won. After all, she had lived and worked in London and New York in some of the most famous shops in the world. But, in truth, the endless bullying throughout her childhood had shattered her self-esteem. She had tried to tell herself that she must have been talented to have been headhunted for the job in New York. But she continued to doubt her abilities each and every day.

When she had first moved out to Manhattan, she had been excited. She imagined *Sex and The City*-type cocktail nights and swanning down Park Avenue with her takeaway coffee, catching the eye of some hunky guy in an expensive suit.

And yet the reality wasn't so dreamy. She had actually felt desperately alone in the big city. Friends had been hard to come by and whenever she had tried dating, it had been an utter disaster. One guy just wanted to hear her swear in her British accent. Another had conveniently forgotten to tell her he was engaged to be married.

So, she retreated back to her safety net of channelling all her efforts into her work and then stayed in each and every night. It was better that way, she told herself. If you hid yourself away then you couldn't be hurt.

But that seemed to make things even worse, she had found. If you're lonely we recommend you join a club, the magazine articles said. Go out and meet new people. But Amber's lack of confidence held her back. So she had tried to remain positive whilst keeping inside her rented room each night and watching box sets on Netflix whilst eating peanut butter out of a jar.

Occasionally, she got cross with herself over her drab existence and would head out on her days off to one of the many museums to study design or to ride the Staten Island ferry, determined to live the New York dream. But it never completely stemmed the loneliness.

A sound on the opposite side of the river made her focus back on the present day. In the distance, she could see that a man had just come out of the Cranbridge Stores. He was the first person she had seen so far in the village. At least it showed her that the shop was actually open.

She was looking forward to seeing Cathy, who had been so unwell during the past couple of years. At least they could catch up before Amber booked her forwarding flight on to New Zealand in a few days' time.

Thinking that her aunt may be beginning to worry about where she was, Amber began to walk across the narrow bridge. It wasn't until she was almost halfway across that she realised that the man who had just come out of the shop was also heading over the same pedestrian bridge towards her. She glanced at his face as he grew nearer and realised that she recognised him. But he also looked to be in an absolutely foul temper. With his leather jacket and five o'clock shadow, he had an air of menace about him.

Amber quickly decided to step to one side to let him by as the bridge was barely wide enough for two people.

However, she was still jet-lagged and not quite with it and so took a misstep as the toe of her trainers got stuck in the raised edge of the bridge. She flailed, her arms swinging around like a helicopter. Beginning to lose her balance, she reached out and grabbed the man's arm in a panic.

Then, as if in slow motion, she dragged the man with her as she fell off the side of the bridge and into the river below.

2

If Josh Kennedy had been in a bad mood only a minute ago, that was nothing compared to his temper once he found himself suddenly falling into the freezing-cold river.

'What the hell!' he shouted out in shock as his bottom crashed into the stony bottom of the river and the whole of his spine jolted in pain.

As the agony slowly faded, he registered that he thankfully hadn't broken any bones. However, he quickly became aware of the cold water seeping into his clothes. He shivered, wondering whether the day could get any worse.

It was nine o'clock in the morning. He'd managed one coffee so far that day, swiftly followed by the normal row with his mum, which was becoming a daily event. Storming out in a fit of pique, he had wanted to cool his anger off. Ending up in the river certainly hadn't helped.

He wiped the water dripping from his hair and face and stared in shock at the blonde-haired woman sitting in the river next to him, who was looking right back at him with brown eyes which were huge in shock.

'Hi, Josh,' she said, to his amazement.

He gave a start. 'Do we know each other?'

'You could say that,' she told him. 'After all, our mothers have been best friends for all of their lives.'

He looked at her, incredulous. 'You're Amber?'

She gave him a sheepish smile, which lit up her pretty face. Josh was almost rendered speechless. He couldn't quite believe that this attractive woman was the same Amber Green who had been a gawky teenager with huge frizzy hair.

Now she was all grown up, with her blonde hair hanging in soft waves around her shoulders. Long dark eyelashes. Pale smooth skin highlighted by freckles and a rosy blush across her cheeks. Her trendy leather jacket was also soaked at the hem and dripping water back into the river.

She nodded ruefully. 'I'm afraid so. Sorry about, you know, taking you into the river with me.'

'That's OK,' he said, standing up, which caused the water to drop from him in a small wave. 'It's almost like old times.'

She looked up at him. 'What do you mean?'

'Don't you remember?' he said. 'You, me and Pete used to play in our paddling pool when we were younger.'

She shook her head as she looked around. As she sat in the river, Josh took in the long legs sprawled out, the jeans as soaking wet as his own.

He shivered in the cool breeze. It was already late September and the weather was turning colder. He supposed he was lucky that it wasn't midwinter, when he'd have either caught a cold or skidded across the frozen river.

He glanced down at Amber who still hadn't got up.

'Are you hurt?' he asked, suddenly concerned at her lack of movement. 'Can you stand?'

'I'm fine,' she told him, standing up next to him with a heavy sigh. 'Just really, really embarrassed.'

'Don't worry about it,' he said, realising that the shock of the cold water had also cooled his temper. 'It'll save me from needing a shower later on.'

She bent down to pick up her handbag, which was also in the water.

He watched as she examined the contents inside, most of which were probably ruined. However the mobile phone she brought out to check seemed to be still working.

Then they both waded across the river towards the bank at the same time. Stepping out of the water, he held out a hand to help her out as well.

Once on the riverbank, she had just thanked him when the front door of the shop was flung open and he heard his mum shout out. 'Amber? Is that you?'

'Hi, Cathy,' said Amber, as his mum strode up to them.

Despite the possibility of getting her own clothes damp, his mum enveloped Amber into one of her bear hugs. 'Hello, darling,' she said, eventually stepping back. 'Your mum sent me a text to say that you'd landed safely this morning. What on earth happened to you both?' she asked, looking them both up and down. 'Are you OK?'

'We're fine,' Josh told her. 'We took a tumble into the river, so we're just a little soggy around the edges.'

'It's all my fault,' said Amber, a blush spreading across her cheeks. 'I'm so clumsy.'

'You're telling me,' said Josh, trying to make light of it.

But Cathy gave her son a stern glance. It was hardly surprising given that he'd stormed out only a few minutes ago after their latest row. It was about the shop, of course. It was always about the shop these days.

'Well, I remember you breaking your wrist on our trampoline all those years ago, but I'd have thought you might have grown out of it. Goodness, you must be freezing. Let's get you sorted before you catch a cold.' His mum wrapped her arm around Amber and led her towards the front door of the shop. 'Come inside, both of you, and warm up.'

Josh followed them across the lane and towards Cranbridge Stores. As always since he had returned two years previously, the sight of the dilapidated shop made him sad. It should never have got to this stage and yet here they were, stuck in an endless cycle of misery with no way out.

He went up the couple of squeaky wooden steps onto the veranda in front of the shop. At one time, his dad had sat there on a rocking chair and played his guitar almost every summer's evening. But that seemed a very long time ago and now the veranda lay empty.

As his mum pushed open the shop door, he heard the ring of the rusty bell that had hung above the door for as long as he could remember. He had always thought that it was supposed to herald the many customers that would come and go. But it was a rare sound. Customers were very infrequent these days.

He glanced up Riverside Lane but, as usual, there was no one around, let alone anyone keen to shop in Cranbridge Stores. And who could blame them, he thought as they stepped over the threshold and into the shop. On a damp and dismal autumnal morning, it seemed to look even worse than usual. The strip lighting that was thirty years out of date was harsh in its glare, highlighting the full-to-bursting shop. Every area, every shelf and almost every aisle was filled with boxes and goods. There was no organisation to it all, just everything crammed in, making the aisles narrow and not easy to manoeuvre around.

As Amber proved by immediately knocking over a tower of biscuit boxes that had been squeezed into the ever-decreasing space.

'Sorry,' she muttered, glancing around wide-eyed, clearly in shock at the state of the place.

Josh knew how she felt. And that Amber's look was exactly the same as any potential customers wore when they popped in. And why they never returned.

'I told you those biscuits would be in the way,' his mum called out over her shoulder.

Josh rolled his eyes as he rebuilt the stack once more. The biscuits had been on special offer at the cash and carry shop. They were cheap and plentiful. But it appeared that the handful of customers that they received each day weren't in need of family-sized boxes of biscuits. They just wanted some milk and a newspaper. If they could find the fridge, that was. It was hidden behind a stack of cleaning goods.

No wonder there was hardly any money, he thought as they continued past the old till at the back of the shop and through to the stockroom beyond. What profit could be made from such a mess?

He supposed that buying the biscuits had only contributed to the problem of the overstocked shop but he was pretty much resigned to the state of the place nowadays.

His mum headed across the stockroom to where there was a small kitchen in the far corner.

'I've got a towel in here somewhere,' she said, searching around near the sink.

The stockroom was fairly large as it ran the entire width at the back of the shop. Two-thirds of the area though was filled with yet more unsold stock. The last third, next to the kitchen area, was taken up with a small ride-on tractor.

As always, seeing the tractor reminded him of his father. Even now, he could see his dad tinkering with it, bending over the bonnet, trying to get the engine going. His dad had used the back room as his garage to build the thing from scratch, but it had never worked.

Both Josh and his younger brother, Pete, had spent their teenage years watching and waiting for the grand day that his dad had promised when the tractor would run and they could take a ride on it out on the lanes of Cranbridge. But that day had never come and now that his dad was no longer with them, it never would. But the tractor remained. Nobody could bear to part with it and the precious memories it held.

'Here you are,' said his mum, handing a small towel to Amber. 'Mind you, you could probably use a change of clothes. You must be freezing. Are your suitcases still outside? Josh, go and fetch them, would you?'

Josh went to turn when Amber said, 'I haven't got any.'

'You haven't?' said his mum, looking astonished.

'Travelling light?' drawled Josh.

She shook her head, blushing. 'Lost by the airline,' she finally told them. 'They've sent them to the wrong destination.'

'Oh! How awful!' his mum replied, horrified. 'Such a pain! But not to worry, I've got something that you can borrow for now. Let's head upstairs and we'll get you warm and dry again.' His mum looked at Amber for a second and broke into a smile. 'It's been too long since I saw you. You know, you look just like your mum did at your age.'

Amber smiled. 'Thanks. She sends her love.'

'I do miss her,' said his mum, still smiling. 'Come on upstairs. Let's have a proper catch-up. I want to hear all the gossip about your fabulous life in New York!'

Josh watched them head up the narrow staircase at the side of the shop to the large flat upstairs. It had been such a long time since he had seen his mum so animated, thought Josh. Had she smiled like that since she had finished her cancer treatment? Maybe when the results had come through that the chemotherapy had worked and that the breast cancer was gone. Although, as always, the spectre of the next check-up scan was just around the corner.

And before that? Well, they had all been deep in grief.

There had been so much to sort out after his father had passed away unexpectedly. Thankfully, his brother, Pete, had been around then to help out. But eager to make his fortune, Pete had moved to Singapore and remained there ever since, working the financial markets.

Pete had told them that he hadn't wanted to leave them behind, but Josh and his mum had insisted that he gave his new life a go. Pete was only younger by two years, but he had always been the baby of the family and treated as such. At least he was living his dream, thought Josh. Pete certainly seemed happy whenever Josh spoke to him, which was pretty infrequent these days.

Life was always so busy that the two brothers hardly spoke. They had always been such a close-knit family in the early days. So much at one point that Pete had tried to persuade Josh to go out there and join him. Josh had even been a tiny bit tempted to go. But then their mum had been diagnosed with breast cancer.

Josh couldn't leave when she was so ill. Somebody had to take responsibility and he was the elder brother. So he had put his successful career as a sustainability consultant in the European business sector on hold and had left London to stay in Cranbridge these past two years.

And he hadn't been happy for a single day since then.

Not that it had been easy for his mum either, he knew. The treatment had certainly taken the strength from her. Not that she ever really complained.

He headed upstairs to the flat, whereupon he heard his mum and Amber chatting in the smallest bedroom.

He sighed as he went into his own bedroom to change out of his wet clothes. He shouldn't have argued with his mum earlier. As always, he felt so guilty when they disagreed. But she just couldn't get past the loss of his dad. Nothing could be changed in the shop. It all had to stay just like it was. Just like it had always been.

And yet, everything had changed. Pete had left. His mum had been ill. Only Josh remained the same, stuck in Cranbridge and wondering when his life was going to start again.

He had just flung open his wardrobe doors to pull out some drier clothes when he noticed the set of mechanic tools at the bottom. Would the tractor ever get working? He had tried so hard to fix the engine, but it felt like yet another failure.

In that moment, he felt the loss of his dad so much he had to blink back the tears. But his dad was gone and it was highly likely that soon the shop would be as well. Cranbridge Stores was on the brink of bankruptcy. He just didn't have the courage to break the news to his family yet.

3

Amber headed up the stairs to the flat above the shop, all the time trying to listen to Cathy chat excitedly in front of her.

But Amber could hardly take it all in, thanks to her inner mortification. She had fallen in the river and, worse still, taken Josh with her! She had never been exactly dainty, but this was a terrible start to her stay.

More than ever, she just wanted this visit over with so that she could run away from her embarrassment. Hopefully she would be booking her onward flight for the following weekend and could escape her total and utter shame.

This was why things never worked out for her, she reminded herself. Because she was clumsy and stupid. Just like those teenage girls at school had told her over and over all those years ago.

She shivered, her wet clothes clinging to her as she followed Cathy across the cosy and homely-feeling living area. It had large oak beams which went all the way into the high apex of the roof. A pile of books and records were on top of an oak dresser. The kitchen cupboards along one wall were also made from oak and in the corner were a couple of comfortable-looking sofas and an upright armchair which was occupied by a tiny old lady.

'Mother! Amber's here!' said Cathy, as they went across the creaky floorboards.

'Welcome!' said the elderly lady, smiling briefly before her face dropped in dismay as she looked Amber up and down. 'Is it raining again?'

'They fell in the river!' Cathy told her, laughing. 'Amber and our Josh. Can you imagine?'

'How extraordinary,' said the lady, slowly getting up to walk over to Amber. 'That's a welcome you'll never forget! You won't remember me, I'm sure. I'm Clotilde, my dear, but everyone calls me Grandma Tilly.'

'Hello,' said Amber, smiling down at her.

Grandma Tilly was only four feet tall, but it was a round and friendly face with surprisingly blue eyes amongst the wrinkles that looked up at her. Amber guessed that Grandma Tilly was in her late seventies.

Amber had a sudden memory of Tilly giving her an extra slice of birthday cake at a party when she had been hiding in a corner, as usual.

'I haven't seen you for many years,' said Tilly, still smiling fondly up at her. 'Always had your head in a book, if I remember. You're a pretty thing, aren't you?'

Amber blushed, unused to receiving compliments.

'Isn't she lovely?' said Cathy, putting her arm around Amber and giving her a squeeze. 'Now, you must get changed before you freeze to death. Follow me. I'm sure I have something that will fit you, although you're a lot slimmer than I am these days.'

They headed out of the kitchen-diner area and into a short corridor from which led two doors on either side.

'That'll be your bedroom,' said Cathy, pointing at the door on the left. 'But this is me.'

Amber followed Cathy into the first bedroom, which appeared to be the largest. It had a double bed and a couple of wardrobes, as well as an old dressing table. The window looked out over the side street.

'Let's have a look at what will fit you,' said Cathy, flinging open a wardrobe door.

Amber was touched by Cathy's kindness, but it really was adding insult to injury that she didn't have her own clothes whilst her suitcases were lost in transit.

'Here you go,' said Cathy, holding out a pair of black leggings and a blue jumper. 'I think this colour would be nice on you. I've got some shoes you can borrow as well as your trainers are soaking wet. Gosh, I can't tell you how lovely it is to have a bit of female companionship around here.' She glanced at the open bedroom door. 'My mother has moved into a smashing little bungalow just down the lane this past summer,' she added, in a whisper. 'The stairs were getting a bit much for her on a daily basis, considering she's seventy-seven now.'

Amber watched as Cathy brought out a large bath towel from a nearby drawer.

'Thanks,' she said, as she took the clothes and towel from her. 'You're looking well,' she added, tentatively.

Cathy's attractive face was more lined than Amber remembered. But of course, the years that had passed had been pretty stressful. Her hair was still worn wavy to her shoulders but strands of grey mingled amongst the auburn.

Cathy's smile faded slightly before being fixed back into place. 'Thank you, sweetheart,' she said in an overly bright voice. 'Six months in remission and counting!'

'That's great,' Amber told her. 'Mum was so worried when you were ill.'

'We spoke almost every day when I was having treatment,' said Cathy, sitting down on the bed. 'And of course she visited when she could. Before they emigrated, of course. I do miss her. I mean, Josh is great, but you don't want to tell your own son about all your aches and pains all the time.'

'Where's Pete living these days?' asked Amber, trying to remember.

'Singapore,' said Cathy in a wistful tone. 'He's got a beautiful flat apparently.'

'Have you been out to visit him?'

Cathy's smile faded slightly. 'Chance would be a fine thing. Anyway, there's so much to do here, with the shop and everything.' She hesitated. 'Now that it's just us.'

Amber nodded. She knew that Cathy had been widowed only a few years previously. Along with the cancer, it had obviously been an incredibly tough time. But none of that had prepared her for the sheer chaos and mess of the shop downstairs. It was all a stark contrast to the glamour and organisation of a huge department store like Saks Fifth Avenue.

Cathy appeared to pull herself together. 'Anyway, I'll let you get out of those wet clothes. The bathroom's just across the hall. You're welcome to have a shower. I'm sure you must be desperate after the long flight. Help yourself to my shower gel and whatever you need. Take your time. Come and find us in the kitchen when you're changed. We'll get the kettle on.'

Amber took the clothes and towel into the bathroom, which had a Victorian bath with an overhead shower. Like the rest of the flat, it was both homely and stylish, with its tiny seaside motifs on the tiles and pictures.

She was grateful to peel off her wet clothes and enjoyed the hot shower, which brought warmth back to her cold skin.

Afterwards, she slipped on the leggings that Cathy had given her. They were a bit short, but she supposed people would assume that they were cropped. The jumper fitted her a bit better and at least it went down to her thighs. Despite the style being a little old on her, she was grateful for the leggings and jumper, which made her feel a bit warmer.

She left the wet clothes drying on the towel rail in the bathroom and headed back down the short hallway, following the sound of Cathy and Grandma Tilly chatting.

'There you are,' said Grandma Tilly, beaming up at her from the table where they were both sitting. 'Tea or coffee?'

'Coffee please,' Amber told her.

'Sit yourself down,' said Cathy, who had leapt up. 'I'll make it. Are you hungry? Would you like a sandwich?'

Amber shook her head as she sat down. 'I had breakfast on the plane, thanks.'

'At least have a biscuit,' said Grandma Tilly, pushing the plate across to her.

'Thanks.' Amber reached out and chose a biscuit coated in thick chocolate.

'Doesn't she look like Denise when she was Amber's age?' Cathy's question was directed at Grandma Tilly, who nodded.

'Oh yes. Spitting image of her, apart from the blonde hair.'

'Well, Denise did try peroxide once, don't you remember?' Cathy smiled in memory. 'Had to cut most of her hair off after that as it was snapping off. In a right state, she was.'

'My mum?' Amber was stunned. 'With bleached hair?' She had only known her mum with her naturally coloured brown hair.

Cathy placed a mug of coffee in front of Amber. 'It looked ghastly! But you've got your father's colouring, so the blonde suits you, thank goodness.'

'You'll be sleeping in my old bedroom,' said Grandma Tilly. 'It's got the best view as it's at the front.'

'Sounds lovely,' said Amber.

'Josh is opposite you and I'm only next door in the double bedroom,' said Cathy. 'So you've got company whilst you're here.'

Amber wasn't so sure that Josh would want her in such close proximity after their dunking in the river earlier.

'It's a lovely room,' carried on Grandma Tilly, in a sort of daze. 'I do miss the view.'

'But not the stairs, eh?' said Cathy, in a bright tone. 'And your bungalow is lovely and you can see the river from your lounge window.'

Tilly nodded, although Amber thought that the accompanying smile was a little forced.

'You might not like my flowery wallpaper though,' said Grandma Tilly.

'I'm sure it'll be fine,' Amber told her, thinking back to the shabby room she had rented in New York.

'Perhaps Josh can give it a lick of paint to cheer it up whilst Amber stays with us,' said Cathy. 'I'll have a word with him.'

Amber was nonplussed. Surely Cathy understood that she was just passing through for a couple of days before flying out to New Zealand to join her parents? OK, so she hadn't booked her onward flight yet as she was just waiting for her deposit to come back from her landlord on the room she had rented in New York. But once she had enough to pay for the airline ticket she would be leaving.

'I'm sure this is all a bit of a comedown after your glamorous time in New York,' said Cathy, with a kind smile.

Amber shook her head. 'Not at all,' she told them, not wanting to admit how distinctly unglamorous her life had been up until that point. She had bought some new clothes in the Manhattan shops, some of which were currently en route somewhere in her lost suitcases, the rest being shipped on to New Zealand. But most of her money had been swept up into the high cost of living in one of the most expensive cities in the world.

'It's so nice to have company, for a change,' said Grandma Tilly, reaching out to help herself to a biscuit. 'We get a bit lonesome around here these days.'

Amber hesitated. 'Doesn't the shop keep you busy?'

They both exchanged a sad look before Tilly turned to face Amber once more. 'At one time, we were rushed off our feet. When I ran the shop with Bill, my husband, it was the hub of the village. But that was a long time ago. After he died, Cathy, Todd and the boys moved in.' Tilly gave a little shrug of her shoulders. 'But times change, don't they? People pass away or move on. Now most of the folk in the village are strangers. They come home from school and work and close their front doors. Time was when you would keep your doors unlocked as neighbours were always popping in and out. But, like I said, that's ancient history. Now it's all deliveries from that big supermarket and Amazon. Nobody comes by that often.'

Amber let them chat on about the business, which all seemed pretty precarious. But they remained cheerful despite the fact that there was a lack of customers. She wondered whether perhaps Cathy's famous husband, Todd, had made so much money from his guitar playing that their lives were relatively comfortable and that the struggling shop wasn't that big a deal.

After they had finished their coffee, Cathy persuaded Amber to head downstairs to the shop once more. 'Josh will show you around properly now that you're all nice and dry. I'll tidy up and then we'll follow you down,' said Cathy.

Amber went down the wooden staircase and stopped, hesitating as she really didn't want to face Josh again so soon after falling into the river.

So she stood and stared around the stockroom instead. She looked at the many piles of boxes, all fighting for space. And then at the rusty tractor as well. What was it doing inside? And what on earth did they need a small tractor for anyway? She couldn't understand the reasoning behind it.

The sound of heavy footsteps clattered down the staircase and Josh nearly ran her down as he rushed into the room beside her.

'Hey,' he said.

Amber noticed that he had also got changed and was now wearing a different pair of jeans and sweatshirt. He must have been changing in his bedroom but hadn't joined them afterwards for coffee and biscuits. He was probably avoiding her, she thought.

His dark hair was still a bit spiky from where it had been wet and she had to concede to herself that he had grown into a good-looking man. She found herself wondering whether he had a girlfriend and what he was doing stuck in such a quiet village.

The silence stretched out as she tried to think of something to say.

'I was just wondering about the tractor,' she eventually said, forcing herself to stop staring at him.

'It was my dad's,' he told her. 'He bought it to try and get it going, but he never got round to doing it up before, you know...' Josh's voice trailed off.

'I'm sorry.' Amber felt bad, having brought up what must be painful memories. 'You must miss him.'

Josh nodded. 'Yeah. Anyway, the tractor's stuck here,' he carried on, before adding under his breath, 'like a lot of other things around here.'

Amber didn't know what to make of this so remained quiet.

Cathy and Tilly were making their slow way down the stairs.

'Haven't you made it into the shop yet?' said Cathy as they finally reached the bottom.

Amber shook her head.

'Come on then,' said Josh, turning away.

So Amber followed him into the shop, with Cathy and Tilly close behind.

As she tried to find somewhere to stand without knocking anything over, easier said than done with everything so crowded, Cathy went over to the long counter which was in the far corner.

'So!' she said, in a very jolly tone. 'What do you think of our little empire?'

Amber smiled and nodded her approval, all the time praying that her face didn't show how she really felt about the state of the place. It wasn't good, she thought, staring around. The interior was so dated that it gave off a very tired and old-fashioned feel and not in a country-charm kind of way either. On top of that, the place was packed with shelving units right up to the ceiling, which meant it also felt very crowded and almost suffocating. Every available surface, including the counter where the till stood, was piled high, but it was all so random. There was washing powder and loo rolls. Then newspapers. Eggs. Plastic toys. It was a real mish-mash of goods. There were also a couple of fridges, but whereas one held a small amount of milk and cheese, the other two were dark and switched off. Presumably so they could hold yet more random stock.

Amber found herself thinking that if she lived in the village, she probably wouldn't come in here either.

But, to her surprise, the bell above the front door jangled as some-body came in. A man in his late sixties weaved his way through the narrow aisles, carefully picking up a newspaper as he moved.

'Good morning,' he said, finally making it to the counter.

'Good morning, Frank,' said Cathy, smiling. 'How are you today?'

'Not bad,' replied the gentleman. 'It's a right miserable day out there though.'

'Let me introduce my goddaughter, Amber,' said Cathy, gesturing towards Amber, who was still standing in the middle of the shop. 'She's staying with us for a while.'

'Lovely to meet you,' said Frank.

Amber nodded. 'You too,' she said, as always somewhat uncomfortable about being the centre of attention.

'She's just flown in from New York,' said Cathy, with a proud note in her voice.

'So good they named it twice.' The gentleman laughed, patting his pockets as if searching for something. 'Good Lord, I've forgotten my pound coin,' he said, with a sigh. 'I'm getting so forgetful.'

'It doesn't matter,' Cathy told him. 'You can pay us tomorrow when you come in.'

But Frank was still frowning. 'I've got my debit card on me if that helps. Don't like not paying my way.'

'We don't have a card system here,' said Cathy. 'Besides, we know where you live, so there's no escaping just yet!'

'Well, if you're sure,' said Frank, picking up his newspaper. 'I'll be in first thing to pay off my debt.'

'It's fine,' said Cathy. 'We'll see you tomorrow.'

After the bell had jangled that the customer had left, Josh went over to the till. 'And that is why we need a new till and contactless payment,' he said in a pointed tone to his mother.

Cathy laughed. 'No, we don't! This works fine.'

From what Amber could make out, 'this' was an extremely old-looking till. It was pretty ugly and not very handy for the modern era, she guessed. Once more, she thought back to Saks Fifth Avenue where nearly every purchase was on a card. But, of course, this was just a small corner shop, not one of the world's biggest department stores.

'The customers can't pay by card at the moment,' said Josh, clearly getting cross. 'Not everyone has cash on them these days.'

'We're not having this argument again,' said Cathy in a firm tone of voice, before glancing at Amber. 'Not in front of our guest.'

Amber shuffled from foot to foot, wishing she was somewhere else.

As mother and son glared at each other, Amber softly excused herself and weaved her way through to the front of the shop, keen to get away from the awkward atmosphere.

The bell jangled as she opened the front door and she stood for a moment on the wooden veranda. Despite the overcast day, the view was sensational. She looked around the riverbanks, the trees all glowing with the warm autumnal colours of gold and red.

At least she was sheltered from the drizzle, she thought, before glancing up and realising that she was standing under a massive gap in the roof of the veranda and that it was leaking. She shuffled away from the leak and looked at one of the large bay windows. Like everything else in the shop, it was packed full of all manner of goods, none of which were remotely enticing. Peering around at the other window, she realised it was equally dismal.

For a moment, she let her imagination run riot, thinking back to the many designs she had created in both London and New York. They had been everything from fantasy to modern and eclectic. Of course, any such design would be totally out of step with sleepy Cranbridge Stores.

And what about the inside of the shop? There were no real displays. It was chaotic. There appeared to be no system or organisation regarding the stock, which was piled up everywhere. Cathy didn't want to update anything. Josh was unhappy. It was a mess.

She wished she could do something to help. But then she remembered that she was only here for a short time as a favour to her mum. She had promised to pop in and ensure that Cathy was well and happy. Perhaps one out of two wasn't bad.

In any case, Cranbridge Stores would continue without her anyway after she was gone. Besides, what difference could she make? Her expertise was with large department stores. It was probably best that she left well alone, she told herself.

But she took one last wistful glance at the windows before she headed back inside.

4

As the day wore on, it became increasingly obvious that Amber's luggage was not going to arrive that day. Or possibly the next day either. Amber was now stuck in Cranbridge with no clean clothes of her own.

'So what are the airline doing about it?' asked Cathy, sat on the chair behind the till. It was almost five o'clock and, as per the rest of the day, there didn't appear to be any sign of an afternoon rush in the shop.

Amber shrugged her shoulders, rereading the email from the airline. 'They've offered reimbursement, but I just want my clothes. They've promised that they're tracking them down and will send on my cases as soon as they find them.'

'Well, I'm sure they'll turn up soon,' said Cathy. 'If you need any toiletries, I've got lots upstairs and you can always help yourself to whatever you find in the shop. In the meantime, you're welcome to borrow my clothes. I know they're probably a bit old-fashioned compared to what you're used to.'

'Thank you, that'll be fine,' said Amber, anxious to reassure her.

There was no denying that her illness had taken its toll on her godmother. The once vibrant woman had an air of sadness about her.

Amber glanced through to the back room where Josh was unpacking some boxes. She wondered where on earth he was going to place any new stock, let alone bring in any customers to buy them.

'I guess it's always this quiet on a Monday?' asked Amber, hoping her question didn't offend.

Cathy gave her a sad smile. 'It's quietened down a bit since that massive supermarket opened up five miles away. Most people shop there instead.'

'What a shame,' said Amber.

'I didn't really take any notice at the time when it opened,' Cathy told her. 'It was just after I lost Todd. I was too grief-stricken to even think about competition and profit lines. But Josh was worried from the first moment he heard about it.'

And possibly with good reason, thought Amber.

'Do many people live in the village?' she asked, wondering about the local customer base.

'About 500 in Cranbridge itself,' said Cathy. 'And a couple of hundred more in the tiny hamlets beyond that. There's Cranley, of course. That's slightly bigger. That's where Willow Tree Hall is. You know, the stately home? That seems to be getting in a whole load of visitors these days. They've diversified, of course.'

'In what way?' asked Amber, wondering whether they could take any ideas from a more successful business

'They've got their own cider press now,' Cathy told her. 'So they're bottling and selling local cider. There's a tea room as well that's just opened. And they hold a monthly market. I took Mum there last month as a treat and there was such a diverse range of stuff to buy.'

'Maybe Cranbridge could do something similar,' suggested Amber.

She inwardly gave herself a little shake. She didn't need to get involved as she was leaving for New Zealand hopefully in a few days.

'I'm not sure who would be up for that kind of challenge,' said Cathy, frowning. 'A market would be a big thing to organise. Anyway, we like things the way they are. My father had the shop laid out differently, of course. But Todd liked it like this and so that's how it should be. How it's always worked. Things will change for the better, you'll see.'

The trouble was that Amber couldn't see how business could pick up with the shop being so overcrowded and unappealing. But it appeared to be Cathy's lifeline to her late husband and Amber could understand how she wanted everything to remain the same.

'Let me go and check that I put a blanket on your bed,' said Cathy, standing up suddenly. 'I don't want you feeling cold overnight.'

'Please don't go to any trouble,' said Amber.

Secretly, the jet lag was kicking in and she longed to lie down and go to sleep, but she hadn't the heart to tell her godmother.

Cathy disappeared into the back room and up the stairs. Amber glanced the same way and realised that Josh had disappeared as well.

For the first time, she was alone in the shop. For a moment, she daydreamed how she would change the look and feel of the place if it were hers. The oak beams would stay, of course. But it would be so much prettier. Warmer. Some fairy lights here and there.

Then she shook herself out of her reverie. Owning and running a shop had never been a dream of hers. Besides, she had no talent for that kind of thing. She was just a window dresser. That was all.

She had figured that nobody would come in so when the bell above the front door jingled, she was somewhat amazed.

She hesitated before standing up, glancing once more at the back of the shop, but Josh and Cathy were still nowhere in sight.

'Good afternoon,' said an elderly gentleman, as he weaved his way through the shop. 'I don't think we've met. I'm Stanley.'

'Hi. I'm Amber,' she told him, a bit surprised at having to introduce herself to a complete stranger.

'Well, it's nice to have some young blood around here,' said Stanley, his grey eyes twinkling as he smiled at her.

'So, what does that make me?' drawled Josh, as he came back into the shop carrying a box. 'Part of the fixtures and fittings?'

Amber relaxed, grateful to see him smile for the first time since they'd met earlier that day. At least he could take over dealing with the customer.

'It makes you both a welcome sight having spent two hours on the bus getting to and from my hospital appointment this morning,' said Stanley.

Josh put down his box and frowned. 'Is everything OK?' he asked.

Stanley nodded and continued to smile. 'Just a check-up,' he replied. 'But thank you for your concern.'

'Well, I thought something was amiss when you didn't come in at half past nine for your newspaper.'

Amber watched as Stanley's smile faltered slightly. 'Yes, my routine was a little out of kilter today. Normal service resumes tomorrow.'

'Glad to hear it,' said Josh, riffling through the box and sighing. 'Otherwise Amber will think that we have no customers at all.'

'And how is your dear lady mother today?' Stanley asked.

'She's fine,' said Josh, looking around as if realising that she was missing. 'Where is she?'

'Upstairs,' Amber told him.

'Good,' said Josh, looking relieved. Obviously, the worry with his mother's health still weighed heavily on him, thought Amber.

'And what brings you to Cranbridge?' asked Stanley, turning to look at Amber once more. 'Not that I'm complaining, of course.'

Amber blushed.

'She's my mother's goddaughter,' said Josh, after a lengthy silence. 'Her best friend's daughter.'

'Indeed?' Stanley's eyebrows shot up. 'Would that be Denise Spencer?'

Amber was amazed and nodded. 'Yes. That's my mum. How did you know?'

Stanley beamed. 'I was the headmaster at the local school. I remember your mother and Cathy too. Two peas in a pod, they were, always getting told off for chatting and not concentrating on the task in hand. But how wonderful that you're here and, might I say, looking just like her. How is she?'

'She's well,' Amber told him. 'She and dad have just emigrated to New Zealand.'

'Gosh, how exciting.' Stanley fixed her with his grey eyes. 'Of course, that's a long way from both you and Cathy.'

'Not so far for me,' said Amber. 'I'm just passing through to see Cathy and then I'm flying on to start a new life with mum and dad.' She didn't admit that she had no idea what that life was going to entail. Everything was so up in the air at the moment and it was rattling her already shaky self-confidence.

'Well, I shall look forward to seeing you in the meantime,' said Stanley, handing over his change for the newspaper.

Stanley left the shop with a small wave and a jingle of the bell over the door.

'Welcome to Cranbridge,' said Josh, as he placed the coins inside the till. 'I'm sure it's a big change from the excitement of New York.'

He headed off to the other side of the shop, leaving Amber by the till counter.

He was wrong, of course, thought Amber. You could work in an amazing, famous shop in one of the biggest cities in the world and people expected it to be fun and life-changing. But in reality it could still be utterly lonely. Working on the windows of the shop, most of the time had been filled with short conversations regarding props and building the vast displays. Nothing personal. Sometimes she would spend the whole day by herself. And when she left work on a Friday afternoon, chances were that she wouldn't speak to anyone until she was back there on Monday morning.

The problem with not really speaking to anyone on a daily basis was that you almost lose the habit, thought Amber. You don't want to go out. You even refuse rare invitations, scared in case you've forgotten how to socialise. And yet, she was lonely. Utterly and completely lonely.

But a brief stay in Cranbridge wouldn't cure that.

Amber checked her phone once more, which thankfully had survived its dunking in the river. And with no update arriving from the airline or landlord, she was stuck there for the time being.

5

It had been a long day, thought Josh, flipping the Open sign over to read Closed in the window of the front door. A day full of dunkings in the river, unspoken words following the argument with his mum that morning and awkward silences. The last thing he felt like doing was keeping anyone company and going out to dinner.

But his mum had found him just as he was bolting the front door locked.

'We should celebrate,' she'd said. 'Go to the pub for dinner.'

'Celebrate?' Josh had found himself muttering, wondering what on earth there was to rejoice about.

'Amber flying over all this way to visit us,' his mum had replied, rolling her eyes. 'A change of company for us all. And, I don't know, why on earth not?'

Because we can't possibly spare the money, Josh had wanted to tell her. But it was the first time in a long time that she had looked so cheerful and what harm could a few more pounds added on to the credit card do?

He knew though that at some point he was going to have to address their overheads and talk to his mum about reducing their buying of goods and trying to sell off what they could. He had been wondering about selling on the internet but had no idea how to start.

Josh stood on the veranda at the front of the shop, waiting for the family to gather. He looked at the Closed sign on the door. His dad had never wanted to be a shopkeeper. Todd Kennedy had been a man full of life and personality. His lead guitar playing antics were still all over YouTube. He had been a huge magnetic force, instantly drawing people to his side as soon as he entered a room. But the rock and roll lifestyle had taken its toll and once Josh's grandfather had passed away, his dad had persuaded them all to move to Cranbridge for a quieter life.

Of course, not even a country village could contain Todd's dazzling personality and he was soon buying all manner of stock from every country fair and market that he could find. The trouble was, it was such a wide range of goods that much of the stock remained unsold and Josh just felt overwhelmed with it all now. Boxes of sellotape jostled for space with long rolls of material. Mounds of front door mats tottered precariously next to tins of baked beans. Garden brooms were alongside wellington boots and children's toys, knitting needles and car engine oil.

His mum and grandma kept saying that it was the supermarket's fault that the fortunes of the shop had altered. Times had changed. But the bizarre range of stock and crammed displays certainly didn't help.

Josh wanted to tidy up the place, get some kind of order somehow. It needed local support. Newer additions, like contactless payment and even online selling. But his mum refused to change anything and so it continued to feel like an impossible task.

In his lowest moments, he dreamt of just taking the whole stock to the council refuse dump and getting rid of it all. But his dad had bought a lot of it, so they at least ought to get some money for it. Besides, it was hardly eco-friendly to add to the global waste.

Indeed, Josh's biggest dream was to make the shop more environmentally friendly and sustainable. It was a cause close to his heart. Growing up, his dad had taken the family to the Great Barrier Reef in Australia. They had paid for a private boat hire and the driver had been passionate about the ecology of the reef and the impact climate change and industry was having on the coral.

It had struck a chord with twelve-year-old Josh and from that moment on, he had become passionate about saving the planet from the population intent on destroying it in his rebellious teenage years, and he had protested on many Greenpeace demonstrations. At university, he had decided to use his brain to back up his arguments and completed his degree in environmental business studies.

He had been lucky in how swiftly his career as a sustainability manager, helping customers bring greener working practices into their companies, had grown. It had been an extremely satisfying job, making the world a greener place one company at a time. He had visited and worked in some of the richest and most exciting cities in Europe.

And then he had received a phone call out of the blue one morning two years previously. His father had suffered a major heart attack and was unlikely to make it through the night. He had driven at speed to the hospital and just made it in time to squeeze his dad's hand and say his goodbyes.

Nothing had been the same since. After the funeral, when he had been preparing to get back to his day job, his mother had become unwell. The cancer was swiftly diagnosed with, thankfully, a treatment available. But she had been too fragile, too upset about the shop, for him to turn his back on Cranbridge Stores.

And so he had given up his job, honouring the promise made to his father that he would take care of his mother and grandmother. He had thought it would only be a temporary measure. But he was still here, two years on. Stuck in limbo. He couldn't update the shop without causing his mum to get upset and she had been through enough. They all had. The trouble was that he was used to being his own boss, but he had absolutely no say in the shop's business.

At some point he knew he was going to have to be brave and tell his mum that he needed to leave for his own sanity. He just hadn't the heart to tell her yet.

And so nothing changed except his growing resentment at being stuck in the village.

The truth was that, deep down, he no longer cared about the shop. It was his prison, his captor and he just wanted to move on. And the guilt about his true feelings made him even more miserable.

Amber was the first to join him downstairs before dinner. She was looking uncomfortable, tugging at the blue jumper which he recognised as his mum's. He felt bad for her that she didn't even have her own clothes to wear at the moment.

What a come down Cranbridge must be after the glamour of New York, he thought. He didn't blame her for looking a little overwhelmed at the mess inside Cranbridge Stores. It was all in stark contrast to the glitzy department stores on the streets of Manhattan.

Once they had all gathered together, the family walked around the corner of the shop and across Riverside Lane. Josh glanced down the road, but there was nobody there. The boarded-up shops along the lane just confirmed that nobody had a reason to visit what was the heart of the village any more.

Apart from the shop, the only other business that was open was The Black Swan pub on the other side of the narrow bridge across the river and even that had seen better days.

'It's a cheerful atmosphere at any rate,' he heard his mum say to Amber as they headed through the front door of the pub.

Josh thought of describing the pub with many words, but cheerful probably wasn't at the foremost in his mind. The Black Swan was pretty run-down these days. It hadn't been updated for the many years since it had been his father's local pub, but at least the oak beams and fireplaces kept it on the rustic side of dilapidated.

Like everything else in the village, it wasn't particularly busy. Only a handful of regulars went in a couple of evenings a week, Josh included. It had become his sanctuary, where he could escape the claustrophobic atmosphere in the shop and flat.

When he had moved into the flat after his father's funeral, he had assumed it would only be for a few short weeks. Two years later and he was still there.

Mike, the mouthy landlord, didn't seem to mind that Josh could nurse a single pint of beer for a whole evening. It was all he could afford and the last thing he wanted to do was start relying on alcohol too much in times of stress. He had seen what the similar addiction had almost cost his father in terms of his health. Or at least that was what his dad had told him when he had described his drunken life touring around the world in a rock band.

They found a table quite easily in the relatively empty pub, despite the lively darts competition going on. Then Josh headed up to the bar to order the drinks.

'Good evening,' said Mike with a nod. 'I see you've got the family with you tonight.'

Mike was a pleasant enough man with a slightly rumpled face who was always friendly to everyone apart from his own wife, with whom he suffered a hate-hate relationship.

'And who else is that over there?' asked Mike, squinting over at the table.

'Mum's goddaughter,' Josh told him.

'Well, I can't remember the last time we had a pretty lady in here,' said Mike, still staring at Amber over Josh's shoulder.

'Perhaps it's the lack of feminine ambience that's putting them off,' drawled Josh.

The swearing and shouting of the darts match was increasing by the second.

'Yeah, probably,' said Mike. But he didn't seem to notice or care about the noise.

Unlike his wife, Angie, who appeared suddenly from behind the bar. She rolled her eyes at her husband before turning to shout across the bar. 'Oy! You lot! Shut it, yeah? We've got ladies in here.'

'In here?' said one the darts players, looking all around him and then shocked at seeing Cathy, Grandma Tilly and Amber sitting in the corner.

Tilly beamed and waved at the gentlemen whilst Amber shuffled in her seat, obviously uncomfortable at the attention.

'Nice to the see the family in with you tonight,' said Angie, her wide smile emphasised by the bright pink lipstick she wore.

Everything about Angie was bright. From her peroxide-bleached big hair, to her pink jumper, blue miniskirt and bright cerise long nails, she was loud and brash.

'Right, I'm going to watch *EastEnders*,' said Angie, pouring herself out a large gin and tonic.

'I wanted to watch the football,' said Mike, becoming cross.

'Tough,' said Angie, laughing almost manically.

'Now wait a minute,' began Mike, following his wife out the back.

The shouting could still be heard by everyone in the pub.

At the end of the bar, their niece, Belle, rolled her eyes and sighed. In contrast to her noisy and quarrelsome aunt and uncle, Belle was always smiling and friendly. That evening, her long black hair was tied back in a ponytail and she was dressed in jeans and a white shirt.

'Have you got a menu?' Josh asked her.

Belle looked shocked. 'A menu?'

'Mum fancied a nice meal out,' Josh told her.

Belle was still looking worried. 'Then I think she's come to the wrong place.'

She had a point. The only food they ever served in the pub was microwaved and even that wasn't particularly pleasant. But Cranbridge was hardly bursting with restaurants. In fact, The Black Swan was the only place to eat without having to get in the car to leave the village.

'It was mum's idea,' said Josh.

Belle blew out a sigh. 'Let me check what's in the freezer.'

As Belle disappeared into the kitchen, Josh looked around. He shouldn't like this grubby pub. The décor was from the 1970s. The food was probably cooked in the 1990s. It was worn and shabby and didn't smell great. And yet he found The Black Swan a comfort. It was a mostly masculine atmosphere which he craved, missing his brother and dad's company so much.

Belle was friendly, despite her aunt and uncle severely lacking in customer service, but there had never been any kind of connection between them, despite her being a similar age to him. He had always had a hunch that she had been attracted to Pete rather than him. So they remained only friends.

His own love life had been put on hold when he had moved to Cranbridge two years previously. Not that he felt he was missing much. He had enjoyed a string of dates over the years but nobody had ever come close to owning his heart. He knew that love existed. He had seen it between his parents over the many years of their happy marriage. He just wasn't sure he would ever be so lucky.

He took a quick sip from the pint of beer that had been placed in front of him and glanced around the pub. Aside from the darts competition and his family, the only other customer in the pub was Del the coach driver. Or Dodgy Del as everyone referred to him.

Del had a good heart and would always manage to find anything that anyone needed, especially at short notice. But most villagers had learnt over the years that it was best to never ask where anything connected to Del came from in the first place.

'All right?' said Del as a way of greeting, between sips from his pint of cider. 'So who's that little beauty you've brought in?' he asked, giving a wink and smile in Amber's direction.

Josh shook his head warningly at his friend. 'Just passing through, Del. So hands off.'

Del laughed. 'Might have known you'd keep a pretty girl like that to yourself.'

'It's not like that,' Josh told him, glancing back over to where Amber was sitting. She had certainly grown up into an attractive woman, shining out like a diamond in the grotty under lit pub.

But Del wasn't listening as he had just switched his attention back to Belle, who had returned with a handwritten note of microwaveable meals.

'No worries,' carried on Del. 'My heart belongs to the lovely Belle here.'

She gave him a grimaced smile. 'I'll try to contain my excitement,' she told him, her voice laced with sarcasm.

'Not on my account, sweetheart,' said Del, grinning.

Thankfully Belle was more than capable of keeping Dodgy Del at arm's-length, such was her strength of character. She rolled her eyes and handed over the list to Josh. 'It's not a great choice, but you already knew that,' she told him.

He sipped from his pint before carrying back the drinks to the table.

'Thanks,' murmured Amber, as she took the gin and tonic from him.

For a second, they locked eyes, her brown to his blue and he felt a jolt deep within. A spark of something. He looked away as he dropped into his seat. So she was attractive, so what? He'd dated pretty women before.

But she most definitely wasn't the type for a fling. And he wasn't stupid enough to upset his mum any further. Or his own Aunty Denise either. Amber's mum was an equally formidable character.

So that was where any small amount of attraction ended, he reminded himself. She was going to leave and join her family in New Zealand. He would never see her again, probably.

And he felt even more alone at that thought than ever before.

* * *

Josh had told them how awful the food in the pub might be, but Amber was surprised at how bad it actually was.

'How can they not be able to cook chips?' she asked, prodding a blackened chip with her fork. It was both charred and burnt on the outside and yet still undercooked on the inside.

'I think Angie has trouble cooking anything with those false nails of hers,' said Cathy, nodding in agreement. 'Still, it's nice to be somewhere different tonight.'

Amber was surprised. From what she had gathered so far, her godmother didn't like any kind of change, especially in the shop. And yet here she was, craving an alternative to what must be some very lonely nights in the flat. Especially since Grandma Tilly had moved out, although Amber understood that the stairs had become too much trouble for her unsteady legs. She had appeared very eager to invite Amber around the following day to her new bungalow for a cup of tea. Perhaps Grandma Tilly was a little lonely too now that she was living by herself.

Amber's gaze wandered on to look at Josh. Did he get lonely as well? There was hardly a vast amount of choice of single women around the village from what she'd seen so far. And it wasn't as if he wasn't good-looking. She studied him for a moment. Handsome face. Nice eyes. Wide shoulders.

He suddenly turned his head, as if feeling her gaze on him, and she quickly looked down at her plate, blushing. Thankfully she wasn't really hungry. Her body clock was still running on New York time and all she really wanted to do was climb into bed and sleep forever and a day.

She suppressed a yawn, which unfortunately Cathy caught.

'You poor thing,' she said, smiling. 'You must be shattered. Let's get the bill and you can head back to the flat.'

'You go ahead,' said Josh, nursing his pint. 'I'm going to finish my drink, so I'll pay up in a while.'

He wished them goodnight and then they left the pub.

Outside, it was dark already and the temperature had dropped. At least she still had her leather jacket, thought Amber, drawing it around her as she glanced up. The sky was clear and full of stars. She had missed seeing them in Manhattan, she realised.

Cathy tucked her hand through Tilly's arm as they went back across the bridge. Amber just prayed that she wasn't so tired that she fell in again, but thankfully they all made it to the other side safely.

As they reached the shop, Amber heard Cathy's soft sigh.

'Is everything OK?' she asked.

Cathy gave her a sad smile. 'I just miss Todd, that's all. Things just aren't the same any more.'

Tilly squeezed her hand and gave Amber a watery smile.

'I don't know,' carried on Cathy, 'the shop seems to have become sadder since we lost Todd. Poor Josh is stuck here with me when he should be living and travelling like his brother.'

'Maybe he likes it here,' said Amber.

But Cathy shook her head. 'He just seems sad and frustrated most of the time.' She gave herself a little shake and then fixed a smile on her face. 'Now, are you sure you'll be all right up there in the flat on your own? I'm going to walk mum home. I won't be long and Josh will be back soon.'

'I'll be fine,' said Amber.

'I'm sure you're desperate for your bed,' said Cathy.

Amber wished them goodnight as Cathy unlocked the back door of the shop and switched on the lights so she could find her way up the stairs.

Amber quickly washed her face before going into the small guest bedroom. She had never been so grateful to see a bed in her life. Regardless of the fact that Cathy had given her a pair of Christmas pyjamas, at least she could be tucked up in the warmth and lying flat on her back, unlike the previous night where she had tried and failed to find a comfortable sleeping position on the plane.

Within seconds of her head hitting the pillow, she was asleep, her dreams full of stars and narrow stone bridges over the river.

6

Amber woke to find sunlight streaming through a gap in the curtains in her bedroom and onto her face. She was amazed to hear birdsong until she slowly realised that she was definitely not in New York any more and was actually in the flat above Cranbridge Stores.

The room she had rented in a shared flat had not been peaceful. In New York, she had endured flatmates that shouted at each other at all times of the day and night, busy streets outside full of traffic, horns and sirens. It had been a constant urban white noise. But not in Cranbridge.

She rolled over in her bed to take a peep around the curtains. Her bedroom overlooked Riverside Lane and she could see the river sparkling under the morning sunlight. Already the seasonal transition from late summer into autumn was well under way. The trees that flanked the river were covered with golden leaves, some of which were drifting down to the ground in a gentle breeze.

It was a lovely day to be outside and yet she saw only one person in the distance walking their dog. She peered left and then right on both sides of the river, but there was nobody else in sight. It was so quiet, she thought. She was so used to being jostled on the packed streets of New York and London, but not here.

Another person came into view, walking hurriedly along the other side of the river. So the village wasn't completely devoid of people. Just customers who didn't want to come into the shop.

She lay back in bed, looking around the tiny room. Apparently it had been Grandma Tilly's room up until recently. Despite the flowery wallpaper, it was a small but quite sweet room, with only a single bed, a narrow wardrobe and a chest of drawers. A pile of Cathy's clothes were folded and lay on top of the drawers.

Amber frowned, remembering her lost luggage and grabbed her phone to check for any updates. She was amazed to see that it had gone past eight o'clock in the morning. She had managed to sleep solidly for ten hours. She hadn't slept so well since she had moved to New York. The noise in the city that never sleeps had unsettled her and so she hadn't been able to do so much either.

A bit embarrassed about her lie-in, she leapt out of bed. At least she had been able to wash and dry her clothes from the previous day, so they were clean. If her suitcases didn't arrive that day, she'd have to head out later to buy some new underwear and other supplies. She couldn't keep borrowing Cathy's clothes.

She left her bedroom and went to the bathroom across the hallway. On the way, she glanced inside what appeared to be Josh's bedroom which was next to the spare bedroom. The door was already open and there was no sound from within. Presumably he was already downstairs at work.

She wondered about Josh. He looked like a broken man at one point during the previous evening when he thought no one was watching him. The shock of losing his dad had obviously taken its toll. From what she'd heard, he had been a successful businessman until a few years ago, so his life had obviously changed dramatically, and, perhaps, not for the better either.

She headed down the stairs and immediately came across Cathy and Josh in the crowded storeroom.

'Good morning,' said Cathy, smiling. 'You must have slept well.'

'Good morning,' replied Amber. 'I did, but you should have woken me up earlier.'

'Nonsense,' said Cathy. 'You obviously needed the rest.'

'It's not like you've missed any customers,' said Josh, gesturing into the empty shop with a sad smile.

Cathy sighed loudly, glaring briefly at her son before saying, 'Amber isn't here to work. She's on holiday. Now, let's get you some breakfast.'

Amber followed Cathy back up the stairs and into the tiny kitchen.

Cathy made Amber sit at the table whilst she rushed around the room preparing some toast and coffee. She appeared almost frenzied, thought Amber, unloading the dishwasher and cleaning the work surfaces.

'Won't you have a coffee with me?' asked Amber, as Cathy placed a plate of toast and a steaming mug of coffee on the table. 'And I can tidy up after myself. Please don't worry.'

'Maybe later,' said Cathy, smiling at her. 'Now don't you rush your breakfast. Take your time. Oh and grab your coat before you come back down. Mum's looking forward to your visit.'

Despite being used to her own company, Amber felt uneasy having too leisurely a breakfast when everyone else was at work.

So she ate her toast, tidied away her plate and then headed back into the shop, with her leather jacket in her hand.

'Oh good,' said Cathy, nodding at Amber's jacket. 'Let me grab my coat and then I'll show you the way to Mum's new place.'

It was only a five-minute walk to the other end of Riverside Lane, past the mill and over the last of the pedestrian bridges to the other side of the river, where a single line of newly built tiny bungalows lay on a small incline. They were built in the same coloured brick as the rest of the village, although perhaps not as pretty as the other buildings. But at least they had no stairs, thought Amber as they headed up the paved path to the front door of No. 1.

Cathy let herself in with a key and called out, 'Coo-eee! It's only us!'

'Good morning!' said Tilly, who was waiting in the narrow hallway with a wide smile. She was wearing her coat already. 'I thought we could have our walk now and coffee later as they're forecasting rain and I don't want to lose my perm just yet.'

'You two go and enjoy yourselves,' said Cathy, giving them both a wide smile. 'I've too much to be getting on with today. Now, Mum, I need to strip your bed and put the bedding in for a wash as well.'

As she rushed off past them and into the tiny bedroom, Amber saw Tilly shake her head slightly.

Amber hesitated before asking softly, 'Is Cathy OK?'

Tilly sighed. 'She's worried about her scan later this week,' she said in a quiet tone. 'It's only another check-up, but it hangs over her like a cloud until she gets the results. She gets a bit manic until it's over with.'

'I'm sure she'll be OK,' said Amber.

'I hope so, love. It's been a tough two years.'

As Cathy rushed past into the kitchen with an armful of bedding, Tilly visibly brightened up.

'Now, how about that walk? Unless I'm needed in the shop, of course.' Tilly sounded almost hopeful.

'Nonsense!' beamed Cathy. 'Josh and I can handle it. You two have a nice walk. I'm sure that'll brush off the last of Amber's jet lag.'

So Amber and Tilly headed back outside. Amber looked across at the river as Tilly slipped on her gloves.

'At least you've stayed in the centre of the village,' said Amber.

'It still feels a little strange to be over this side of the river,' said Tilly, linking her arm with Amber's as they began to walk. 'I've always lived over the shop, you see.'

They continued down the lane until they were standing opposite the shop, which was on the other side of the river.

They both stood and looked at it for a while. It was a very attractive building with its sandy-coloured brick and pointed roof, thought Amber. But the veranda was too bare. It needed a bit of colour and, truth be told, a lick of paint or wood resin to make it look a bit less shabby.

'I remember the first time I ever clapped eyes on the place,' said Tilly. 'It was the prettiest place I'd ever seen.'

Amber nodded. 'I'm sure it was.'

At one time, she added silently to herself.

'Bill my husband, had grown up here. In fact, it was first owned by his great-grandfather. Then his father and then it passed to us to take care of. Over 100 years of Kennedys have run the stores. I thought that perhaps the line of succession would stop there when Cathy married Todd, who began to make a name for himself with his music. I mean, what's a rock musician going to do in little old Cranbridge?'

Amber joined in her soft laughter. 'But he came anyway?'

'Aye, that he did,' said Tilly nodding. 'To my great surprise, I must confess. He was never the country village type. But he was starting to have a few heart problems and, truth be told, I think he was growing weary of the lifestyle. So he packed up the family and came here.' Her smile held sadness though. 'So Todd and Cathy took over the shop once I was widowed.'

'Was it busier in those days?' asked Amber.

Tilly sighed. 'In the start, yes it was. It was a little shop full of everything that the villagers needed. But Todd was so enthusiastic that he used to carry on buying anything that he could lay his hands on. Toys, tools, stationery, it all began to pile up. As you can see, he carried on buying stock right up until...' Her voice trailed off.

Amber squeezed her hand, which Tilly absent-mindedly patted. 'Come on, love. I promised I'd show you the village and we haven't got beyond the shop yet.'

Tilly led Amber across the river, but then turned away from the shop and further down Riverside Lane.

'This used to be the haberdashery,' she said, as they went past the shop next door to Cranbridge Stores. It was a replica of their own shop and equally as shabby from the outside, albeit with an empty room inside.

'Beautiful material Mavis used to have in there too,' said Tilly. 'So Todd bought off the remaining rolls before they left. That was a long time ago now, of course. But I've heard a rumour that the local newspaper's going to be moving in there.'

'Really?' Amber was stunned. Surely they would have been better off in a town somewhere.

'Well, Frank Conway owns the newspaper, you see. Have you met him yet? He lives next door to me. Anyway, he runs a whole bunch of local papers and apparently they've had problems with the offices they're renting.' Tilly shrugged. 'Anyway, it will be nice to have someone next door after the shop lying empty all this time.'

Amber stepped forward to peer inside as there were no curtains or boards on the windows. She was amazed at the space inside. It was huge and now quite obvious to her how impractical and full Cranbridge Stores really was.

She rejoined Tilly and they continued walking down the lane.

'That was the hairdressers,' said Tilly as they went past the next shop. 'Only shut last month. I've been desperately hanging on to my perm ever since. And this last one was the bakery,' she said as they reached the last shop before the mill. 'It's been years since I had a proper home-made loaf of bread. Such a shame because the mill is lovely when it gets going. Not that it has for years, of course.'

The old bakery was another shop that appeared to be the same design as the other three before it. Large door in the middle with two huge bay windows on either side. A flat above the shop that narrowed into a pointy roof.

The mill was built in the same warm-coloured stone, but there were a few spokes on the wooden wheel that appeared to be broken.

They stopped and turned around to look at the river as it made its way through the centre of the village. Once more, apart from the bird-song, it was quiet.

'Where did all the villagers go?' asked Amber.

Tilly looked at her. 'You mean, why's it so quiet?'

Amber nodded.

'There's only me and a few other creaky old folks hanging on in there from the original villagers.' Tilly smiled. 'So places get sold and new people move in. Most of them commute into the nearby towns, from what I've heard. Either by car or the train station which is in the next village. Or they work from home, shut up inside with their broad-band. At the weekends, they're on their mountain bikes or they get into their 4 x 4s and head to Aldwych town, which is ten miles away. They've got a cinema, a big shopping centre, sports centre, the lot. It's a real shame, though.'

'What about the church?' asked Amber, looking across the river to the tiny church on the end of the lane opposite.

'Glenda's our new vicar,' said Tilly. 'Arrived last summer. She's done a marvellous job with making Sunday morning service a bit more interesting. She's real fun. But times change and religion has changed along with it.'

'But people still live here so they must need to shop in the village occasionally,' said Amber, trying to think of some kind of solution.

'I don't know, love,' said Tilly, blowing out a sigh. 'It's hard to describe, but it used to be bustling here. A community. Everyone looked out for each other. People need somewhere central to gather around.'

Amber looked down the river to The Black Swan pub. 'So, if not the church, what about the pub?'

Tilly laughed. 'You've tasted their food, haven't you? Mike and Angie don't exactly give off a welcoming ambience either, wouldn't you say? And last night was one of their milder rows, trust me.'

'And yet it is isolating when you work from home,' said Amber. 'Or when you just stay indoors all day.' She spoke from personal experience.

'It certainly is.' Tilly gave a whisper of a sigh and Amber realised that perhaps the move into the bungalow wasn't perhaps a happier solution after all. Tilly gave her a sad smile. 'Don't you mind me, love,' she said, squeezing Amber's hand. 'It'll be nice to have some company whilst you're here. Cathy and Josh are always so busy that I hardly see anyone these days. So I stick on the television and get knitting, just to keep my hands active.'

They walked across one of the narrow pedestrian bridges to the other side of the river. All the time, Amber was racking her brains, trying to think of how they could bring everyone out and into the fresh air. The village was so pretty. It just needed a central point, other than the river. Somewhere for people to gather and meet. Somewhere like Cranbridge Stores, she mused.

She wished she could help the family and in turn help the shop to flourish before she left. But her skills were limited and she had no idea what could be done to make a difference in the meantime.

7

Josh stood at the front door of the shop, looking inwards and wondering where on earth to begin.

He had intended to start getting some kind of organisation in the shop that day, hoping that Amber's visit would cause a distraction for his mum. Perhaps even get her out of the shop, for once. She had stopped going anywhere recently, desperate, it appeared, to stay inside. But Cathy had sent Grandma Tilly out with Amber instead, leaving them bonded in the awkward atmosphere together.

'What's this?' His mother's voice broke into his train of thought.

He turned his head and saw her holding an envelope that he had deliberately left on the counter the previous evening.

'It's the paperwork for a contactless payment system,' Josh told her, trying with all his might not to roll his eyes. 'I sent off for the details last week.'

'What do we need that for?'

'Mum, most people want to pay with a card these days.' When they bother to come in, he added silently to himself, glancing around the empty shop.

'People don't seem to mind the till,' said his mum, gesturing at the ancient huge till.

In Josh's eyes it was a monstrosity from a bygone era, totally unsuitable for the modern age.

'People need to be able to pay with a card,' he repeated.

'It makes a lovely sound when the drawer opens,' his mum carried on, touching the edge. 'That's why your dad liked it so much. It was your grandad's, you know.'

Josh took a deep breath. 'I know it was Grandad's. But it doesn't work for us as well as it could. It's obsolete.'

'Just like me, I suppose,' said his mum, any sign of a good mood quickly disappearing.

He knew why his mum was like she was. She was still desperately trying to preserve his dad's memory. The trouble was, Josh felt as if he were failing both of his parents each and every day.

He turned away to face the front of the shop. It was the same conversation they had every day. Round and round. And nothing ever changed. The theme of the argument was always the same. He wanted to change the shop. His mum didn't.

The business was failing and there was no room for sentimentality. Tough decisions needed to be made. But he knew his mum didn't want to listen to any of his reasoning. She was still viewing the business through the rose-tinted glasses of the past. From the happier days when his dad had been alive, when everything had been safe and secure. But now all that had changed and she was struggling to face the new reality.

'I think you forget that I let you change the windows and doors, didn't I?' his mum added.

This time, Josh did roll his eyes. 'They were rotten and it was draughty.' He had also managed to get the electric circuit board updated so that he no longer feared a fire every time he flicked a switch. It had been a minor victory amongst so much failure.

The rest of his hard-earned savings had gone into paying off the hefty second mortgage on the place, a burden he had shared with his brother. Unknown to anyone other than Josh and Pete, their dad had remortgaged the shop many years previously. Even their mum wasn't aware that Todd had gotten himself into financial difficulties. He had been a great father but not so good a businessman. The debts had been quite substantial on top of the mortgage. His dad had bought anything and everything from fairs and warehouse sales, filling the shop with who knows what. There was so much of it and most of it rubbish. But the money problems had remained, so Josh had used up the last of his money to ensure that his mum and grandma had a roof over their heads. Unfortunately he didn't have enough to cover the shop's day-to-day debts, which were mounting at an alarming rate.

'You've spent too much money on all the updates,' said Cathy, obviously not wanting to give up the argument quite yet. 'You didn't need to get the central heating done in the flat above the shop as well.'

He didn't reply, merely turning away to look outside of the window. It was just another row in a long line of them and he felt so helpless, trapped in Cranbridge with none of his business savvy even close to helping out his family. He had been desperate to get away when he was younger, although he loved his family. He wanted to follow his own path and make something of himself. He had turned his passion for battling climate change into a real business. He had worn nice suits, enjoyed being someone whose opinion counted for something. A grown-up with a career.

But now he was back in the village and it was as if he had stepped back in time. He was even in his childhood bedroom in the flat above the shop. These days he felt like a teenager again, with no room to breathe or grow.

'Your father didn't like technology,' he heard his mother say.

Josh drew in a sharp breath to steady his tone of voice as he continued to face the window. 'He bought an electric guitar,' he reminded her. 'He used that as well as his acoustic one.'

'Humph. That was music.'

'Well, he was a musician.' He finally turned to look at his mum. 'The shop needs to change,' he told her in a gentle tone. 'Otherwise...' His voice trailed off. Even at the age of thirty-five he couldn't say what needed to be said.

His mum crossed her arms. Defence shields up, he thought.

'It's fine the way it is,' she finally said.

No, it's not, he thought as she turned to straighten a pile of biscuits next to the till. Did she know how bad it really was? He sometimes thought she did.

'I came back to run the shop,' he reminded her.

'No, you came back because your father was ill.'

'And then you were ill,' he said. 'And Grandma couldn't do it all by herself, so here I am.' Stuck in Cranbridge, he added to himself.

She looked at him, lifting her chin a little. 'I could have coped.'

'With all the chemotherapy making you so sick?'

'Well, not on those days, but all the others,' said his mother quickly. 'Anyway, I don't want to talk about the chemotherapy. Or any of it.' She swiftly walked out from behind the counter. 'I'm going to make a cup of tea,' she said, rushing through to the back room and up the stairs to the flat.

Josh sighed. He knew that his mum preferred to stick her head in the sand than confront the reality of their situation. He also knew that she was stressed about the scan results later that week. The doctors had been hopeful last time about the future and yet his stomach was still clenched in fear.

His mum had fallen ill way too soon after losing his dad, but they had got through the worst of days, hadn't they? But there always seemed to be another appointment to stress about.

And he couldn't face telling her the truth and cause her yet more hurt and worry. So he stayed silent and frustrated, unable to see a way out of their predicament.

He turned back to look out of the window and watched as Grandma Tilly and Amber slowly walked along the other side of the river.

He looked at Amber. Her long dark blonde hair shone in the dappled sunlight peeping through the trees. It was almost the same colour as the changing leaves on the oak trees, he thought.

Perhaps Amber could help his mum see that the shop needed to be reorganised. She was calm, thoughtful. Maybe she would be more gentle than him in persuading his mum to see the light.

As he continued to watch them, he wondered briefly what Amber's life had been like since their teenage years. She'd always been so quiet when they had been growing up. That much hadn't changed. But she had done so well for herself, working in both London and New York.

The bell above the door rang as Grandma Tilly pushed it open.

'It's lovely out there,' she said. 'I love this time of year.'

'Me too,' said Cathy, appearing from the back room holding a cup of tea. 'I saw you both out of the window and I've made a cuppa. Do you want one?'

'Thanks,' said Grandma Tilly, heading over to the seat behind the till. 'What have I missed?'

'Just your grandson's daily nagging session,' said Cathy.

Grandma Tilly hugged her coat around her in the cool air of the shop. 'I timed our walk just right then, didn't I?' She gave Amber a large wink before looking innocently at Josh.

'Apparently we need updating,' said Cathy, in a sarcastic tone, looking at Amber. 'Can you believe it?'

Amber shuffled from foot to foot, obviously embarrassed about being put on the spot. 'I don't know anything about shops,' she eventually said. 'Only the windows.'

'Maybe you can do something with ours,' said Grandma Tilly. 'I've always loved the big bay windows here.'

Amber looked startled at the suggestion. 'Oh, I don't know...'

'They couldn't look any worse,' carried on Grandma Tilly.

'Excuse me, I did those windows this summer,' said Cathy, looking slightly affronted.

Grandma Tilly grinned. 'I know you did, my darling. I just think we've got this amazing window dresser in our midst for a while. Don't you think we could use Amber's talents?'

Everyone turned to look at Amber, who was now very pink in the cheeks. 'If you think it would help,' she muttered. 'Of course I'll redecorate them for you.'

'Excellent,' said Grandma Tilly, grinning.

'See?' said Cathy in a triumphant tone of voice as she looked at Josh. 'And you said I couldn't make changes around here!'

Josh went to speak but found no words coming out. It was hardly the massive changes that were required. He supposed it was a start, but how could two windows change their fortunes for the better?

8

Amber had agreed to create a new window display for Cranbridge Stores, mainly because it made her godmother happier than she had seen her since she'd arrived.

'I'm so pleased you can do this for us,' said Cathy, putting her arm around Amber's shoulder and giving it a squeeze before looking up at Josh. 'What do you think?'

'If you think it'll help,' he said, with a shrug.

Despite being riddled with self-doubt, Amber felt a small flush of indignance. Was he questioning her expertise? 'The point of any kind of window dressing is to draw in customers,' she found herself saying in a prim tone of voice.

'There!' said Cathy, with a firm nod. 'What she said. Amber, you do whatever you want with the windows. After all, you're the one with the training and talent.'

Amber saw Josh's face drop at his mother's words.

'I think I'll just go and see it from the outside,' she said, anxious not to get in the middle of yet another argument. So she headed outside to get a view of the windows from the road in front of the shop.

It was a beautiful morning, with not a single cloud in the pale blue sky. The low sun was peeping through the yellowing leaves of the trees lining the riverbank. The dappled light danced off the slow-running river as it carried on through the village.

All around there were the telltale signs that autumn had begun, from the rustling of the dried leaves picked up by a soft breeze to the trees ablaze in golden and crimson hues.

Heading down the steps from the veranda and onto the lane, she couldn't resist bending down to pick up a bright red maple leaf that had caught on her trainers.

'Good morning,' said a voice.

She turned round to find Stanley walking slowly towards her. 'Good morning,' she replied.

'Isn't it a beautiful one?' he said, smiling appreciatively at the view all around them.

She nodded. 'It is. Are you heading in for your newspaper?'

'Plus a couple of extra tins for the harvest festival at the church this weekend. It seems to have come around so quickly and all I appear to be is another year older.' He paused and looked at her. 'And what are your plans for this fine day?'

'I've been tasked with decorating the front windows,' she told him.

'How lovely,' he said, nodding his approval. 'I cleaned mine just last week.'

As Stanley went up the stairs and into the shop, Amber gave the two large bay windows a proper look.

Stanley had a point. Both windows were dusty and grimy, which was hardly the right starting point for a big display. So her first job was going to be cleaning them inside and out.

She went back inside and began to clear the clutter of goods that were in front of the window. Thankfully both Josh and Cathy appeared to be busying themselves elsewhere in the shop and flat so she was left to her own devices which suited Amber just fine.

Amongst all the tins and boxes on the windowsills, she found a few dead bugs as well as some dried leaves which had obviously been swept in when the front door had been open. The leaves were quite pretty as they were obviously from the large oak tree, so she put them to one side.

Once cleared, she was pleased to find that the window ledges were quite wide so would hold a substantial display. Once she had decided on the theme, of course. That piece of inspiration was still eluding her.

For now she decided to concentrate on the cleaning. Grabbing a bucket from the back room, she filled it with washing-up liquid and hot water before beginning to soap down both the windows and ledges.

'Here,' said Grandma Tilly, handing her a shammy leather once she had finished. 'I'm sure all of this is a bit of a comedown from that fancy department store though.'

'It was never that glamorous,' Amber told her.

And it was true. The majority of her work had been toiling in the tight window spaces, using sellotape, glue and anything else that would hold the elaborate displays together. From the front window, they were fabulous and artistic, but from behind they were far less glamorous.

As she wiped down the window ledge, she realised that it would be seen from both inside and outside the shop and therefore she didn't have the luxury to hide any staging. It would have to work from every angle.

'So sad that you were made redundant,' carried on Tilly. 'You must have loved that job.'

Amber's smile faltered. Had she loved that job? Only the actual design part. The head of window dressing had been a difficult woman who took the credit for a number of Amber's ideas. She had been sour to work with and there had always been an atmosphere. In retrospect, it had been a small relief to have been made redundant, although it had left her both jobless and homeless.

Something must have shown in her face as Amber realised that Tilly was studying her. She quickly carried on polishing the glass.

'This is a super space to use,' said Amber, changing the subject. 'Really wide and deep, which will be great.'

'I've always loved these windows,' said Tilly. 'I used to pop a small Christmas tree in one of them when Advent arrived.'

'You should do the same this year,' Amber told her.

Tilly made a face. 'Think I'll leave that kind of thing to you, dear. I should probably just stick to my knitting. After all, I'm surplus to requirements these days.'

But Tilly's words had no pleasing tone and Amber wondered whether she felt at a bit of a loose end now that she had moved out of the flat upstairs.

When she had finished cleaning, Amber went outside to look at the windows once more, this time from the veranda. At least the light now bounced off the newly polished glass. The problem now was what to fill the space with.

Deep in thought, she stepped down from the veranda and back onto the lane. She stood and stared around the village. Autumn, she thought. Lots of yellows, oranges and reds. Nature. A time of harvest moons and storing up for winter. She thought about the leaves that had been swept inside onto the windowsill. Then she remembered what Stanley had said about the harvest festival. Perhaps that was an idea.

She had a sudden vision of checked red and white cloth, on top of which were some pumpkins. Apples, as well. Some rosy, some green. Leaves, of course, in all the autumnal colours. Maybe some twigs. Fairy lights for the darkening days.

That was it! She had her theme. She just hoped it would look as good in real life as it did in her mind.

Feeling excited, Amber headed back into the shop for supplies. The shop was surely full of things that she could use?

'Is it OK if I borrow a few bits and pieces from around the shop for the display?' she asked Cathy.

'Of course,' said Cathy, beaming. 'What kind of things are you looking for?'

'Glue, string, fairy lights,' said Amber.

Cathy looked surprised. 'I think that kind of thing is in the back room.'

'Have you any kind of spare material as well?' asked Amber. 'Like an old tablecloth or something?'

Cathy and Grandma Tilly looked at each other. 'Aren't there a couple of rolls of material in the corner near the stairs?' said Tilly.

'I think so,' Cathy replied.

'I'll have a look,' said Amber, heading out into the back room.

As usual, it was full of boxes and very tight to move around. She almost fell over a couple of times, clambering over to get to what she needed. But she soon found the rolls of material that Tilly had mentioned. They were a little dusty, but, to her delight, one of them was a gingham red and white check. It was perfect for the display.

She found the string and sellotape in the toolbox next to the old tractor. She was just about to head through to the shop once more when she spotted a couple of old wicker baskets, propped up in a dark corner. She grabbed those as well before heading towards the window.

Amber spent a very happy couple of hours brushing down the cloth of dust and cleaning the wicker baskets ready for the display. All the time, her mind was racing with ideas for the display.

In addition, she went outside and found a couple of short, thin branches which were laying on the ground near to the river. She also picked up many leaves, selecting those which were whole and mud-free.

Once back inside, she began to stick the leaves onto the string and let them dry before winding them around the fairy lights that Cathy had found for her from the Christmas decorations.

'You're working ever so hard,' said Cathy, popping a biscuit and cup of tea on the windowsill next to where Amber was gluing the leaves onto the stick.

'Thanks,' said Amber, thinking that it was the most enjoyable day she'd had at work for a long time.

The lack of anyone overseeing her designs had made her feel far more relaxed than she could remember being at work. With nobody judging or criticising her choices, she had been free to bring her own ideas to life.

Cathy was still watching her and smiling. 'Oh, I knew that you coming to stay with us was going to change things for the better.'

Amber hoped that Cathy wasn't investing too much hope into what could only be a couple of small window displays. But at least it was nice to see her godmother cheerful. She just hoped she could produce a display that the whole family liked, even Josh.

But, as usual, her work was tempered by her own nagging self-doubt that she would never be as talented as she hoped she could be.

9

Josh had been somewhat bemused by his mother's suggestion that Amber dress the windows of the shop. In the scheme of things, it was a drop in the ocean compared to all the other changes that needed to be made. But if it kept his mum in a better mood than she had been in lately then who was he to argue?

Before he went to the cash and carry to pick up the meagre supply of milk and cheese for the shop and home, he had watched as Amber had gone to and from the stockroom. String, tape, old crates and even a pair of old wicker baskets had all been commandeered from their hiding places before being cleaned up and taken down to the front of the shop. A red and white checked cloth had caused Amber to smile more than he had seen her so far.

Even so, his expectations were low as to what she could pull off with such low-impact supplies. After all, their shop hardly had the similar budget or resources of a New York department store.

Late in the afternoon, just as he was bringing in the last of the purchases from his van, Amber came into the back room, where his mum was pouring herself yet another cup of tea. What else was there to do with little or no customers?

'Well, the windows are done,' said Amber, blushing and wringing her hands together with nerves. 'I hope it's OK.'

Cathy clapped her hands in glee. 'Oh, I've been so desperate to take a peek, but I promised you I wouldn't! I can't wait to see what you've done.'

Josh followed them somewhat less enthusiastically. They headed through the shop, weaving their way through the muddle and out to the veranda before turning to face the bay windows.

But what Josh saw made his mouth drop open in surprise. For a start, he'd had no idea how big the windows really were. They seemed enormous now that they were clutter-free and decorated. And how!

Inside, the windowsill was covered by the gingham red and white checked cloth, on top of which were placed various wooden crates, vases, the wicker baskets and even some conkers and acorns. Bare branches had been wrapped in pale fairy lights bringing an almost festive feel to the whole display. Amber also appeared to have glued many different-coloured dried leaves and strung them across the tops of the window. Both windows were a mirror image of the other.

Even better, he noticed that inside the wicker baskets, Amber had placed some of the biscuits and tinned food that he was desperate to sell. He was impressed that she knew about the power of product placement.

The whole arrangement was excellent, he had to concede. It looked warm, full of countryside charm. Pretty but sophisticated as well, although he couldn't for the life of himself think how she had achieved that with such simple items.

'Hasn't she done well?' said Grandma Tilly, beaming with what appeared to be pride.

'Oh, Amber!' cried his mum. 'It looks wonderful! I knew you could do it!'

She stepped forward to give a clearly embarrassed Amber a hug.

Then his mum stepped back to give Josh a stern look as if to prompt him to say something nice.

'It's pretty good,' he finally said, with a nod. He looked back at the windows once more. 'Remarkable, in fact.'

Amber shrugged her shoulders, still embarrassed. 'It's easy when you know how,' she told them.

'But we don't, if you haven't already realised,' he told her, grinning. 'So take the compliment and run with it.'

Her smile faltered for a second before she was swept inside with his mum and Grandma Tilly.

Amber was obviously talented but the complete lack of confidence in herself was something else altogether. The question was why? What had happened to her to make her think that her obvious talents were so lowly?

* * *

Later on, Amber went with his mum to watch a girly film at Grandma Tilly's bungalow. Josh left them to it. In a way, it was nice that his mum had some female company. She didn't get out much since recovering from her illness, which worried him. She had always been so full of life. It was a stark contrast to the almost angry woman that she had become.

Once he had closed up the shop, Josh stayed in the back room to tinker with the tractor's engine. But it brought him no pleasure.

He could still remember the first time that his dad had appeared with the small red tractor in the lane behind the shop.

'What's that for?' his mum had asked, looking horrified at yet another one of Todd's wild ideas.

His dad was beaming from ear to ear. 'I dunno what we're going to do with it,' he'd said, grinning. 'But isn't it a beauty? It's a David Brown 25! Do you know how much these things are worth?'

The family had stared as one at the faded bodywork, riddled with rust and with various pieces almost hanging off.

'Does it work?' Pete had asked, his ten-year-old eyes wide with excitement.

Josh, hitting his cynical stride early in his teens, had drawled, 'It's arrived on the back of a trailer,' to his younger brother. 'What do you think?'

'Listen, it's about the opportunity, the dream!' their dad had said, his eyes gleaming.

His mum had sighed. 'That's what you said when we all moved here from London.'

'And that worked out for the best, didn't it?' his dad had replied, with a wink to his sons.

Back in the present, Josh's sigh was remarkably similar to the one his mum had all those years ago.

In one way, it had worked out, moving the family out of London and into the village when Josh had been in his early teens. For a start, the pressure of modern life was well away from them, as well as the temptations that the bright lights of the city had also brought. His dad had remained clean of alcohol for the remainder of his life once they had moved to Cranbridge. He had embraced living in the country, taking the boys fishing and visiting the local pub for a Diet Coke. Best of all, he had taken up playing his guitar again. On a Sunday, when the shop was shut, he would sit on the veranda in the front and play. If Josh closed his eyes, he could still hear that sweet music.

The rest of the time, there was always music playing somewhere. On a radio or the record player. But the shop and the flat were quiet now. Too quiet.

With his dad gone and Pete having moved abroad to work, it felt as if the spark had gone out of their lives. And Josh couldn't see how it was ever going to return.

He turned the key in the ignition and waited for the tractor to splutter to life. Once it had got going for only the briefest and loudest of moments, the engine cut out almost immediately.

He flung down the old rag he was holding in despair. The tractor needed a major overhaul, but he just couldn't afford the expensive parts. It would cost hundreds, maybe even thousands, to get it going once more. Maybe that was the point. Maybe it should be left and sold for scrap. After all, it had been his dad's dream, not his, to repair the tractor.

But getting rid of it would mean another piece of their lives going and he just couldn't face any more heartache at the moment. All he could face was his pint of beer in the pub. So he shrugged on his leather jacket and wandered through the dark shop, bumping into various boxes as he went. If he got rid of the tractor then there would be more space for stock at the back of the shop. But what was the point without any customers?

Drawn to the light in the front of the shop, he realised that the fairy lights were still switched on in Amber's window display. Intrigued, he went out through the front door and, after locking up, headed out into the lane before turning around to face the shop.

He was startled to see how different it appeared to normal. Rather than dark and somewhat uninviting, he had to admit that the windows were attractive, pretty even. They drew the eye in with their autumnal display. It was cosy without looking too twee.

She certainly had a gift. Of course, Amber was used to drawing in the crowds in fancy department stores in the city. Josh glanced around. As usual, there were no crowds in Cranbridge. Her window display would certainly appeal to anyone who was passing. The trouble was that nobody ever did.

Although the thought of losing the shop to bankruptcy upset him, he wasn't perhaps as sad as he should be. It just felt like a terrible burden that he wanted to be rid of. He wanted his old life back. He wanted freedom to make his own decisions. But the thought of abandoning his mum and Grandma Tilly to face the music reaped by his dad was too much to bear. It would break their hearts to know that Todd had possibly bankrupted the shop and home that the family had kept for so many years.

He wanted his whole family to move on from the pain of the past. He just didn't know whether saving the shop was a big enough deal to ensure their future happiness as well.

10

Amber woke up the following morning with a spring in her step.

Her jet lag had faded after another good night's sleep and, wonder of wonders, the airline had sent her an email to say that her luggage had been found and would finally be arriving that day.

So she was feeling more cheerful than she had done since arriving in the village. Also, she had found that working on the windows of the shop the previous day had given her an incredible sense of satisfaction. Design had always been her favourite pastime and to make a career out of it had been a dream come true.

To her surprise, a greater joy had come from the couple of customers who actually came in the shop later that morning and commented on the window displays.

Yes, it was only Cranbridge, but still, she had never had feedback from actual real-life customers before. Hidden away in the depths of huge department stores, the only reviews she had ever received had been from her managers. And she had always felt they were barbed.

So she felt a small burst of confidence from the praise that she received.

Frank was particularly complimentary. 'I spotted the new window when I headed past last night. It looks really super.'

'Thank you,' said Amber, blushing as she helped to pack his pint of milk into a bag. Cathy had gone to check on Grandma Tilly, so Amber had offered to help out in the shop as she had no other plans.

'That should draw in a few more people anyway,' he added to Josh, who was standing nearby.

'Let's hope so, eh?' said Josh, fixing a smile on his face.

'Speaking of new customers, have you heard the latest?' carried on Frank. 'As you know, I own the *Cranbridge News*. Well, the building they're currently leasing for their offices has just been sold off to be converted into flats.' He rolled his eyes. 'As if we need any more of those. Anyway, I've leased the empty shop next door. It should work, I think.'

'What was it before?' asked Amber, trying to remember what Tilly had told her.

'A haberdashery. Not that my editor Tom needs to know that,' said Frank, laughing. 'Anyway, it'll be company for you all. There's half a dozen staff coming, so at least we'll start to get a bit of young life in the village, eh?'

But after he left, Amber thought Josh looked more depressed than before. 'Not sure six people are going to make that much of a difference,' he muttered, almost to himself.

It was as she had suspected. The shop was definitely in trouble. 'Does your mum know how bad it is?' she asked.

He shook his head. 'Not really. If she's guessed, then she really doesn't want to know the truth. She's had enough bad news these past two years.'

'Was the business failing before you lost your dad?' she asked.

Josh nodded. 'You know what he was like. He wasn't much of a businessman. He just liked buying stuff and chatting to the customers. When we had some, that is.' Josh sighed. 'I think I've just made everything worse these past two years.'

Amber frowned. 'How?'

'Because she's unhappy,' he told her.

Amber shook her head. 'She's unhappy because she lost her husband. You can't do anything to change that.'

He looked at her with bleak eyes. 'But I'm failing him too. I can't save the shop.'

Amber felt so sad for him and looked around at the place, trying to think of something positive to say. 'It's still the prettiest shop I've ever seen,' she told him. 'Somewhere under all this stuff, I mean.'

'That's not enough,' said Josh, his voice hoarse with emotion.

'But it's a start,' she told him. 'We'll try and think of something, OK?'

He nodded. 'Thanks,' he said, blowing out a sigh. 'Sorry. I guess Mum's appointment at the hospital this afternoon is rattling me more than I thought.'

'Are you going with her to get the results?' asked Amber.

Josh shook his head. 'She always says it's better if she goes on her own.' He looked at her, his blue eyes filled with sadness. 'She never got over losing dad so fast. And then we never had time to grieve because we went straight from that into the cancer treatment. It's been hard for her.'

Stuck in the crowded, almost claustrophobic shop probably didn't help her mood either, thought Amber.

'Maybe she could get away at some point,' she said. 'Take a break away from everything.'

'Pete says he's invited her to Singapore for a holiday, but she refuses to leave.'

'Maybe I can have a word,' said Amber.

'I'm not sure how far you'll get, but thanks,' said Josh, smiling gratefully at her.

At that moment, a courier arrived with both of Amber's suitcases. Amber was so relieved to see them that she didn't even mind that the delivery driver had managed to knock over stacks of boxes and goods when he had dragged them inside.

'I'll take them upstairs,' said Josh, grabbing one suitcase. 'I'd better do one at a time, otherwise the whole shop will end up on the floor.'

Amber giggled, just pleased to finally have all her clothes and possessions back.

'What's this?' asked Cathy, who had just returned from visiting Tilly.

'My suitcases have finally arrived,' Amber told her, beaming.

'About time!' said Cathy. 'That is good news.'

She seemed to wait until Josh had disappeared upstairs with the first suitcase.

'Perhaps it'll be a good-news day for all of us,' she added, almost to herself.

She looked so frightened suddenly that Amber found herself hurtling across to give her a hug.

'Thank you, love,' said Cathy, leaning on her for a moment before straightening up once more. 'I needed that.'

'Perhaps I could come to the hospital with you?' Amber suggested. 'For a bit of company.'

'You don't want to do that,' said Cathy, shaking her head.

'I wouldn't have offered otherwise,' Amber told her. 'And I've got nothing else to do today.'

Cathy squeezed her arm. 'That's kind of you, but I don't want to upset Josh.'

'Upset me how?'

They both jumped at the male voice behind them and turned around to find Josh standing there.

'I was offering to go with your mum this afternoon,' Amber told him, getting her words in before Cathy could speak.

'I think that's a good idea,' he said quickly.

'You do?' Cathy looked amazed.

'Of course,' he told his mum.

Cathy looked at Amber. 'Are you sure? The idea was for you to come for a bit of a break. Not work on windows and go to miserable hospital appointments.'

'I'll be fine,' said Amber.

If anything, Cathy was even more nervous on the way to the hospital. So Amber found herself chatting more than she had ever done before to fill the silence. She talked about New York, her clothes and the work she had displayed in the windows.

Thankfully she was only just running out of things to say when they arrived for Cathy's appointment.

Amber respected Cathy's wishes to be left alone and therefore sat on the chairs outside the consultant's room whilst she met with the doctor. She kept everything crossed as she waited for Cathy to reappear.

In the meantime, she saw many patients in the Oncology wing who weren't looking half as healthy as Cathy. It was hard to see so many people who were so obviously unwell. For the first time, Amber thought how difficult it must have been for Josh to go through that as a son, as well as Cathy herself.

Finally, after what felt like a very long time, Cathy left the consultant's room. To Amber's horror, her aunt's face was shiny with tears.

She was just thinking of something, anything, to say, when Cathy broke into a wide smile. 'It's OK,' she said, laughing and crying at the same time. 'They're happy tears. The consultant doesn't want to see me for a whole year.'

Then they were both laughing and crying with relief as they hugged each other.

'I'll ring Josh and then shall we have a cup of tea in the café before we head home?' said Cathy. 'And a piece of cake to celebrate. I don't want to go back yet.'

Once they had bought their lemon drizzle cake and tea, they sat down on the edge of the busy café in the hospital.

'Cheers,' said Amber, holding up her cup to chink it against Cathy's.

'Thank you,' said Cathy, still beaming from ear to ear. 'I think I'm in shock. I've worried about this appointment for weeks.'

'Well, now you can relax and not worry about it for a whole twelve months,' said Amber.

'They said they'll sign me off for good after that,' said Cathy, leaning back in her chair and sighing with relief. 'It's felt like my whole life has been on hold for so long.'

Amber nodded as she glanced around the café. 'Me too,' she found herself blurting out. Being in the hospital and seeing so many ill people had made her realise that she ought to be making the most of her life and not just let it slip by.

Cathy was startled. 'You too?'

'It doesn't matter,' said Amber, instantly regretting her words. 'Today is all about you. Not me.'

'Tell me,' urged Cathy.

Amber took a deep breath. 'My whole life seems to have stagnated. I really wasn't that happy in London or New York, to be honest.'

'A lot of people find a city overwhelming. Especially if they're a little shy.'

Amber nodded. 'I just don't know what to do next.'

Cathy leant forward to take a bite of cake. 'So why don't you stay in Cranbridge until you work out what it is you want?' she said, wiping the icing from her lips.

Amber smiled at her godmother. 'I think Mum might have something to say about that.'

'Well, I've been thinking about her as well,' said Cathy with a sheepish grin. 'Maybe I can offer your mum an alternative.'

'A different daughter?' said Amber, laughing.

'A different visitor,' said Cathy with a gleam in her eyes. 'Me.'

Amber was stunned as she remembered Josh's words from earlier. 'You want to go and see Mum?'

'I miss her so much. And Pete too. I thought I could go to Singapore and then on to New Zealand. What do you think? I feel the need to spread my wings a bit.'

Amber found herself nodding enthusiastically. 'I think it's a great idea,' she said. 'I'm sure Josh can cope in your absence in the shop and keep an eye on Tilly as well. He'll be pleased that you'll be having a break. And mum's going to be thrilled to see you.'

'I did have one more idea,' said Cathy, reaching across the table to hold Amber's hand. 'It's a huge favour to ask. Could you help out in the shop whilst I'm away? It would only be for a month, I think.'

Amber blinked at her. 'A month?'

'That would give me enough time to see Pete in Singapore before heading on to see your mum and dad,' said Cathy.

Amber was stunned. A whole month?

'It'll go really quickly, I'm sure,' Cathy added. 'Then you can leave as soon as I'm back.'

Amber really wasn't at all certain about the plans that had been suggested. But her godmother looked so happy that she found herself nodding her head in agreement.

'OK,' she said. 'Of course.'

As usual, she was sacrificing her own plans for everyone else. Except she had no plans, she reminded herself. And if anyone deserved a break, it was her godmother.

'I knew you coming to see us would make everything better,' said Cathy, squeezing her hand and smiling.

Amber nodded and smiled as well. It was a sacrifice on her part, to be sure. However, she was certain it was the best thing for Cathy to get away for a while. She was less sure about being stuck in Cranbridge with Josh for another few weeks though. But, it wasn't forever and surely the time would fly by?

She just hoped Josh would be happy about her staying on.

11

Josh had spent most of the afternoon trying not to think about his mother's appointment at the hospital.

Grandma Tilly had also come into the shop in the middle of the afternoon looking concerned.

'I didn't want to be by myself today,' she had told Josh.

But they were both climbing the walls with worry about the results by the time Cathy finally called.

However once he had passed on the good news, they had both waited for his mum to return, smiling in their joint relief.

'I come bearing great news,' said his mum, breaking into a wide smile when she finally came through the front door with Amber.

'I can't believe it's all over,' said Grandma Tilly, bursting into tears.

His mum rushed over to draw Grandma Tilly into her arms. 'Yes, Mum. They don't even want to see me for another year. And, no offence after all the wonderful work that they've done, but I don't particularly want to see them either!'

She looked over her mother's shoulder and stared at Josh. For a moment they locked eyes as they shared the relief of getting the all-clear from the hospital.

Josh found himself slumping against the counter, the realisation of how worried he'd been washing over him. It was over. Finally they could all move on from her illness.

But to what? That was almost a bigger fear than the cancer. But he wasn't going to put a dampener on things at that moment when everyone was so relieved.

'I have other good news,' said his mum, glancing at Amber. 'Well, it's an idea actually.'

'There's room for more good news?' said Tilly, bringing out her handkerchief and wiping her cheeks. 'What else is there to come?'

His mum looked at Josh. 'I've talked it over with Amber and I want to go and see Pete in Singapore.'

Josh was staggered. He'd only shared a brief conversation with Amber about his idea for his mum to have a holiday, but she appeared to have worked wonders.

He looked at Amber, who gave him a small nod as if to confirm that it was indeed true.

'I rang Pete after I talked to you,' his mum continued. 'He even wants to pay for the plane ticket over there.'

Thank goodness, thought Josh because he didn't really have any more spare money to play with. Of course, had he any savings, he would have spent them all on his mum. She deserved this.

Tilly clapped her hands together. 'Oh, what a splendid idea! I'd come with you if I had a passport.'

'You can always apply and come with me,' his mum suggested.

But Grandma Tilly was shaking her head. 'Oh no. I never enjoyed travelling on planes at the best of times. I couldn't travel that far.'

Josh was pleased for his mum, but his mind was reeling with the practicalities.

'I know what you're thinking,' she said, looking at him. 'You're worried about the shop.'

I'm always worried about the shop, he thought but stayed silent.

'Well, I've got good news on that too,' his mum continued. 'Amber has kindly agreed to stay on whilst I'm away.'

Josh was stunned. He looked across at Amber, who was blushing furiously and not making eye contact with anyone.

'Don't you want to head on and see your parents?' he asked, thinking it was too much of a sacrifice. Surely she didn't want to hang around Cranbridge when she could be making a fresh start in New Zealand?

But his mum beat her to the reply. 'It'll be a bit crowded, seeing as I'm hoping to hop on a plane when I'm over in Singapore and go and see them as well! Look, it's all sorted. I'll talk to Denise tonight when the time difference is a bit better. Amber's offered to stay here and keep you both company and then she can leave when I return.'

'I think it's a marvellous idea,' said Grandma Tilly, reaching out to squeeze Amber's arm.

Josh was trying to think of a downside, but his mind was reeling with the sheer amount of information he'd received in the past five minutes. Not least the fact that his mum was going to Singapore and New Zealand.

'Well, it seems as if you've got it all figured out,' he finally said.

Mother and son locked eyes once more. He wanted to say more, but there were too many people around.

'Well, this calls for a proper celebration,' said Tilly.

'I agree,' his mum said. 'Let's go to the pub for a drink!'

'Twice in one week? I'd better change my cardigan.' Tilly smiled. 'I can't wear this old thing. Amber, be a dear and walk me back, would you? I feel a little unsteady after all this excitement.'

'Of course,' said Amber.

As they left the shop, Josh thought that his remarkable grandmother was many things but not particularly subtle. But he was grateful for the chance to be alone with his mum for a moment.

'I'm sorry to land all this on you,' she told him as soon as it was just the two of them.

'That's OK,' he said. 'I've been trying to get you to go and see Pete for a long time.'

'I know,' she said, sighing heavily. 'I just wasn't ready, I guess. I needed to know that the damn stuff was gone for good before I could move on. Finally it feels as if I can have a clean break.' She studied him. 'You need one too, I think. From me.'

He slumped down on the stool behind the counter. 'I'm sorry,' he said, shaking his head. 'I've been so angry these past two years. I didn't mean to take it out on you.'

'I'm sorry too,' she told him, coming over to stand on the other side of the counter. 'I should have realised that it's been all about me.'

He shrugged his shoulders. 'So it should. You were seriously ill.'

'But we were both grieving,' she said softly.

There was a pause and the shop was silent for a while.

'I miss Dad,' he found himself saying.

'Me too,' his mum said, nodding.

The silence stretched out between them, but for once it was comfortable.

'I think it's a good idea that you go and see Pete,' he finally said. 'Get a break from all this.' He waved his arm around at the crowded shop.

'About that,' his mum began, taking a deep breath. 'You said you've got some ideas about how to best update things around here. Well, perhaps you could get on with all that whilst I'm away.'

Josh looked up at his mum. 'Are you sure?'

'It's time.' She appeared to gulp back some tears. 'I had a good chat with Amber at the hospital. I've been holding on to this place for so long, trying to keep it as it was in the past. But the past is just that, the past. I think we could all do with moving on.'

'I don't want to upset you by changing things too much,' he told her.

'I believe in you,' his mum said. 'You'll do what's right when the time comes.' She hesitated before adding, 'If you think it will save the shop, then do whatever you think necessary. It's been in the family for so many years, I couldn't bear it if we lost it like this.'

It was then that he realised that she had always known how treacherous their financial situation was. But that the fear of her illness returning had stopped her from having the strength to face it.

'I'm not sure what I can do to stop us from losing this place,' he said.

'Just do your best,' she told him, with a soft smile. 'That's all you can do. Besides, I'm sure you grandmother will keep an eye on you.'

Josh took a deep breath and stood up. 'One more throw of the dice then,' he said.

His mum's smile grew wider. 'Now you sound just like your dad.'

'Good,' he said, trying to sound stronger than he felt. 'We could do with a bit of his nerve and self-belief around here.'

'Yes, I think we could,' his mum replied, nodding. 'But we have you, which is even better, I think.' She stepped forward and they hugged each other.

'I'm so pleased it's all gone,' he murmured into her shoulder.

There were tears in his mum's eyes when she finally stepped back to look at him. 'Me too. And now we have Amber to help us as well,' she said, reaching out to stroke down a stray lock of his hair.

'Are you sure that she really wants to stay on here?' he asked.

'She assures me that she does,' said his mum.

Josh wasn't so sure about that. Amber seemed happy to please everyone but herself. It touched his heart that she was doing this for his mother, but to sacrifice herself to be stuck in Cranbridge for another month was really pushing it, he thought.

'She's got a real eye for design,' his mum added, glancing over at the front of the shop. 'Those windows are lovely. Maybe she can do something with all this as well.'

Josh laughed. 'That's a bit of a tough ask, to be honest, Mum.'

'Come on,' she said, giving him a nudge. 'Let's lock up early and meet them both out in the lane. No one else is coming in today.'

After he had drawn the locks across on the front door and flipped the sign over to read Closed, they weaved their way through the shop.

'I haven't wanted to leave you alone, but you're ready,' said his mum over her shoulder to him. 'And you've got a partner in Amber.'

Josh gave the shop one last glance. He wasn't sure what either of them could do to make a real difference to the shop's income, but in a small way he was grateful that he wasn't facing it alone. And he realised that he was actually a tiny bit glad that Amber was going to stay on in Cranbridge, if only for the next four weeks.

12

'It's just for a month.'

Amber looked out at the river, which was flowing much faster that morning after some heavy overnight rain. She adjusted the mobile which she was holding up to her ear and looked up at the grey sky. More rain was forecast that day. At that moment, the sunny skies of a New Zealand summer seemed even more appealing than before.

'And anyway, you can't stay with us at the moment,' her mum carried on. 'Now that Cathy's coming over to stay for a couple of weeks, the spare bedroom will be taken. You don't want to sleep on the sofa at your age. Gosh, I've still got so much to sort before she arrives. We've barely unpacked yet and the sheep haven't even arrived yet.'

Despite her panic, there was excitement in her mum's voice and Amber realised just how thrilled she was about Cathy's visit.

It had only been a couple of days after her hospital appointment, but Cathy's airline ticket to Singapore had been booked for later that afternoon. As it was still during the school term, Josh's brother Pete had managed to find his mum a last-minute single-way ticket at a heavily discounted price.

'Cathy's left her flight open-ended in case she wants to stay out here a bit longer,' carried on her mum.

'As long as I arrive in time to decorate the Christmas tree,' said Amber, thinking that Cathy's holiday was suddenly sounding a lot longer than a month. So much for spending some quality time with her godmother. But she knew she was just being selfish because this trip would be just what Cathy needed.

'Oh, I don't want to think about Christmas at the moment,' said her mum. 'How am I going to roast a turkey in this summer heat? And your father is so busy with the farm that I barely see him.'

'Maybe we can do a barbecue instead,' said Amber. 'You've got to go with the flow now that you're not in England any more.'

'Don't remind me,' muttered her mum.

There was a short silence. 'Is everything OK over there?' asked Amber.

'Of course! Now, what was I saying? Oh yes, do you think Cathy would like the pink or the pale blue duvet cover? She'll be shattered from the long journey anyway.'

As her mum carried on chatting about how much she had to do, Amber focused on the view. Autumn was rushing in with a vengeance as the leaves changed from cool greens and sunny yellows to rich oranges, fiery reds and earthy browns. There were worse places to be, she considered, other than a pretty village in the countryside.

Of course, New York had Central Park, which had been lovely in the various seasons. But having grown up in mostly country villages, the constant hum of the traffic and sirens had always slightly unsettled her. So Cranbridge's peace was welcome, if still a little eerie in its emptiness.

Perhaps the peace and quiet would give her time to plan what her future held, thought Amber. She could decide what the next chapter of her life would be once she left the village.

As she turned on the spot to face Cranbridge Stores, her positivity faltered somewhat. It was, and there was no other word she could think of to describe it, quite a depressing shop. So muddled, so full, the air felt musty and sad.

But, like her mum said, it was just for another month. Hopefully.

And Cathy was so excited about her upcoming holiday that she didn't have the heart to say anything about not wanting to stay. In fact, the last couple of days had been spent in such a whirlwind, with Cathy giddier than Amber had ever seen.

It had all been swiftly arranged that Cathy was going to stay with Josh's brother, Pete, and then on to see Amber's parents in New Zealand for a while.

'It makes sense seeing as I'm already halfway across the world in Singapore,' she said, beaming. 'I've got lots of shopping in those markets to do whilst I'm out there though.'

'Not too much!' protested Josh, even though he was smiling. 'We don't have room for anything else in the shop!'

Amber thought he was far more attractive when he smiled rather than when he was in default grumpy mode.

Cathy giggled and gave Amber a wink. Amber thought that the fresh air and seeing her youngest son and then her best friend would do her godmother the world of good. Cathy had even been talking about taking a dip in the Pacific Ocean and heading up into the mountains.

But, in addition, getting the all-clear from the hospital seemed to have opened Cathy's eyes up to a whole world of possibilities at home as well as on holiday.

'At least it'll give you both a chance to tidy up the shop a bit once I'm out of your way,' she had told them the previous evening as the three of them ate their dinner in the flat.

Amber had looked surprised as she'd turned to Josh. 'I'm sure we could think of something,' she'd said slowly.

Josh had appeared to take a deep breath before speaking. 'Even if we have to rearrange most of the shop?' he'd said in a soft tone.

The silence rang out for a while as Cathy looked at her son. Finally, and to his obvious relief, she had nodded her head. 'I don't see why not.'

Josh's mouth had dropped open and he'd looked at Amber for confirmation. But she was feeling as stunned as he was. Having been so adamant for so long that no changes were to be made to the shop, the last thing she had been expecting was for Cathy to have a complete change of heart.

Cathy had looked over at Amber, her face suddenly worried. 'What do you think?'

Amber had flicked a quick look at Josh. 'I think that it's a good idea,' she'd said tentatively. 'Much like getting new clothes for your holiday. Everyone and everything needs a refresh every once in a while. Even the shop.'

'Well then,' Cathy had said with a firm nod, turning to look at her son, 'I'll give you both carte blanche whilst I'm away.'

Josh had laughed. 'Are you sure about that?'

His mum had reached out and squeezed his arm. 'Quite sure,' she'd told him. 'I trust you. You won't let me down.'

Amber had watched as mother and son exchanged a tender look before Cathy straightened up. 'Now, I've been thinking that I may need another suitcase to take with me,' she'd said.

'For more clothes?' Josh had said, still smiling as he raised his eyebrows in mock surprise.

Cathy had been rushing around packing up the new clothes that she had treated herself to in Aldwych town.

'It's only Primark,' Cathy had said the previous afternoon, bundling the massive brown paper bag quickly out of sight.

Not only had Cathy picked up a few different clothes, she had also dyed her hair and treated herself to a haircut. She was suddenly looking a lot younger than she had appeared until recently and Amber had found herself realising that Cathy was still only in her mid-fifties.

Josh had spent a lot of time muttering about the petty cash going missing, but he was definitely smiling a bit more. It was hard to stay grumpy with Cathy so cheerful and the excitement about the holiday all around them.

On the day of her departure, as Josh placed the suitcases inside the van, Cathy took a long look around the shop before smiling at Amber.

'I'll miss the old place, of course. But I feel like I'm coming alive again,' said Cathy, drawing her into a hug. 'Like I've been stuck on pause for the past few years.'

Amber nodded. 'Have an amazing holiday. You deserve it.'

She felt somewhat homesick for her parents, but she knew that she would be heading out to New Zealand to join them in a month's time so she knew it wouldn't be for long.

'I'm sure I've forgotten something,' said Cathy. 'I'll just check one last time.'

As she rushed upstairs, Amber went to where Josh was standing with Grandma Tilly next to the van.

'Where's she gone now?' asked Grandma Tilly, a little impatiently.

'Just double-checking that she hasn't forgotten anything,' Amber told her.

Grandma Tilly sighed. 'I'll go and hurry her up. It would be a fine to-do if she missed her flight after all this fuss!'

Amber stood next to Josh as they waited outside on their own. It would be awkward, to be sure, to be left alone with Josh. But there was a tiny bit of excitement deep within as she wondered what on earth they could achieve between them.

'Your mum's going to have a wonderful time,' she said.

He nodded. 'Yeah. She deserves a break.'

'Absolutely. You never thought about maybe heading out to see your brother in Singapore?'

He blew out a sigh as he turned to face her. 'Can't afford it,' he said. 'Besides, there was no one to help run the shop with Mum if I went away.'

'Of course,' she said, then hesitated before saying, 'it's a good thing I'm here then.'

He looked up at her in surprise and smiled. 'Maybe it is.'

'I guess the pay is invisible, right?' she joked.

'Free bed and board though,' he added, before his smiled faded. 'Is this all OK with you? I get the feeling that Mum kind of railroaded you into staying.'

'I need somewhere to stay,' she told him. 'And your mum wants me to decorate the shop before she gets back.'

'If you can find a clear surface somewhere in there,' he said, turning his head as his mum and Grandma Tilly finally came out of the shop.

'Are you sure you'll be all right here on your own?' Cathy asked Josh for the twentieth time as she came up to them.

Josh rolled his eyes. 'Yes, Mum.'

'I know! I know!' she said, smiling. 'You won't miss my nagging, will you?' She then stepped forward to give her son a hug. 'You know you've been my rock these past few years,' she murmured. 'Thank you.'

Amber watched as Josh remained quiet for a moment but squeezed her back in return.

Finally they straightened up. 'Anyway, I won't be on my own, will I?' said Josh. 'Grandma's told me that she's going to keep an eye on us.'

'I'll keep an eye on them both,' said Grandma Tilly, with a wink. 'Don't fret.'

So it was a happy round of teary goodbyes, bear hugs and 'I'll text you when I land' from Cathy.

Grandma Tilly was also beaming and looking excited for her daughter. 'First stop, duty free!' she said, laughing as Cathy got into the van.

Then with a final wave and shout of 'goodbye', Josh started up the van engine and off they went around the corner, disappearing from sight.

Amber stood in the chilly autumnal air and wondered just what she'd let herself in for. The future of Cranbridge Stores had been left in her and Josh's hands. She just hoped she was up to the job.

13

It had been a slightly awkward evening with Amber, thought Josh. They had made a bit of small talk when he had arrived back from dropping his mum off at the airport before they had both gone to their separate bedrooms.

Luckily Cathy's plane took off only ten minutes late and he had woken up that morning relieved to find that it had landed safely in Singapore.

He had already received a number of texts and photos with his mum and brother grinning in some kind of tropical garden.

He was pleased. They were safe and happy.

He was also slightly envious of the blue skies and change of scenery. After all, he was still stuck in Cranbridge with the shop.

But at least he could finally change the inside. So he found himself feeling slightly more optimistic than he had done for a while. Staring around the shop, he tried to imagine how different it could look. For a start, there was too much clutter in the space. Boxes definitely needed to be removed, but where to put them? The back room was just as full as the shop itself.

He had no idea what to do next and was almost grateful when Grandma Tilly came into the shop.

'How are you getting on?' she asked.

'I honestly don't know where to start,' Josh told her.

Grandma Tilly nodded as she looked around the crowded space. 'It's certainly a bit busy in here. Of course, it never used to look like this.'

'How did it look?' asked Amber, coming in from the back room.

'Oh, it was quite different,' said Tilly. 'My father-in law ran a tight ship. Of course, it was all loose goods and branded items on the shelves come the 1950s. Myself and my mother-in law weren't even allowed on the shop floor. Anyway, it's best we've got equality these days. Women's lib and all that. I hated being stuck upstairs. I used to sneak out to go to the dance hall in Aldwych.'

'Such a rebel,' said Amber, with a soft smile.

Grandma Tilly's smile grew wider. 'I really was.'

'So, it didn't look like this?' said Josh, waving his arm around.

'It was far emptier in those days,' said Grandma Tilly. 'Thanks to the rationing after the war. There wasn't much food about. Or money either, to be honest. My father-in law would sell things on credit. Folks weren't getting paid so they had to borrow.'

'That doesn't sound like very good business,' said Josh.

Grandma Tilly shook her head. 'We were a community in those days. We knew everyone and they knew us. It was a matter of trust. They were Cranbridge families. We knew every name and person who came through that door.'

'Times change,' said Josh, feeling almost sad that he didn't have that kind of connection with the village.

'As long as kindness doesn't,' said Grandma Tilly.

'So, when did the shop become more full?' asked Amber. 'After rationing had stopped?'

'Oh yes,' said Grandma Tilly, nodding. 'It was all so exciting in the sixties when I was growing up. Your grandfather had changed the shop. We lost the big downstairs kitchen and moved everything upstairs. Then all the little kiddies would come in for their sweets.' Grandma Tilly smacked her gums together in memory. 'It felt like a proper corner shop with tubs of sweets behind the till.'

Josh had a sudden memory of Grandma Tilly giving him and his brother a paper bag full of sweets. He could remember the excitement even now. How had he forgotten?

Grandma Tilly picked up her handbag. 'Right. I'd best get off. My morning soap starts in half an hour.'

After she had left, Josh couldn't help but smile and raise his eyebrows at Amber. 'Are you sure you haven't changed your mind about staying? My grandmother will want to tell you all of her stories.'

'I think she's a little lonely,' Amber told him.

Josh nodded. 'Village life can be pretty quiet.'

'I'm sure it can be,' she said, looking at him for a longer moment before looking away.

Did she mean him? Josh wasn't sure. He wasn't lonely, as such. He was just a bit restless. That was all.

But doing up the shop would at least keep that at bay for another month whilst they updated the place.

He dragged his hand through his hair, somewhat overwhelmed. He had dreamed of this day for so long when he had free rein to sort out and clear the shop. But now he was coming up with a complete blank, as if frightened that he would make things even worse.

He looked at Amber. 'So, what do you think?' he asked. 'I mean, where do you think we should start in sorting out all of this?'

Amber sighed as she looked around the space. 'It's so hard because it's so, er...' Her voice trailed off.

'Busy? Packed? Completely overcrowded?' he said.

She smiled. 'Just a little bit,' she told him. 'If you look past all this stuff in the middle of the shop, it's actually quite wide. In fact, when Tilly showed me the empty shop next door, which is the same layout, I was amazed at the actual amount of space that you really have in here.'

'Come and show me then,' he said, leading the way out of the shop.

They walked to the empty place next door and peered in through the windows.

'It's big,' he said, surprised as he stared at the space. 'Really big.'

'There's actually plenty of space,' said Amber, as she straightened up. 'You've got tall ceilings, so there's plenty of room at the sides of the shop for some high shelves. It's just the rest of the room is so cluttered. It feels pretty oppressive in there.' She stopped and blushed, as if she had gone too far with her words. 'But that's just my opinion,' she added quickly.

'Good job that I agree with you,' he told her, causing a smile to light up her pretty face. 'So, where do we begin?'

'Let's head back,' she said and they went back inside Cranbridge Stores.

It looked even worse than usual, with the damp dreary weather outside not giving any extra light.

Amber sighed. 'It's so hard when everything is in the way,' she said.

'I think we should just start from scratch,' he said. It was an idea that he had often dreamt about. 'Clear everything out from in here.'

Amber looked startled. 'The whole shop? You mean giving it a total overhaul?'

'I think we should start with a blank canvas.' He shrugged his shoulders. 'It could certainly do with a lick of paint in here and I can't do that until everything's out. We could move it to the back room and just operate out of there.'

Amber frowned. 'But won't it be a bit tight for space in there with the tractor. It's already pretty crowded back there.'

Josh blew out a sigh. 'Yeah.'

Amber hesitated before speaking. 'Look, I hope you don't mind, but I had a look online at the value of this kind of tractor. Being a classic vehicle and all that. It could be worth quite a bit of money. You know, a couple of thousand pounds.'

Josh looked up at her in surprise. 'Really?'

Amber nodded. 'That could pay for the renovations that you want to do around here.'

The silence stretched out for a beat whilst Josh struggled with his inner turmoil. Finally he sighed. 'Maybe it's time it went.'

'But I understand that it has huge sentimental value to both you and your mum?' said Amber.

'More to me than Mum, to be honest,' he lied, his heart feeling heavy. 'But we can't move back there. I thought I could get it dragged out the front of the shop.'

'What's wrong with the back door?' said Amber, looking a little alarmed.

'When I replaced the doors back there, I thought we could do with a single one. So we've blocked up the rest of it with the bricks.' He rolled his eyes. 'I didn't think about the tractor at the time.' He looked at the front door. 'So that's the only entrance with double doors and the only way we'll be able to get it out of here.'

'And then what will you do with it?' she asked.

'I don't know,' he said, in all honesty. 'Drive it around the shop and leave it outside in the back lane until Mum gets home. Perhaps I can persuade her to sell it.'

Amber bit her lip, frowning in worry. 'It seems a bit drastic,' she told him.

'It's like you said,' he told her. 'We need the space. We'll have to clear a bit in here first, of course. There's some stuff that we'll need to get rid of to make space. It's like some kind of puzzle, but we'll work it out.'

He had been semi-joking, but his heart almost broke with the thought of his dad's beloved tractor being sold. It wasn't much, but it had been such a big part of their lives for so long. But he had to be honest with himself. It was in the way and, anyway, if the shop was going to get repossessed by the bank, it would still need to be moved out.

The sooner the better, he thought. Like a plaster needing to be ripped off, the tractor had to go. He just hoped the remaining scar left behind on his heart wouldn't be too deep.

14

Keeping her promise to Cathy to look out for Grandma Tilly, Amber walked up Riverside Lane to visit her.

She was anxious to keep out of Josh's way whilst he worked out what could be done with the shop anyway. After all, it was his responsibility and she would probably just get in the way.

The weather had turned a little and Amber was glad that her suitcases had arrived as she was able to pull on her black parka coat to keep out the rain and cold wind.

As she walked, she noted that nobody was around. Stanley and Frank had been the only customers in the shop so far that day.

'Good morning,' she said, as Tilly opened the front door.

'There's a welcome face,' said Tilly beaming. 'Good morning to you too. Come on in.'

Amber followed Tilly into the bungalow. To her surprise, the kitchen table was piled up with boxes.

'What's all this?' asked Amber, as she took off her coat.

'I'm still sorting out from my move,' said Tilly, flicking on the kettle. 'Those boxes had been piled up in the corner of the bedroom and I nearly tripped over them this morning. I thought perhaps you could put them on top of the wardrobe for me.'

'Of course,' said Amber, peering inside one of the open boxes. 'Are they all photo albums?'

Tilly nodded. 'Oh yes. Some are years old. Would you like to have a look at a couple? If you have the time, of course. I know you and my grandson are busy in the shop.'

Amber heard Tilly's soft sigh as she poured out their coffee.

'I've got plenty of time,' Amber told her. 'Shall I pick out a couple of albums and take them into the lounge?'

Tilly smiled again. 'That sounds like a plan. I'll find some biscuits.'

Once they had settled down on the armchairs in the lounge, Amber opened up the first photo album. It was full of photographs from when Josh and his brother were young boys.

'How sweet,' said Amber, showing Tilly a photograph of the boys paddling in the river. 'Is that Cranbridge?'

'Yes,' said Tilly. 'They always used to visit us every summer. Then when my husband passed away, they all moved in.' She smiled to herself. 'The flat was suddenly full of life, shouting and laughter. I do miss those times.'

Amber thought that the bungalow was perhaps even quieter than the shop these days.

'There's Todd,' said Amber, looking at a photograph of him playing his guitar. 'I barely remember him, I'm afraid. Except that he was fun and sort of animated all the time.'

'Absolutely,' said Tilly, nodding. 'He had such an enthusiasm for life. He had a big hearty laugh that you could hear three doors away. He was so gifted as well. He used to sit on the veranda on my husband's rocking chair and play his guitar. Such a talent.'

'Have the boys inherited his gift for music?' asked Amber.

'Pete has,' said Tilly. 'He's really good, although I haven't heard him play for years. Not Josh, I don't think. I mean, he's a good lad but not particularly creative in that way.'

'But he was good at his job,' said Amber.

'Oh yes,' Tilly told her. 'Earned quite a bit of money as well, from what I heard. He was always going on about climate change and trying to be greener.' She frowned. 'He doesn't do that so much these days.'

'I guess he's had a lot on his mind,' said Amber.

'I suppose.'

The next album they looked at was much further back in time.

'This was Bill's,' said Tilly, as Amber peered at the faded black and white photograph dated 1900.

'How amazing,' said Amber. She looked more closely at the photograph. 'And that's the shop?'

Tilly nodded. 'Those were the days,' she said. 'They sold black twist tobacco by the inch.'

Amber couldn't believe how different it looked. 'So much of the food was loose produce,' she said, studying the crates and baskets full of fresh fruit and vegetables.

'Even the flour and butter had to be measured out. Nothing was in tins or plastic in those days,' said Tilly. 'Not until later on, before the Second World War. Then it all changed again.' She flicked through a few of the pages to a photograph that read 1938. 'There, you see? How everything is more mass-produced?'

Amber peered at the photograph. The shop had definitely changed.

'Only the bell above the door is the same,' she said.

'And me,' said Tilly before frowning. 'Or rather not when I think about my grey hair. And that I'm not part of it any more.'

Amber saw that Tilly was looking upset. 'I'm sure you could come and help out whenever you wanted to in the shop,' she said quickly.

Tilly shook her head. 'I tripped and almost broke my wrist last year. Cathy and Josh don't want me hurting myself, so they said.'

'Then perhaps once we've tidied the place up a bit you could come in,' said Amber.

'Perhaps,' Tilly replied, with a small smile. 'It would be nice to feel useful again.' She sighed. 'Otherwise I'm just sitting here with the television on. I haven't even got anything to knit at the moment.'

She pointed to what appeared to be a bag full of knitting needles and balls of wool.

'What do you normally make?' asked Amber.

'Blankets for cots, little hats and scarves.' Tilly shrugged. 'Anything really.'

As Tilly retreated into a bit of a gloom, Amber thought quickly as to how she could keep her busy.

'Tell you what,' she said. 'Maybe you could make me and Mum a blanket each. It would be lovely to have something home-made for a change.'

Tilly's face brightened up. 'You'd want something like that? A bit old-fashioned, don't you think?'

Amber shook her head. 'Traditional,' she told her. 'That's the difference. And I'd know that you'd made it. Think how chuffed Mum would be when I show it to her when I arrive. It could even be a Christmas gift.'

Grandma Tilly's face faltered for a moment. 'Well, hopefully we can keep you for a bit longer before then.'

However, by the time Amber left, Tilly looked far more cheerful and was talking colours and patterns for the blankets. As Amber walked back down Riverside Lane, she at least felt as if she had helped in some small way to cheer Tilly up. She was hoping it would be as easy with Josh, but she very much doubted it, given the scale of the shop's problems.

15

After returning from visiting Grandma Tilly's bungalow, Amber grabbed a sweatshirt to put on.

Although it was a brighter day, the sun had less warmth now and the nights were beginning to grow colder. In fact, she had had to find an extra blanket on the bed the previous night.

She peered out of the shop window, where there was a cold mist rising from the river in the low sunlight. Autumn had definitely arrived. Although not, unfortunately, many more customers.

Despite the shop windows looking vastly improved, there hadn't been a rush of people actually come in. She had spotted a couple of people stopping and staring at the new window display but they appeared hesitant to make the first move and come over the threshold.

Was it any wonder? she thought, shivering in the cool air of the shop.

'Isn't there ever any heating in here?' she asked, stamping her Uggs on the wooden floor to get some warmth in them.

Josh looked up from the box that he had been opening. 'All the old radiators are hidden behind all of this,' he told her, waving his arm around at all the stock piled high. 'I guess I'm sort of immune to it by now. I think Grandma wears thermal underwear, if you wanted to go down that route.'

His grin was positively flirtatious and she found herself blushing furiously in response.

'I think we'll leave my underwear out of it,' she muttered. 'How come you've never thought to sort out the heating in here before now?'

Josh carried on smiling which unnerved her slightly. Grumpy Josh she could deal with. She found smiling Josh was a little unsettling.

'To be honest, I've always thought it was such a health and safety nightmare in here that the whole lot would go up in flames if I tried to switch the radiators back on,' he told her. 'But I had a new boiler installed upstairs, so at least the flat stays warm.'

Amber looked around at all the cardboard everywhere. 'So, where do we start?'

Josh blew out a sigh. 'I have no idea, to be honest. I've dreamt of this day for so long, but now that we're here I can't think straight.'

His easy demeanour had dropped suddenly.

Amber looked around, trying to see a clear way through the muddle. 'Look, how about we just start in the middle,' she finally said. 'We'll just take it one pile of stuff at a time.'

She was surprised that Josh was a bit nervous about tackling the shop, but it wasn't hard to see why. The sheer amount of stuff in the shop was incredible and overwhelming.

She looked out at the teetering pile of baked bean tins that were piled up on top of a cardboard box. 'So, we've got tinned goods,' she said.

'Better check the dates,' said Josh, with a grimace. 'I'm not sure how long they've been here.'

Thankfully the beans were in date, as were the tinned tomatoes and jars of coffee that they found in the next few boxes.

'So how about we get all the food together?' she suggested.

Josh nodded. 'Sounds like a plan.'

Amber placed them all on the counter for the time being, leaving a space so they could still reach the till.

She suddenly remembered what Grandma Tilly had said about Todd playing music all of the time and looked around at the shop, empty and silent apart from Josh. 'Why don't we put some music on whilst we work?' she asked.

Josh straightened up from the pile of stationery he had been sorting out. 'Music?' he said, before clearing his throat.

'Grandma Tilly said there always used to be music playing somewhere in the shop and flat,' said Amber.

Josh looked downcast. 'I don't think Mum likes to hear it any more.'

'But your mum's not here at the moment,' said Amber, keeping her voice gentle. 'Anyway, it's just an idea. I thought it might help pass the time a bit quicker.'

Josh nodded thoughtfully but didn't say anything, so Amber peered into the next crate.

'Paint?' she said. 'What do you want me to do with that?'

'Paint?' Josh came over to have a look. 'White emulsion,' he said, rolling his eyes. 'God knows where he got this from. Hardware stuff pile, I think.'

'So your dad was the main buyer?' she asked, carrying some stock cubes over to join the rest of the food pile.

'Yeah,' said Josh, blowing out a sigh. 'He loved the randomness of stuff. His brain was always a bit helter-skelter, you know, going here there and everywhere. It certainly made the school holidays fun.'

'In what way?'

Josh smiled in memory. 'He would announce we were going away and we'd have ten minutes to pack up the car. There was a big tent that we used to use and pitch up whenever we found somewhere decent to camp.'

'Who ran the shop whilst you were away?' asked Amber.

'Grandma Tilly,' he said. 'She never used to mind. Said it kept her busy after she'd been widowed.'

He frowned suddenly.

'What is it?' said Amber.

'Do you think that's what Mum's been doing these past two years? With the shop, I mean?' He looked at her.

Amber nodded. 'I think so. When times are difficult, it's sink or swim for most people. Your mum chose to deal with her grief and illness by keeping busy in the shop. It was her safety net.'

'What's yours?'

The question startled her. 'What do you mean?'

'I mean, Mum's is the shop. I try and get the tractor going,' he told her, with a grimace. 'Although I've pretty much failed with that as the engine doesn't seem to run for very long at all. What do you do in stressful times?'

Amber hesitated before speaking. After all, it wasn't a huge deal. 'I draw. Ideas for shop windows, that kind of thing.'

'That's right,' said Josh. 'You were always drawing, even when we were young.'

'That's my safety net,' she told him.

He looked down at the pile of stuff in his hands. 'I've got screw-drivers and screws so that's for the hardware pile.'

Amber was grateful to concentrate back on tidying the shop. Being the centre of anyone's attention was never her idea of calm, especially with Josh, she found.

The randomness of the goods that they found staggered even Amber. There were biscuits, some out of date. Balls of wool. Books. Wrapping paper. Light bulbs. Sweets.

'Why do we need five boxes of plain paper bags?' said Josh, after a while. He blew out a sigh. 'Well, at least they can be recycled, I suppose.' He gave a snort of derision. 'My God, if my former clients saw this place, they'd never employ me again. This place is the least sustainable place I've ever come across and that's saying something, believe me.'

Amber tipped out some out-of-date biscuits into a compost bag so that they could recycle the box and plastic they were wrapped in. 'Would you ever go back to it? Your consultancy work, I mean.'

Josh shrugged his shoulders. 'I've been thinking about it, you know, if or when the business fails.'

His eyes dropped and Amber could feel how sad that made him.

'Perhaps it won't come to that,' she finally said.

He gave her a sad smile. 'Perhaps.'

By late afternoon, they had begun to clear about a quarter of the clutter in the middle of the shop. There was now a large pile of food by the till. Another pile in the corner by the window which was hardware. A third pile was paper goods and stationery. And the last pile was stuff that they had no idea what to call, made up of wool, wellington boots, umbrellas, rolls of material and even sunglasses.

'At least we can recycle all these empty boxes,' said Josh, carrying out yet another pile of flattened cardboard onto the veranda. 'I hate the thought of all of this going to landfill.'

But as they began to clear, it soon became obvious that some of the stock couldn't be sold. There were packets and tins of food that were almost out of date.

'I'm sure Grandma Tilly said something about a tombola at church,' he said. 'I must remember to ask her so we can donate them.'

So they boxed up those items and put them to one side upstairs so that they wouldn't get muddled up with all the other food.

With the shelves in the middle of the shop now empty, they each took an end of one of the shelving units and shuffled towards the front door. Josh pinned open both doors so that there was just enough room to carry it out onto the veranda and then around to the lane that ran alongside the shop.

As they put it down on the ground with relief, Josh said, 'I'll put it back once we've cleaned it and maybe given it a coat of paint.'

But when they went back into the shop, he appeared to change his mind.

'Maybe we shouldn't replace the centre shelves when we've cleaned up.'

'I agree,' said Amber. 'It feels so much bigger now that we can see the middle of the room.'

It was still far too cluttered, she thought. For a moment she remembered how it had looked in Grandma Tilly's photographs in 1900. It had seemed so warm and welcoming, full of character and life. But that was in a different time. Things had to change, she supposed.

They decided to carry on clearing the area in the middle of the shop, leaving the shelves up against the two opposing walls for the next day. As it was Sunday, the shop shut at four o'clock in the afternoon so they were able to carry on uninterrupted. Although, in truth, they hadn't seen a single customer since before they started cleaning.

It was dusty and grimy work, but Amber was finding it hugely satisfying to begin to organise the clutter.

As she removed yet another tall pile of boxes, she realised with pleasure that there was an attractive wood-burning stove and fireplace on one wall that had been completely hidden from view.

'Oh, it's so pretty,' she said.

The bricks in the fireplace had been left in their original bare state, with a thick oak beam running across as a mantelpiece. Underneath the black stove was a large slab of grey slate for the hearth.

Josh stared and blew out a sigh. 'I'd forgotten it was here, to be honest,' he told her.

'It would certainly help with the temperature in here,' she said. 'And it's a great feature.'

'You think?' asked Josh, looking surprised.

'Maybe if it's not so cold, people might linger in the shop a bit longer and spend a bit more money,' she told him.

Josh laughed. 'Amber Green! You're secretly a hard-nosed businesswoman!'

She smiled. 'Not really. I'd just like to bring back the feeling in my fingers and toes on a daily basis.'

They carried on clearing a few more boxes until finally, as it grew dark outside, they decided to stop.

'Thank you,' Josh said, turning to face her. 'I don't think I'd have had the courage to even start sorting out this place if you hadn't been here.'

'You're welcome,' she told him, blushing.

'Maybe Mum's right,' he said.

She looked up at him for clarification and found his blue eyes burning into hers.

'Perhaps things have changed for the better since you've arrived,' he added.

'I'm not so sure about that,' she told him, brushing off the faint praise. 'Well, what do you think about baked beans on toast for dinner?'

'Only if they're in date,' he said, still watching her.

She quickly walked away and up the stairs. Sometimes the way he looked at her made her catch her breath. But he probably looked at everyone like that. He was quite an intense person.

And she was almost sure that her quickening pulse was nothing to do with the fact that he was becoming more good-looking in her eyes with each passing day.

16

Later that week, Amber had just finished clearing yet another pile of goods in the shop when Josh handed over his mobile for her to take a call.

'I hope you're both not working too hard,' said Cathy, as soon as Amber had picked up the phone.

'We're fine,' said Amber. 'Don't worry.'

Josh rolled his eyes at her, having already endured a lengthy phone call of concern.

'How's Singapore?' asked Amber, eager to change the subject.

'Oh, it's amazing!' said Cathy. Amber could feel her smiling down the phone line. 'Pete's taking me to Raffles Hotel for tea at the weekend when he finishes work.'

Amber had already got the impression that both the brothers were equally hardworking.

'I heard from Mum last night,' Amber told her. 'She's so excited.'

'Me too,' said Cathy. 'I've got another ten days here and then I'm heading on to New Zealand. I'm not sure how long I'll be staying there.'

Amber nodded thoughtfully to herself. As she had suspected, Cathy's holiday was stretching out longer than originally planned. But she found she didn't mind. She was enjoying helping Josh reorganise the shop.

After they had finished chatting, she handed the phone back to Josh.

'She sounds as if she's having a nice time with your brother,' said Amber.

Josh glanced around the messy shop. 'Lucky her,' he said. 'We'll both need a holiday after all of this.'

Amber looked around. They appeared to have made more mess than when they had started, or so it felt.

'Maybe I'm not very good at this,' she said, her fears and doubts bubbling to the surface as usual.

Josh looked at her. 'Yes, you are. Don't lie.'

'It's not a lie,' she told him. 'It's just the truth.'

He frowned. 'Look, if you were so rubbish at your work, they wouldn't have given you all those amazing jobs.'

'Which I then lost.'

'That's redundancies and a downturn in the market,' he told her, coming to stand in front of her. 'That's not your fault.'

She hung her head. 'No. I guess not.'

Was he right? Perhaps. Or perhaps not.

She was startled when he suddenly touched her chin and lifted her face up to his. 'You have a smudge on your cheek,' he said.

Amber found she was holding her breath as he brushed her cheek with his thumb.

'Occupational hazard these days,' she managed to finally say as his blue eyes locked onto hers.

He stared down at her for a second before he abruptly let go and Amber could finally breathe out once more.

'I thought I'd head over to the pub to see the England match after dinner,' he said, his voice casual. 'Do you want to come with me?'

Amber was surprised and pleased to be asked but was still trying to get over her reaction to his touching her cheek so she shook her head. 'Thanks, but I'm pretty weary,' she told him. 'I think I'll have a shower and then put my feet up here, if that's OK.'

He shrugged his shoulders. 'It's your home too,' he told her.

Amber smiled to herself when he left an hour later. It did feel a little like home, although she wasn't even sure where that was these days. When was the last time she had felt at home anywhere? Certainly not in New York. And not even in London before that.

Probably growing up, but even then their houses had been many. Moving around the country chasing her parents' next dream meant that they had never settled anywhere. But even a temporary home had turned into a sanctuary from the bullying girls who had been her class-mates at secondary school.

One girl had been particularly vicious. Catherine Hooper had been relentless in her sniping and bullying, always laughing at Amber's awkwardness. The mocking laughter still haunted her to that day.

Amber shook her head as if to erase the painful memories of the past as she finished the washing-up and glanced in the bathroom. She had rushed through her daily showers since arriving in Cranbridge, aware that two other people might be needing the bathroom each time. Her flat share in New York hadn't been any more relaxed when everyone needed to get into the bathroom. But now she was alone. And there was an actual bath in there! Cathy had even suggested that she treat herself to a bubble bath and had shown her where everything was.

Josh wouldn't be back in the flat for hours, she reminded herself. So she decided to go for it.

Sinking into the hot bubbles that had almost filled the tub ten minutes later, Amber gave out a cry of satisfaction. Wow, she thought, smiling in the steamy sweet-scented air. This was amazing.

Lying back in the bath, her mind drifted to, of all places, the shop. The windows had been easy, but the layout and look of the shop was something else.

She tried to think about other things, but her imagination was now running riot, filling her head with colour choices and looks for the shop. She dismissed too flowery a look. It didn't seem to fit with the overall feel of the place.

So what was Cranbridge Stores? It was a country village shop which had been in the family since the 1900s. It just needed something to reverse its declining fortunes.

She thought back to Grandma Tilly's photograph and, without the present-day clutter and muddle, she focused on the positive points of the building. What had it retained from all those years ago? It had beams. It was a large space. The veranda was certainly another plus. It had character. Or it could have if she could just find some...

Suddenly she saw it. A clear vision as to how amazing the shop could be. She sat bolt upright in the bath, slopping bubbles over the side. She saw clean white walls, showing the uneven original plaster. In front, some tall shelving units. Painted dark oak to match the beams. The floor too needed a coat of varnish and would be shiny. The leaves and decorations in the window could be extended to the shelves. Fairy lights and strings of autumnal leaves lay across the top and could even be hung around the beams as well.

Feeling excited, she quickly got out of the bath, grabbed her towel and rushed across to her bedroom. She found her drawing pad and sat down on the bed as she drew, her pencil flying over the page.

She then grabbed her coloured pencils and coloured in the shelves and fireplace that they had only discovered that day. The decorative leaves were added, as were a few other touches.

She finally stopped and looked down at her design. It worked! Almost, she realised. What was missing? She wasn't sure. The walls of the shop looked good. She had sketched in the pretty fireplace. But there was a gap in the middle of the floor. What display could it hold there?

Amber bit her lip, but she couldn't think of anything.

She stood up and paced up and down. What was wrong with her? She normally discovered the missing piece really quickly.

She went to the doorway, listening out for any signs of movement. But Josh was still over at the pub.

She just needed to look at the shop one more time. So she grabbed her drawing pad and pencil before rushing downstairs, still only dressed in her towel.

* * *

The argument behind the bar in the pub was getting even louder.

'I told you the satellite dish needed looking at!' shouted Angie.

'No, you didn't!' hollered Mike. 'You nagged me about everything other than that!'

'I did! You just weren't listening as per usual!'

Josh drained the last of his pint. So much for a beer in front of the football match. BT Sport had stopped working and the television only showed an error message.

He shrugged on his coat and made eye contact with Belle, who was standing behind the bar and looking as if she were wishing she were anywhere else but there.

'Thanks for the relaxing drink,' he said.

She gave him a small smile. 'Love may be blind, but it's marriage that's the real eye-opener,' she told him, glancing behind her as the shouting became even louder.

'Will you be OK?' he asked.

'Oh yes,' she told him, with a weary smile. 'They were due a good argument, otherwise it's all just simmering tension and veiled threats. I'll head up to bed soon and leave them to it.'

'Goodnight then,' said Josh, heading over to the door.

'Goodnight,' he heard her call out.

In the cool night air, he felt calmer once more. At least his parents' marriage had been a happy one, he reminded himself. Certainly not the shouting awfulness of Mike and Angie's wedded unbliss.

Heading back across the pedestrian bridge, he thought he saw a light on in the shop, but he figured it must have been the reflection of the fairy lights. He was also incredibly tired. It had been an emotional few days, saying goodbye to his mum and then beginning to clear the shop. He was grateful for Amber's calm presence to keep him company as they worked through the mess.

He unlocked and then pushed open the back door and stopped suddenly upon hearing a sound. There was definitely somebody in the shop.

'Who's there?' he called out, switching on the light.

He heard a gasp and, grabbing a nearby hammer from the toolkit next to the tractor, he surged forward, expecting to come face to face with a burglar.

He came to an abrupt halt when he found Amber standing in the middle of the shop wearing only a short bath towel which barely covered the tops of her legs.

She was staring at him wide-eyed and clutching a drawing pad.

He tried to think of something witty to say, but he was too mesmerised by her still damp shoulders in the overhead light, as well as the blush on her cheeks.

'I thought you were out!' she moaned, clutching the paper even closer to her chest. Her brown eyes were blinking rapidly in shock.

'The satellite TV stopped working,' he replied, trying desperately not to stare at her long bare legs.

He watched as she grabbed the pencil even tighter in her hand.

'What's that?' he added, trying to change the subject by nodding at the pad and then abruptly realising that he was actually gesturing at her chest.

'It's nothing,' she told him. 'It's just a silly drawing.'

'I'd like to see it,' he said.

But she was violently shaking her head. 'Forget it. It was just a stupid idea.'

'Look—' he began.

But Amber had finally found her feet and was rushing past him. 'I'd better go,' she told him as she headed up the stairs to the flat. He heard footsteps and then her bedroom door slam shut.

He wondered what on earth she had been drawing down in the shop. Forget it, she had said. But he was going to have real trouble forgetting how incredible Amber looked in that short towel.

17

As Amber headed downstairs the following morning, she knew she had to try and be brave when seeing Josh face to face.

'Good morning,' she managed to say to him, with a cheery smile on her face.

His eyebrows raised at her overly bright tone of voice, but he merely smiled and said, 'Good morning' in reply.

There, she told herself. *That wasn't so bad, was it?* At least she'd been able to speak.

If only she could do something regarding the absolute mortification she felt about being discovered in only a bath towel in the middle of the shop the previous evening!

What on earth had she been thinking? She couldn't believe she could have been so stupid. She had been so wrapped up in her ideas for the shop that she hadn't even contemplated the notion that Josh might come home early.

As it was, she had just about managed to stay hidden whilst he had his breakfast that morning, trying to keep her blushing face out of view.

Thankfully, she could hide her bright red face in one of the many boxes that still needed clearing.

She was hoping they would get a chance to redistribute the stock that was obsolete but found herself distracted by the bewilderment and somewhat bemusement of their intermittent customers.

'Have I taken a wrong turn somewhere?' said Stanley, looking around in wide eyed wonder when he came in at his normal time of 9.30 a.m.

Some of the boxes had already been moved out of the way, others were stacked even higher. It might not have looked any better, but it was some kind of progress, thought Amber.

'We're having a bit of a clear-out,' Amber told him.

'Well, if I hadn't seen your lovely window designs on the way in, I wouldn't have known it was the same shop,' said Stanley, looking a little startled. 'Then again, it's certainly a little easier to move around. If you could tell me where I can find the newspapers now.'

'They're here in the back,' called out Josh, bringing out *The Times* newspaper to hand over to Stanley. 'I didn't want to bring them in here because, well...' His voice tailed off as he waved his arm around.

'I meant to say to you how the windows look even better at night,' carried on Stanley, before looking concerned. 'Dear me, that came out wrong. What I meant to say was that I was going for a walk yesterday evening and I saw a couple of people walking their dogs and looking at your windows. It looked ever so pretty all lit up.'

'Do you think so?' said Amber, blushing. 'How kind you are to say so.'

Stanley picked up his newspaper. 'It certainly makes Riverside Lane more cheerful in the dark evenings. Good day to you.'

With a nod, Stanley walked his way back through the shop and out of the front door, the bell ringing out as he left.

'I think you've got an admirer,' said Josh, waggling his eyebrows at her.

'Rubbish,' muttered Amber, hurriedly looking away to the door, where the bell had just rung once more.

'A bell to announce Belle,' said Josh, who appeared to be in a very good mood that day, thought Amber.

Belle rolled her eyes. 'Yeah, like I haven't heard that one before.'

'And how are your softly-spoken aunt and uncle today?' asked Josh, still grinning. 'Still screaming their love for one another?'

'If the television wasn't broken before their argument, it certainly is now!' Belle blew out a sigh. 'I'm here for a couple of light bulbs,' she said. 'Two of the corner lamps were also casualties in last night's row.'

'I'll have a look out the back for you,' said Josh. 'I think there was a box somewhere.'

As he disappeared, Belle leant on the counter and stared around. 'Is it me or does it look even worse than normal in here?'

'We've just started to reorganise it all so it looks a bit of a mess,' Amber told her.

'So you're staying for a while, I heard,' said Belle, giving her a friendly smile.

Amber nodded.

'Well, it'll be nice to have a bit of female company around here,' said Belle. 'Come over to the pub one night and we'll have a chat over one of my famous gin and tonics. It would be nice to have some female company, to be honest.'

'Thanks,' said Amber, as Josh returned holding a large box. 'I'd like that.'

'That's an idea,' he said, putting the box down on the counter. 'Poor Amber only has Stanley for company around here.'

'He's just lonely,' muttered Amber, blushing. 'I'm not sure who else he gets to talk to for the rest of the day.'

'Stanley does like to chat,' said Belle, nodding in agreement. 'He comes into the pub once a week on a Wednesday night. I think he struggles for company since his wife died.'

'That's so sad,' said Amber. 'He only seems to come in at half past nine each morning.'

'Maybe it's his routine that keeps him going,' said Belle, nodding thoughtfully. 'Mind you, sometimes he's the only person I really talk to on a Wednesday night as well.'

It struck Amber that perhaps Stanley wasn't the only lonely person in the village. Even someone as confident as Belle appeared to struggle for companionship.

'Any ideas which type you want?' said Josh, rattling the contents of the box.

Belle peered inside. 'Those two,' she said, reaching in to pick out a couple of light bulbs. 'Right, how much do I owe you?'

Once she had paid up, Belle pocketed the two bulbs.

'Don't forget about that gin,' she said, smiling at Amber before she headed towards the door. 'By the way, the windows look great. Didn't recognise the place when I saw them.'

'Not sure I recognise it myself these days,' said Josh, as Belle closed the door behind her. He looked around the mess. 'I think we've made it worse not any better.'

Amber thought about what Stanley had said about the people out and about in the evening. 'By the way, why don't you open a bit later each night?'

Josh shrugged his shoulders. 'Nobody does late-night opening around here, apart from the pub. I mean, there's no point. It's like a ghost town.'

'I see,' said Amber, wondering whether to question him further.

Josh picked up on her tone. 'What?' he asked.

'Grandma Tilly mentioned that some people commute from the village into the towns and cities for work,' she began. 'Perhaps they don't get home until after 5 p.m.'

'Perhaps,' he said, still looking at her. 'What's your point?'

'I've done the long commute when I worked in London,' she told him. 'You come home late at the station and just want to grab some food.'

Josh grimaced. 'Well, they're not grabbing it from here, according to my sales figures.'

'Because you're not open after five o'clock,' she reminded him.

'And we don't have any kind of convenience food like ready meals,' he added.

She nodded. 'That too.'

He shrugged his shoulders in response. 'Look, until we clear the shop, I can't even think about opening hours and all the rest of it.'

'I know,' Amber told him. 'The trouble is that I'm beginning to run out of places to put things.' She hesitated before going on. 'I think maybe it's time for you to move the tractor to clear some space in the back room.'

Josh almost looked ashen in the light. 'Yeah, you're right. I'll move it after we close up this evening.'

* * *

Once the shop was closed later that day, Amber began to wipe down the dust on the fireplace which they had uncovered.

But Josh quickly told her to give up. 'There's no point cleaning anything in here until that stinky old tractor has come through,' he told her. 'Chances are that it'll leave a trail of oil anyway.'

She grimaced. 'Let's hope not.' She glanced over to the front door. 'How are you going to get it down the steps on the veranda?' she asked.

'I've set up a ramp with some sheets of plywood,' he told her.' Hopefully they'll hold the weight.'

'Hopefully?' she asked.

He shrugged his shoulders. 'Just keep your fingers crossed,' he said, doubt filling his voice.

Amber pushed as many boxes as she could to one side whilst Josh went into the back room to fiddle with the tractor.

'Keep out of the way,' he called out. 'This could get messy.'

'How messy?' she called back.

But he didn't hear her because he had just turned the key in the ignition. After a couple of splutters, the engine sprang into noisy life. He looked up at her, amazed, as if he hadn't expected it to continue to turn over. Although the shop was immediately filled with both grey smoke and the immense racket of an ancient engine that hadn't been started for a very long time.

Amber was horrified. Was this even safe?

'OK,' she just about heard Josh shout above the noise. 'I'll try and steer it through.'

Amber crossed her fingers and prayed that he wouldn't end up crashing through the double front doors, which she had already wedged wide open. Or, in fact, any of the walls.

The noise of the engine changed to become even louder as Josh crunched the tractor into gear. With a massive jolt, it leapt forward by a foot and she saw him swear to himself in shock.

Amber pressed herself up against the fireplace, as far back as she could go, severely concerned about her personal safety at that point. Not only was the noise awful, the floorboards were shaking beneath her feet. She held her hand over her nose to stop herself from breathing in too much of the smoky fumes coming from the engine.

With another, smaller jolt, Josh wrenched the steering wheel over to one side, forcing the wheels to straighten up and aim for the middle of the shop floor.

This was a bad idea, thought Amber, feeling like she was in the middle of an earthquake. The whole shop was liable to fall down on top of them.

Trouble was, it was probably too late to point that out now to Josh who was busy hanging on to the steering wheel for dear life as it began to make its juddering roaring journey into the shop.

If the noise and shaking were bad enough, the smell was horrendous. The whole air was filled with a smoky, oily fug. She wasn't even sure a good airing would sort the shop out when the tractor was outside.

If the place didn't fall apart first, she thought, hanging on to the fireplace for dear life as the tractor slowly made its way through the shop.

This was a terrible idea, she told herself. She just hoped it didn't end in disaster.

* * *

Josh was using all of his strength to keep the steering wheel straight. The whole tractor was fighting him every inch of the way as if it had never wanted to leave the back room. He was now thinking that it had been better off in there too.

The noise was horrendous, as was the smell of burning rust, which could be coming from either the exhaust, the engine or possibly both at the same time. He was in serious trouble here.

He glanced at Amber, whose own horrified face mirrored his own worries as she clung on to the fireplace. But he couldn't look at her for very long as his whole view kept juddering as the floor beneath him was shaking.

He glanced down at the wheels. Should he have checked the floor-boards were strong enough to hold it? Well, it was too late now, he thought, hanging on with grim determination to get this over with.

On top of the worry and stress, he felt emotionally drained. The tractor belonged inside. He didn't want to move it, but he knew that life had to move on. He had to move on with it, but it brought him no joy that he had finally got the thing going, albeit in juddering, huge jolts.

Somewhere, his father was watching him either laughing hysteri-cally or with his head in his hands in despair.

He had just drawn level with Amber at the fireplace when the tractor gave a massive bang somewhere in front of him and wheezed to a halt, the engine cutting out.

In the silence, his ears continued to ring as the smoke poured out from the engine in front of him.

Amber straightened herself up. 'What happened?' she said, waving her hand in front of her face as a combination of steam and smoke streamed out from under the front bonnet.

'I don't know,' said Josh, turning the key once more.

But the engine made a loud clanging noise and refused to switch on. He tried the key over and over again, desperately hoping to get it going, but to no avail. In fact, each time he tried, the engine sounded worse and worse. Metal was crunching together, clangs and rattles rang out.

He climbed out of the seat and went around to open the bonnet. But even that wouldn't open so that he could try and see what had gone wrong.

It was an utter disaster. Instead of being stuck in the storeroom, the tractor was now stuck in the middle of the shop!

Josh felt a white-hot fury of frustration. 'I don't believe this!' he shouted, kicking the fender in his anger. To add insult to injury, it fell off onto the floor with a clang. He stared at it in shock. How had his life gone so badly, terribly, wrong?

He looked at Amber, who had come to stand next to him. Hoping he hadn't frightened her with his anger, he turned to placate her. But, to his amazement, she looked like she was trying not to smile.

'It's not funny!' he said, his voice louder than normal with his despair.

'I know it's not,' she said, before pressing her lips together to stop the smile from spreading across her face.

'This is terrible!' he carried on, the anger suddenly fading as quickly as it arrived.

'Yes, it is,' she nodded, smothering a giggle.

'We've got a bloody tractor stuck in the middle of the shop!' he said, pointing out the obvious.

And then they both burst out laughing at the same time. On and on they laughed until Amber clutched her stomach.

'This is crazy,' she said, still laughing.

'Oh God! What have I done?' he said, still feeling the absolute horror of the situation.

They both kept laughing at the ridiculousness of it all.

Finally, Amber managed to get a hold of herself. 'What are we going to do?' she asked, wide-eyed as she stared at the tractor.

Josh looked at her for a long moment, but he was out of ideas.

'Grab your coat,' he found himself saying. 'Let's go to the pub and get drunk.'

He had almost expected her to refuse, but, to his grateful surprise, she nodded and said, 'Yeah. Definitely.'

And so they switched off the lights in the shop, locked up and headed across to the pub, leaving the broken-down tractor still in the middle of the shop floor.

18

Amber shivered as they went from the cold dark air of an October's night to the warm and somewhat welcoming Black Swan pub.

She hadn't thought to change her clothes since the tractor had stopped working and felt filthy, probably looked it too, she thought. She checked Josh's appearance and saw that he had various smudges across his face and clothes. She instantly knew that she probably looked just as bad.

'What the hell happened to you two?' asked Belle, behind the bar and goggle-eyed, confirming Amber's suspicions. 'I only saw you a few hours ago and you looked, what's the word, oh yeah, clean!'

'Don't ask,' Josh told her, shaking his head. 'And for God's sake don't mention this to my grandmother. Wine, please. Make it a bottle, would you?'

Belle looked surprised as she continued to take in their smoky and dishevelled appearances. 'White or red?'

Josh looked at Amber in question.

'White, please,' she told him.

'Go grab those armchairs by the fire and I'll bring it over,' he said.

The battered leather armchairs were surprisingly comfortable, thought Amber as she sat down. Or perhaps she was just so tired and shocked that she didn't care any more.

As Josh walked back from the bar, she noticed that his jeans were covered in oil and various dirty marks. She supposed if he didn't mind, then she shouldn't fret over her appearance either. But it was always a battle to fight her inner critic.

'No beer tonight?' she said, as he shrugged off his jacket and sat down in the battered chair on the other side of the table.

'I fancied a glass of wine and if you've tasted the house wine they've got behind the bar, you'd understand that it'd be safer to go for an unopened bottle,' he told her, placing the wine and glasses on the small wobbly wooden table between them. 'Besides, I need a big drink after that little incident.'

Despite the dark lighting and quiet atmosphere of the pub, it was cosy sitting next to the flames as the logs crackled.

As he poured out their drinks, Josh carried on, 'I've also ordered chips and a pizza to share. If they're undercooked, we can always heat them up here on the fire.'

'Thank you,' she said. 'I'm starving.'

'Yeah, it's thirsty work ruining a shop.' He handed her a large glass of wine. 'Cheers,' he said, raising his own glass at her.

She smiled. 'Cheers,' she replied and took a sip of the crisp white wine. 'Mmm, I needed that.'

'Me too,' he said with a grunt as he leant back against the cushions.

'I don't think you've entirely ruined the shop,' she told, him although she couldn't stop herself giggling. 'Sorry,' she said, blushing as he looked sharply at her.

'You're OK,' he said, after a beat, his blue eyes softening as he continued to look at her. 'I'd probably be laughing too if I wasn't weeping with despair on the inside.'

'Maybe it isn't as bad as you think,' she told him.

'The bank is threatening to repossess the place unless we start making a profit,' he told her. 'We have no customers and the small amount that we do have now can't even come in because there's a bloody tractor in the middle of the shop floor.'

'I never said it was perfect,' she muttered, giving him a sheepish grin.

She was grateful to see him smile at her joke. 'Yeah,' he said, before blowing out a sigh.

'Is it really that bad with the bank?' she asked.

He nodded in reply.

'Does your mum know?'

Josh looked up at her. 'No. Not the whole hideous picture anyway.'

'You've been protecting her from it all this time because she's been ill,' said Amber, thinking out loud.

Josh shrugged his shoulders in reply.

'I get it,' she told him. 'We always protect our parents from the bad stuff so they don't worry about us.'

He raised an eyebrow in question. 'You had problems in New York?'

She hesitated. It had started a long time before New York, she thought.

'It's OK,' he said quickly. 'You don't have to tell me if you don't want to.'

But he'd been so honest, she thought to herself. After all, he had trusted her with his problems. She took another large gulp of wine before speaking. 'My boss in New York was pretty awful.'

'Pervert?'

She almost spat out her drink, laughing in shock. 'No! Not that!' She wiped a bit of wine from her chin. 'No, she wasn't very good at her job and preferred to take credit for everyone else's work. Including mine.'

He studied her for a moment. 'And she kept her job whilst you lost yours in the redundancies.'

'I was the outsider,' she told him. As usual, she added to herself.

'Didn't you have any work colleagues who could stand up for you?'

She shook her head. 'I was pretty isolated over there. First in, last out, that kind of thing.'

'So in a way it was a blessing that you got made redundant,' he said.

She laughed without humour. 'Yeah, I've got no job and no home either because my parents emigrated whilst I was abroad and they've gone to a place where I can't possibly carry on with my career.'

'I admit, it doesn't sound great,' he told her. 'Look, you've got a job whilst you need it here. You know that. It just doesn't pay very much.'

'Does it pay at all?' she asked him in jest.

'Not really.'

She laughed once more. 'And there was me thinking that you couldn't wait to get rid of me.'

He stared at her for a beat. 'I never said that. Anyway, I liked your window displays,' he said.

She blushed and looked at her feet. 'It's easy when you know how.'

'Rubbish,' he said, frowning. 'I think you've either got an artistic talent or, like me, you most definitely haven't. You need to have more confidence in yourself.'

She picked up her wine glass. 'That's easier said than done, believe me.'

When their pizza and chips arrived, they were both delighted that, for once, the food was actually cooked all the way through. Probably because Belle had taken charge of their meal, Amber suspected.

They ate in a comfortable silence, with Josh filling up their glasses once more.

'I mean it,' he told her, after they'd finished eating. 'You can stay here as long as you want. It'd mean a lot to Mum.' He paused. 'And I need the help too.'

'Thank you.'

She was touched. Was he actually reaching out to her?

'Is that why you keep drawing?' he suddenly said.

She was confused. 'What do you mean?'

'You said the other day that drawing and designing were your safety net. I get that you had a bad time in New York. But why did you need one when you were growing up?' he asked, before shaking his head. 'Sorry. None of my business.'

Amber took a large gulp of wine. And then another before answering. 'Growing up can be hard sometimes. We moved around a lot. That makes it difficult to make friends. And some of the other girls, kids, can be mean.'

The silence stretched out as Josh studied her thoughtfully. 'I see. That must have been tough.'

'It didn't do wonders for my self-confidence,' she told him.

'So why were you drawing last night?' he asked. 'You know, when I found you in the shop.'

Amber gulped, her cheeks suddenly filled with heat as she remembered standing there in just a towel. She took another large glug of wine but managed to spill most of it down her chin.

'I thought you were a burglar,' he told her, smiling. 'Albeit slightly underdressed.'

'What would I be stealing?' she muttered, still blushing.

'You've got a point there,' he said.

Thankfully his line of questioning was interrupted by the entertainment that Mike had booked for the evening. Amber and Josh gave up all hope of a conversation for the next hour as they struggled to hear themselves think over the ever-increasingly out-of-tune Coldplay fake singer. So they finished off the bottle of wine instead.

During an all too brief pause in the singing, Josh went and bought another bottle.

'It's not like we've got to rush to get up in the morning,' he told her, refilling her glass to the brim. 'The shop is empty.'

'Apart from the tractor,' she reminded him, before taking a large glug of wine. Her head was beginning to go fuzzy, but she didn't care. The alcohol was dulling the pain of the singing.

'I'd almost forgotten about that! What are we going to do?' said Josh, running a hand through his hair.

'I think we should leave it there,' she told him, laughing.

'We may have to if I can't get the damn thing going,' he replied, also starting to laugh.

She took another sip of wine. 'If only it were prettier,' she thought out loud.

'Excuse me, but that is, was, my dad's prize tractor,' he told her, in a fake haughty tone. 'I'll have you know that it's a classic.'

'A classic pile of rusty junk,' she replied, feeling brave with a few glasses of wine inside.

'Hey,' he said. 'That tractor meant everything to my dad.'

'I know,' she told him. 'I was only joking. Maybe if it were painted it would look better.'

Josh stared into the flames. 'My old man loved tinkering with that thing. Every spare moment. "We're going to get it working", he would say. Every time. There was always hope that it would be useful to us. But it doesn't work.'

'Maybe it doesn't need to,' said Amber, staring at the flames as she tried to think of a solution.

'You're not seriously suggesting that we keep the tractor where it is,' he said, shaking his head. 'You're going to feel pretty silly in the morning when you sober up.'

'You just need a bit of vision,' she told him.

'All I need are earplugs if that singer starts again,' he replied.

Josh was looking a bit drunk, she realised as she glanced across at him. He had closed his eyes in exhaustion and she noted what a handsome face it was.

When his eyes suddenly flew open to look directly at her, she quickly looked away, hoping he hadn't caught her staring.

'We'd better get home,' he said. 'Before I fall asleep in this chair and they start singing again.'

'The chairs are nice and comfy, aren't they?' she said.

'Must be the wine talking,' he said, smiling. 'Come on.'

They said goodnight to Belle and made a somewhat uneven path across the pub and out the front door.

Once outside in the colder night air, Amber realised how drunk she really was.

'Sorry,' she said, snagging her boot on a loose bit of pavement and bumping into Josh.

'I think we'd better link arms,' he told her, putting his arm through hers as they began to walk over the narrow pedestrian bridge. 'Otherwise I'll end up in the river again.'

'It was an accident,' she said, laughing. 'Now I've got to know you a bit better I would totally push you in on purpose next time.'

'Ha!' he said, as they reached the other side. 'Next time, I'll make sure you go in first.'

He opened up the shop, which looked softer, lit only by the fairy lights in the window.

Josh walked through first and immediately bumped into the tractor, having forgotten it was there. 'Ow!' he said, hopping around and holding his knee.

'Are you OK?' Amber asked, rushing up to him.

When he straightened, up, she realised how close he was standing in front of her. She had a sudden impulse to kiss him. It must be the wine, she told herself.

'Well,' she said, her voice trailing off in the awkward silence as they stared at each other. The familiarity that they had shared in the pub suddenly seeming a long way away.

'You go up. I'll make sure we're locked up down here,' he told her, looking into her face.

She nodded. 'Yeah. You don't want anyone stealing the tractor.'

He smiled. 'My thoughts exactly. Goodnight.'

'Goodnight,' she replied, turning to go upstairs and away from Josh before she did something really crazy that she may regret in the morning.

19

Amber woke up the following morning with a raging hangover. Exactly how much wine had she had to drink the previous night?

She moved her head and groaned at the pounding headache. She desperately tried to remember what had happened. Then her fuzzy brain finally began to figure it all out. She had gone to the pub with Josh after the tractor had broken down. They had drunk quite a bit, from what she could even bring herself to remember. Rather more than a bit of wine, she realised as her head continued to ache. And then what? She clutched her head and forced her brain to remember what had happened.

Finally, her brain cells slowly clunked into gear. Nothing had happened. She slumped back onto her pillow in relief.

But there had been something. A moment. When Josh had looked at her and she had really wanted to see what it felt like to be kissed by him. But that was ridiculous, utterly crazy. Besides, it was just the wine talking. She didn't feel like that about him at all.

Getting showered and dressed was a painful process, involving much swearing and moaning as she bumped her head on the low ceiling but finally she felt able to head into the kitchen. The flat was quiet. The door to Josh's bedroom was open, meaning that he had already got up and gone downstairs to open up the shop.

Tea and toast helped to start to clear her fuzzy head and afterwards she slowly and carefully headed downstairs.

As she walked from the back room into the main shop, the low sunlight was streaming through the windows. It was so bright it made her gasp and cover her eyes with her hands.

'Oh God,' she cried. 'Somebody switch off the lights.'

'I've been trying, believe me,' groaned Josh from somewhere nearby.

She peered through her fingers and saw that he was actually sitting on the driver's seat of the rusty tractor, which was still in the middle of the shop. Despite still feeling awful, she couldn't help but laugh at the ridiculous sight.

'I'm not sure you should be driving in your condition,' she told him, walking over to stand next to the tractor.

He looked at her with bleary eyes. 'Are you feeling as bad as I look?'

She nodded. 'Oh yes.'

'Good.'

'Gee, thanks,' she told him.

He smiled, although even that looked a bit painful. 'Misery loves company,' he said.

She looked at the tractor. 'Well, here we all are,' she said.

'Yeah.' He reached out and grasped the steering wheel. 'I was just trying to work out how we can get it towed out of here. And I am completely and utterly clueless as to how to make that happen.'

He looked sad for a moment and Amber remembered their conversation in the pub about how restoring the tractor had been a dream of his late father's.

'Maybe it doesn't need to go,' she found herself blurting out.

He looked up at her. 'What are you talking about?'

'When I was down here the other night drawing, you know, in my, er, towel,' she began, blushing furiously.

Josh grinned. 'I remember,' he said, his eyes gleaming.

She gulped and forced herself to carry on. 'Yes, well, er, what I was doing was designing the shop. But there was something missing.'

'You're telling me that the thing missing in your wonderful professional design was a filthy broken-down tractor.' He laughed. 'Are you still drunk?'

'No, I'm serious,' she told him. 'Look, if you really think that the engine can't be fixed, then why not restore the bodywork instead. Paint the sides, polish the rest of it.' She began to walk slowly around it, thinking out loud. 'It could work. I think it could really work.'

'Amber,' he began to say.

But she held up her hand. 'I know what you're going to say! Look, let me show you the sketch so you can see for yourself.' She looked at him and couldn't stop herself from smiling with excitement at the idea.

However, Josh wasn't smiling back. 'Look, I don't know about this kind of stuff,' he said.

'But I do,' she told him, for once filled with confidence. 'Just think. It's different. It's unique.'

'It's certainly something,' he drawled, rolling his eyes.

Despite her hangover, Amber felt sure that she was on the right track. 'It could make a really nice display.' Her mind went back to Grandma Tilly's old photographs and suddenly she was full of ideas. 'We could get some of those crates at the back and place them around the tractor. Make it really farmhouse pretty. Country.'

She was getting more and more excited.

But Josh wasn't joining in with her enthusiasm.

'What?' she asked him. 'Why can't we do this?'

'Because it's not going to change anything,' he said, climbing down from the battered leather seat of the tractor. 'Maybe we should just quit while we're ahead. Or rather, before the bank closes us down.'

'Don't you think your mum would be upset about that?'

To her surprise, he shook his head. 'This shop wasn't her dream. It never was. This was just another selfish act from my dad, dragging us all out to the middle of nowhere. We were just following him.'

'Maybe he was right,' she told him.

'Maybe he was wrong, as per usual, and now he's not here and I am. Stuck here every day, watching all his dreams die.' His voice caught. 'Just like him.'

Amber stayed quiet. He was clearly upset and all she wanted to do was, surprisingly, give him a hug.

'I had dreams too,' she heard him say.

'Like what?' she prompted, gently.

He shrugged his shoulders. 'I wanted to run my own business. To make something special. Make a difference and try and educate people regarding sustainable living.'

'You could still do that,' she told him.

But Josh shook his head. 'Not here. It's too late.'

'No, it's not.' She stepped forward to grab his arm. 'Maybe this wasn't quite what you had in mind, but I think we could really make something special here. A country store. The Cranbridge Stores. It could be really something.'

She saw him hesitate and open his mouth to speak.

'Let me show you how good it could look,' she said quickly, before he could say anything else.

He lifted his palms up. 'Why not? Things can't get any worse.'

'Gee, thanks for the encouragement,' she said.

But as she ran upstairs to find her sketchpad, she realised she was filled with a dogged determination to prove him wrong. To show him that Cranbridge Stores could be something very special indeed.

In her bedroom, she picked up her sketchpad and immediately began to fill in the blank middle of her original drawing. She pencilled in a rough outline of the tractor before adding in some boxes to represent the crates. Then she grabbed her coloured pencils to show the different goods that could be displayed.

Finally, her hand hesitated before she grabbed the bright red pencil to colour in the tractor.

With a feeling of both excitement and trepidation, she went back downstairs to show Josh.

She shuffled nervously from foot to foot as he stared down at the paper and then up at the shop around him. Then he looked down again and up once more.

Finally, he turned to her with his eyes blazing. 'It'll never look this good,' he said, holding out the pad for her to take from him.

'It can and it will,' she told him, feeling bolder than she had ever felt in her life. 'Give me a week or so to change things around in here. To make it different. If you hate it, then it can go back to how it was. I'll even work out a way to get the tractor moved. But give me a little time and I'll show you how amazing it could really look.'

A silence stretched out between them before finally, he nodded his head. 'OK,' he said. 'But I'm not making any promises.'

'Nor am I,' she told him. 'But let me see what I can do.'

'It'll take us a week to carry on sorting through all this stuff,' he said, pointing at all the boxes of goods everywhere.

'Just trust me,' she found herself saying.

He smiled unexpectedly. 'Funny, I never saw you as a confident person before now.'

She returned his smile. 'I'm not. I don't know where all this is coming from. Maybe it's the fumes from the tractor.'

'Well, be my guest,' he said, waving his arm around the shop. 'Lord knows, it can't get much worse.'

'That's what you think,' she said, with a wink.

At least he was smiling in response as he left to head into the back of the shop.

Amber stood alone in the centre of the shop and did a slow 360 turn on the spot. With a loud gulp, she tried to suppress her fears and doubts about her ability to make the place look good.

Could she really do this? She'd promised Josh she could, so she supposed she had better get on with it. She just wasn't really sure, deep down, that she could, despite the faith in her own skills.

But she didn't want to let Cathy down. Nor Grandma Tilly. Not even the memory of Todd. Most especially, she didn't want to disappoint Josh, because she was beginning to care for him.

And that worried her even more than the sheer magnitude of over-hauling the shop.

20

Josh stood by the front door and looked out, and saw that the recent sunshine had given way to more rain.

The yellow leaves that had already fallen to the ground beneath the trees were looking as sodden as the muddy riverbanks. The river was also running quite high. Yet more rain and storms were forecast over the coming weeks.

Of course, that was nothing compared to the tempest that had hurtled through Cranbridge Stores since his mum had left, he thought, turning slowly around.

He blew out a long sigh. The shop was in utter disarray. Although he knew that the piles of boxes in each corner were in some sort of order, removing the large shelves from the middle had left a mess on the floorboards.

Although, of course, the worst of it was the horror of the dirty old tractor that was now in the middle of the shop.

For the life of him, he couldn't see Amber's point of view regarding leaving it where it had broken down.

He could see a patch of oil that had leaked onto the floor. And there was still a smoky, metallic tang in the air. He quickly opened the front door, anxious to air the shop out, and came face to face with Stanley.

'Good morning,' he said, with a nod.

'Morning,' said Josh, wondering what on earth was good about it.

Josh watched as the smile slowly faded into something akin to shock on the elderly man's face.

'Good gracious!' exclaimed Stanley, staring at the tractor with wide eyes. 'Have you become a garage mechanic overnight?'

Josh shook his head. 'A temporary glitch,' he said. 'Now, the papers have just been delivered out the back. I'll get yours. You're a bit earlier than usual this morning.'

'I've got a doctor's appointment later this morning,' said Stanley, stepping carefully into the shop. 'The perils of getting old, I'm afraid. The company I desire is not exactly to be found at our local health care centre.'

Josh stepped over various boxes and weaved his way around the tractor before heading through to the back room.

When he returned, he found Stanley studying the tractor.

'I must say, this takes me back,' said Stanley, who had been peering at the dashboard. 'My father had one of these when we owned our smallholding on the edge of the village when I was growing up. A good solid make, the David Brown 25.'

'Solid being the operative word when it's stuck in the middle of a shop,' drawled Josh.

Not even Amber with her obvious design talents could make the tractor look any good. But right now there was no plan b so he would just have to trust her.

Stanley handed over the coins for his newspaper. 'Well, you can't say it's not unique,' he said, with a smile. 'I shall watch what appears to be something of a facelift with interest.'

Josh smiled despite his reservations. A facelift? The shop needed a full makeover, complete with major heart surgery.

As Stanley left, Josh took the coins over to the till, which he could just about find behind a new stack of boxes. He sat down heavily on the stool behind the counter. It had been quite an exhausting few days and he was feeling low on energy. He had got spectacularly drunk with Amber, which didn't help as it had been a later night than usual. He thought of her standing in the darkness, looking up at him. He had almost been drunk enough to kiss her. Almost.

Besides, he knew that she would probably run a mile if he made a move on her. Which he most definitely wouldn't. Even if a small part of him was seriously tempted.

He gave his head a little shake. He didn't need temptation right now. He needed the shop to look like a shop again. With a groan, he slumped forward and put his head in his hands.

'I'm not surprised you're feeling like that after the amount of wine you two put away last night.'

He looked up to find Belle standing in the open doorway, staring wide-eyed at the mess in the shop before her eyes flew back to the elephant in the room. Or, rather, the tractor.

'Morning,' he said, with a nod.

'Good morning,' said Amber, coming into the shop, looking far more cheerful than Josh felt.

'What the hell happened in here last night?' asked Belle, walking slowly around the tractor.

'We had a design meeting,' said Amber, with a grin.

'I lost,' said Josh.

'Yeah, well,' said Belle, still looking around in shock. 'I've got to say, I'm rendered almost speechless.'

'First time for everything,' drawled Josh.

'What do you think of the tractor?' asked Amber in a hopeful tone.

'Do you have to put 10p in it to make it work?' asked Belle, peering into the driver's seat.

'What are you talking about?' asked Josh.

'Isn't it one of those rides for kids?' said Belle, straightening up. 'You know, like a Noddy car or something?'

Josh shook his head. 'No. It's an actual tractor.'

Belle looked at Amber and then back at Josh. 'You two aren't high on the fumes, are you?'

'I wish,' groaned Josh.

Belle picked up her pint of milk and placed her money on the counter. 'Well, you've got to admit. It's going to be the talk of the village! See you later.'

As she left, Josh turned to raise his eyebrows at Amber. 'Was that the reaction you were expecting?'

To his amazement, Amber shrugged her shoulders. 'Didn't you get the most important bit?' she told him. 'That we'll be the talk of the village. So people are going to come in here and see the tractor, aren't they?'

'And then they're going to turn back round and run away in horror,' he told her.

She frowned. 'Then let me try and convince you again.'

Amber unfolded a piece of paper from the pocket of her jeans and lay it out on the till counter between them. She turned it around so that the drawing was the right side up for him to look at it.

'What's the problem?' she asked, coming around to stand next to him.

'That,' said Josh, pointing at her drawing of the tractor in the middle of the shop floor.

'I see,' she said, turning to lean up against the counter so they were face to face. 'Let me tell you what I know. A shop needs staging. Like a window display, in that respect. Only bigger.'

He frowned. 'Staging?' he asked, raising his eyebrows in question.

'You're trying to entice people inside,' she told him. 'That's what the fancy window displays are for. You know, in the massive department stores anyway. So I don't see why it should be any different here. There's no use having a pretty window display to entice people inside if the place looks, well, like this inside.' She waved her arm around at the mess surrounding them.

'You do remember that it didn't look like this a few days ago,' he told her. 'It was just messy. Now it's a garage and rubbish tip.'

'It was always going to look worse before it looked better,' she replied.

'It wasn't supposed to be this much worse,' he said. 'With a tractor in it.'

She shrugged her shoulders as if the fact that a dirty old farm vehicle in the middle of the shop was a mere trifling inconvenience. She held up her hand to stop him interrupting. 'Yes, it's a tractor. But it's a small one, not the usual size. This one is only waist height, so you can still see across it. The space still works. I think it'll make a great feature.' She pointed at the design on the paper once more. 'Look at it. It looks bright. Modern. Fun. Interesting. Enticing.'

He looked at her drawing and wondered how best to make his point without upsetting her. For once, she seemed determined and brimming with confidence. He really didn't want to burst what little self-belief she had in her abilities, but her ideas were just too far.

'Look, they're good ideas,' he said. 'Apart from the tractor, obviously. I mean, I like your window displays. They're great. But all this…?'

'The pretty windows are designed to draw customers in, which would affect sales. That was the point.' She looked at him. 'I know you're concerned, but I've done this before. I've done displays throughout shops. Successful ones. This is on a much smaller scale, but it doesn't have to be.'

Josh stayed silent, looking at the paper once more. Her drawing looked amazing, but he couldn't see how it was ever going to achieve anything.

'Let's stage the shop whilst we're sorting it out,' Amber went on. 'It needs better lighting. This strip lighting is so harsh and awful. And it definitely needs painting and brightening up. It's so dull in here. And we'll need decorations to match the autumnal ones in the window.'

Josh sighed. 'All that? We've only got until the end of the year, otherwise we're going to lose the whole place anyway.'

'Then we'd better work quickly, don't you think?' Amber broke into a smile which lit up her whole face. 'I really do think we can make it pretty.'

Josh ran a hand through his hair. 'I'm no good at the prettying bit.'

She laughed. 'Yeah, I think you should probably leave that stuff to me. But you know some DIY, don't you?'

'I've done some building work as well to make ends meet over the years,' he told her. 'So I can paint and fix the place up.'

'Good,' said Amber. 'Let's get started.'

She looked as if she was going to bolt, so Josh reached out and held her arm. 'Not so fast,' he said. 'The trouble is that you can make it pretty, but what are we going to sell?'

'The stock we've got already,' she replied.

'Sellotape and rolls of material?' he reminded her. 'You saw all that stuff yesterday. It's so random.'

'Yes, but nobody could find anything or see what they wanted to buy because it was all such a jumble.' Amber tapped her chin in thought. 'It shouldn't just be a convenience shop. It's a lifestyle shop as well.'

He rolled his eyes. 'Could you sound any more New York?'

She smiled once more and he was reminded how beautiful she was up close.

'Shall we see what paint we've got out the back?' she said. 'We might as well use what's available.'

Josh sighed. 'Am I going to have any kind of say in any of this?'

'No,' she said. 'And I can always ring your mum if you're going to make trouble. She'll be totally on my side.'

He shook his head. 'I can't believe you pulled the mum card to get your own way.'

She was still smiling as she walked away, her ponytail swinging behind her as she went.

Josh remained sitting down and looked at Amber's design once more before staring up and around the shop. He just couldn't see it ever looking any better. But what did they have to lose?

Deep down, he still didn't feel as heartbroken as he should be over the possible closure of the shop. What was bothering him more was that he didn't want to upset Amber.

21

Amber stared around the shop and then down at the different pots of paints that Josh had brought out, trying to see how it could best be decorated. She was still quite amazed that Josh had run with her idea of redecorating the place. She just hoped he hadn't overestimated her limited abilities.

'They're all various shades of white,' said Josh, raising an eyebrow at her.

Amber nodded. 'White will do. Especially if we can paint some of the shelves as well.'

'The aluminium ones?' he asked.

Amber shook her head. 'They're a bit 1970s, don't you think?'

'They're probably older than that.'

'You've got all that wood in the back lane,' said Amber, glancing at the back room. 'Can't we add to the existing wooden shelves? We can sand them down. They'll look nice and rustic. Plus they'll match the wooden beams.'

Josh glanced up. 'I thought maybe we could paint them white as well.'

'No!' Amber was horrified. 'They're warm and give the place character.'

'OK.' Josh blew out a long sigh. 'You're the boss.'

She blushed. 'Well, I'm not. That's you.' She bit her lip. 'Am I being too much?'

'Yes,' he told her before smiling. 'But I quite like it.'

She looked at her feet, finding herself tongue-tied for the first time with Josh in a few days.

'So we need to concentrate on the walls and ceiling first,' he carried on. 'What about the fireplace? Shall we hide it again? We could use the storage space.'

But Amber shook her head. 'I was actually thinking of making it a feature.'

'Of course you were,' he drawled.

'If you want, we can always place something in front of it later,' she said, keen to appease his concerns. 'But in the meantime, to be honest, it's pretty cold in here so the extra heating would be nice.'

He went over to peer into the large wood-burning stove that had been installed in the fireplace. 'I can remember Dad lighting this when we first came here,' he said. 'I'll see if I can get a chimney sweep out to check the flue. I don't want the whole place to go up in flames, or die of carbon monoxide poisoning in my bed.' He laughed. 'Unless it's for the insurance money of course. Kidding!' he added, at Amber's horrified face.

'Just warn me before you light it,' she said. 'I don't want to go up in smoke either.'

She looked at the long wall on the far side of the shop. Without the interruption of the chimney and fireplace, it was actually far longer than she had realised and could probably hold almost six shelving units along the whole stretch.

But Josh insisted that he wanted to paint the wall before they placed the oak shelves back against it. So whilst Amber sanded them down, Josh began to prepare the ceiling and walls.

Along with the tractor, it meant that the shop was even more crowded than normal when a rare customer came in.

'Have my cataracts got worse?' said Grandma Tilly, standing at the front door to the shop and staring around in wide-eyed disbelief.

She hadn't been in the shop for a couple of days and hadn't seen it since the tractor had been moved.

Josh frowned down at her from the top rung of his stepladder. 'Is everything OK? I said I'd pop in and see you later.'

Grandma Tilly smiled. 'I just needed to get out and have some fresh air,' she said. 'So, am I allowed to ask what's going on?'

'We're having a mini makeover,' Amber told her.

Tilly smiled. 'It looks a tad more than "mini" to me, I would say.'

'I agree,' said Josh, as Amber knocked over a pile of tins that had been tottering precariously only a few moments previously.

'Gosh, I'd forgotten about that,' said Tilly, weaving her way through the mess to look at the fireplace.

'Isn't it pretty?' said Amber.

'My husband installed that many years ago,' said Tilly with a knowing smile.

'I don't remember Grandad being good with his hands like that,' said Josh.

'Oh yes,' said Tilly, turning to look at the tractor. 'Mind you, it was your dad that loved this old thing. I don't remember it being quite so prominent in the shop before though. Although I could be losing my marbles, of course.'

'No, that's just us,' Josh replied, giving Amber a pointed look.

She waved his concerns away with her hand. 'It's going to look worse before it looks better,' she told Grandma Tilly.

'Then perhaps I think you're at rock bottom now, my dear,' said Tilly, with a wink. 'But I'm sure you young folks know what you're doing.'

'But maybe don't tell Mum about all this quite yet,' suggested Josh.

Tilly nodded. 'I agree.' She looked around at the mess. 'Is there anything I can do to help?'

'We can't have you hurting yourself,' Josh told her. 'It's such a mess in here.'

Grandma Tilly looked downcast. 'Well, if you're sure, I guess I'd better head home and see what's on daytime TV.'

Amber realised that Tilly needed to feel useful even though the shop really was too much of a mess at the moment for her to be safe.

'How's my blanket coming along?' asked Amber.

'Nearly done,' said Tilly, brightening up a little. 'I'll have to start on your mum's after that.'

'Great,' said Amber.

'I'll swing by later,' shouted Josh as she left. His phone bleeped in his pocket so he checked his messages after climbing down the stepladder. 'So, I've heard from the chimney sweep,' he told Amber. 'But it's going to cost at least £100 for him to come and service the thing. Maybe we can just leave the wood-burning stove for show or something.'

'Look,' said Amber. 'You may not feel the cold in that nice leather jacket of yours, but it's always freezing in here and you want people to linger and shop. I thought that was the point. To make money? So you need to encourage people through the door, which hopefully I can do with some different and more enticing kinds of window display. But then they need to stay put in here for a while, which we're both trying to sort out. Then they shop. Linger. In the warmth. Maybe even pick up more things to buy.'

'OK. You wore me down,' he told her, holding his hand out to stop her going on any further.

'The white looks good though,' she said, looking up at the ceiling. 'Much better than that cream colour. Especially on a gloomy day like today.'

He glanced outside. It hadn't stopped raining for a few days and the forecast said it was likely to continue. But, in a way, it was perfect that it was a dark and dismal autumnal day. The shop needed to be shown in its worst light in order for it to be dressed.

'I'll call the chimney sweep when I head over to the cash and carry,' said Josh, bringing out his van keys.

'Oh! There were a couple of things I needed,' said Amber quickly.

'No worries,' said Josh. 'We'll close up the shop.'

Amber looked alarmed. 'Do you think we should?'

Josh rolled his eyes before grabbing his van keys. 'Yeah, Harrods is really concerned about the competition right about now.'

Amber enjoyed the journey out in Josh's van. Being a little higher meant she could see over the hedgerows and enjoy the countryside, although everywhere was looking muddy and wet.

First of all, they visited the builder's merchants and bought some more white paint. Amber insisted they didn't get the cheapest paint as it would be too thin.

'Less time painting many coats means the quicker it'll dry and then we can start putting the stock back on the shelves,' she told him.

It was a bit like coming up against a brick wall, she thought. She knew they didn't have much money and she wasn't deliberately being extravagant, but she also knew that it had to be done properly if they were to maximise the look of the place.

As they headed next door to the cash and carry, Josh asked, 'How come you aren't as confident about yourself as you are with the shop?'

'Because it's not personal,' she told him, after a pause. 'Designing shop windows is always easier.'

She followed him into the cash and carry and was amazed at the sheer volume of goods available.

'It's all good quality,' he told her, picking up a few bales of loo rolls and kitchen paper. 'That should keep us going until Christmas.'

She hesitated before nodding.

'What?' he asked, turning to face her. 'Why am I sensing disapproval?'

'No, no,' she said, shaking her head. 'I understand why you shop here.'

'But...?' he prompted.

'I don't know,' she said, feeling uncomfortable. 'It's just not very, er, countrified?'

He looked at her. 'What do you want? Straw on the floor and hay bales to sit on?'

'Not that,' she said. 'It's just all this stuff is cheap, and that's great. But it doesn't feel very individual. Original, I mean.'

'We can't afford original,' he told her. 'This stuff just about keeps our head above water.'

He picked up some pints of milk and added it to their large trolley.

She hesitated before deciding to speak up. 'What about your ecology credentials?'

He looked at her. 'What do you mean?'

'How much of this is recyclable? Sustainable?'

He frowned. 'We don't have the luxury of profits to be sustainable unfortunately.'

His good mood seemed to have completely evaporated, so Amber kept quiet for the rest of their trip.

Josh had been running the shop for a very long time so he obviously knew what he was doing profit-wise. She just wasn't sure in her mind's eye that the vision she had for decorating the shop quite fitted with the generic goods he was buying.

But what did it matter? She gave herself a strict talking-to as she helped load the van. She was helping with the decoration, that was all. What stock they held was nothing to do with her. Anyway, another month and she'd be on her way.

But, deep inside, she found herself secretly hoping that perhaps she could stay on for just a few more weeks to see if the shop succeeded once they'd finished the redecorating.

22

Josh huddled over his pint of beer, deep in thought.

'You're not very chatty tonight,' said Mike, polishing a glass over and over with a grubby tea towel.

'It's been a bit hard to hear myself think let alone speak above that lot,' said Josh, nodding at the band who had been playing nearby. 'They don't seem to have improved over time.'

Thankfully they had just stopped for a cigarette break. Although to Josh's mind it was only metaphorically playing.

'I said I'd give them a try for a month,' said Mike, with a grimace. 'Thought they'd be better than me having to talk to Angie for any length of time.'

'At this point, I'll take the peace and quiet,' said Josh, taking another sip of beer.

'No chance of me ever getting that with my wife,' muttered Mike.

Josh put down the pint glass and looked at his hands, which were still splattered with paint. He probably still had lots in his hair as well, but he was so tired that he was past caring.

In all honesty, Josh wasn't in the mood to chat anyway. He had received a phone call from his mum sounding somewhat alarmed.

'Grandma Tilly says the tractor is in the middle of the shop!' she'd said.

'It's a temporary thing,' Josh had replied. 'How's Pete? Are you having a good time?'

But she didn't accept the change of conversation tack he had tried and he'd spent the next ten minutes trying to placate her.

'I know I said I'd give you carte blanche,' his mum had said. 'But it's sounding a bit of a mess.'

'Amber seems to know what she's doing,' Josh had offered, pulling out his ace card.

'Amber's OK with the tractor?' his mum had asked, sounding shocked.

'It was her idea,' Josh had told her.

It was only then that his mum began to be somewhat reassured.

'Well, I'm sure she knows what she's doing,' Cathy had replied.

Josh sincerely hoped so. He had tried to go along with Amber's enthusiasm, but privately he was having severe doubts as to the whole refurbishment of the shop.

'Can't you pay them to shut up?' said Dodgy Del, who had just come in and sat next to Josh at the bar. 'I've had a hell of a day and I'm not in the mood for a bad version of Coldplay tonight.'

'You know what? I'll tell them to take their money and hop it,' said Mike, grimacing. 'I've got a splitting headache myself.'

'I'm not surprised,' said Josh, turning to look at Del. 'What's up?'

'This weather,' said Del, gesturing through the murky window to the darkening sky outside. 'This rain had better ease up soon or else the roads are going to start flooding. I've already had my fill of pensioners moaning today about how wet they've got going round their gardens and parks. It doesn't help that the tea rooms were all full up because of the bad weather. Wasn't my fault.'

'Glad somebody's full of customers,' muttered Josh. 'Maybe I'll open up a garden instead.'

There was a small pause whilst the band began to pack up their set in a somewhat noisy fashion.

'How's the makeover going?' asked Del. 'Still can't believe that trac-tor's stuck in the middle of the place.'

'Me neither,' said Josh. 'It's going far too slowly for my liking. And expensive to boot.'

'Well, she's from New York, ain't she?' said Del, between sips of beer. 'Used to living the high life in her fancy Manhattan loft. Yeah, I've seen *Sex and the City*. Although there weren't enough sex in it for my liking. Just women chatting all the time and I can get that from my sister and mum all evening. Why do you think I come in here to escape?'

'Amber's not like that,' said Josh, shaking his head. 'Anyway, she's from England.'

'How would I know?' said Del. 'She's not said one word to me yet.'

'Wise lady,' said Josh.

'By the way, is she single?'

Josh turned to look at his friend. 'Leave well alone,' he warned him. 'She's too sweet and innocent for the likes of you.'

'Ha!' said Del, laughing into his pint. 'So you're keeping her to yourself.'

'I'm not keeping her for anyone,' Josh told him. 'She's only here for a few more weeks. And it'll be my mum and grandma you'll have to contend with if you upset Amber.'

Del gave a mock shudder. 'I'm right scared at that!'

'You should be,' said Josh, draining his pint. 'I've seen Grandma Tilly threaten the turkey with a carving knife at Christmas and she's pretty good.'

'All right,' said Del. 'I suppose you've got more than enough women in your shop already. There's only so much feminine chatting you can cope with, am I right?'

Josh nodded but deep down, did he really agree? He was actually enjoying Amber's company. She was quiet, yes, but not so much with him. They'd got drunk the other night together, but that was just about needing to blow off some steam.

Life had just got on top of him, he felt. He had been struggling to take care of his mum as well as shielding her from the truth about the situation they were facing with the shop. In a way, it was nice to have the company and some positive spirit about the place. Whether the redecoration would make any difference, he wasn't so sure. But what harm could it do? Of course, if they lost any more customers, nobody would come in at all.

'So you've done the ceilings, have you?' asked Del, breaking into Josh's reverie.

'Can't you tell?' said Josh, running a hand through his hair and feeling the spots of paint still caught in the strands. 'Just all the walls, shelving and floor to go.'

He still had no idea what Amber had planned for the tractor. But at least she had spent the day wiping it clean of grease and muck before covering it up with a large plastic sheet.

'I can always give you a hand, if you like,' said Del.

Josh knew that his mate never did anything for free. 'What's in it for you?' he asked.

'The goodness of my kind heart,' said Del, with his cheeky grin.

'What else?'

'A date with Amber?' asked Del hopefully.

'Not a chance,' said Josh firmly.

'OK then. How about one of those boxes of beers I've seen lying around the place.'

'Done,' said Josh, with a nod. 'You can have two if you're any good with a paintbrush.'

'Nah, mate,' Del replied, shaking his head. 'But I can wire in those new LED strip lights you were asking me about the other day.'

* * *

At least the lighting would be up to date, thought Josh the following day as he watched Del tear out the old strip lighting and start to hang the new ones across the ceiling. Hopefully painting and plugging the many holes in the ceiling would make it look better, he thought, catching Amber's horrified face.

'Does he know what he's doing?' she whispered.

'Of course,' lied Josh. 'Anyway, at least it's warmer in here. You can't complain about that.'

He nodded to where the wood-burning stove finally had a fire crackling away inside. It had cost him to pay the chimney sweep but he had to admit that it was definitely a feature worth having.

'Mind the tractor!' he called out as a shower of dust came down as Del drilled through the ceiling. Thankfully it was still covered with a plastic sheet.

'Yeah, I'd hate for a museum piece like that to get mucky,' said Del, laughing to himself.

Josh had quietly asked a mechanic who frequented the pub to check out the tractor to see if there was any way it could be moved. But he had taken one look at the engine and told Josh that it had totally seized up, as well as the axle. Towing wasn't an option and it was more likely to need a crane to get it moved.

When he told Amber, he was surprised that she began to smile.

'So it will have to stay here after all,' she said, looking pleased.

'That's not what I said,' Josh told her.

But he was having to reluctantly admit to himself that the tractor was probably stuck in the shop for the foreseeable future. In a way he was pleased that it wasn't going to the great scrapheap in the sky quite yet. In another, he still didn't know what anyone, especially his mum, was going to make of it all when they'd finished redecorating the place. He just hoped that the business would have picked up by the time she came back from holiday. Thankfully that appeared to be slightly later in the year than she had originally intended.

'It's just for a few more weeks,' she had told Josh the previous day. 'I'm having such a lovely time in Singapore. It's just delaying heading out to New Zealand, that's all.'

So it sounded as if Amber was going to be staying at least until the end of November. To which Josh was secretly pleased.

Amber's mention the previous day about the sustainability of the business had him wondering though. They still had all the stock to use up that wasn't out of date or broken. Her suggestion about it being a lifestyle shop and having it all out on display might mean they could shift the odd item. But it was the lack of sustainable items that was making him think. Was there a way to run the shop and sell environmentally friendly goods?

At least his new light bulbs were low energy and the heating came from a wood-burning stove, of which there was a plentiful supply nearby of fuel. But the rest of it? He had no idea.

But, in truth, it wasn't that which was keeping him awake at night. It was the thought of Amber leaving him to decide all this for himself. He was enjoying keeping her counsel and her companionship. To his astonishment, they were making quite a team and he was actually beginning to enjoy himself.

Del tried and failed to flirt with her when he worked on the new lights. She smiled at his jokes, but there was clearly no attraction there. At least that's what Josh was hoping. Because he could feel a growing attraction to her himself that was becoming harder to deny. The trouble was that he had no idea if she felt the same way.

23

Amber was finding the redecoration of the shop a lot more fun than even she had imagined.

She had thought she had bitten off more than she could chew initially, but it was actually quite interesting working out where everything should go and the layout of the whole shop.

It all appeared so much bigger now that the space was beginning to get cleared. Once she had told herself that it was really just a big shop window, it had started to click inside her brain that she was up to the task.

Thankfully, Josh had mostly gone along with her ideas, although he was still not convinced about leaving the tractor in the middle of the shop.

'At least you've covered it up,' he'd said, when he saw that Amber had placed a cloth over it.

Luckily, he never thought to peek underneath at any point as Amber had begun to think of the tractor as her secret project. In the evenings, whenever Josh headed over to the pub for his pint of beer, she used the time to continue to transform the tractor. She buffed and polished the silver lights and used leather wax to clean up the interior. She had also begun to prepare the main body of the tractor for its final coat of new colour. She just hoped Josh would like the finished result when she finally revealed it to him.

In the meantime, they were both busy getting on with the renovation. The new white paint on both the ceilings and walls had certainly given the place a fresher feel. And despite her concerns about the quality of Dodgy Del's electrical skills, the new lights were also brighter. The whole shop felt less turgid and yellow and far more modern.

They finished cleaning up the oak shelving units and placed them back against the wall. Amber was pleased to see that they looked more in keeping with the new feel of the shop. It would be far easier to display all the goods now that the customers could actually see what they were buying.

Their idea of splitting items into appropriate sections was certainly a good one, she thought. Thus one part of the wall next to the fireplace held all the food, as well as the tall refrigerators, which had been thoroughly cleaned and disinfected so that they gleamed white once more. On the opposite side was the household section, which displayed the toilet rolls and cleaning products. Towards the back of the shop were the DIY goods, such as the string, screwdrivers and various sized nails and fixings. Finally, nearest to the till was a wide range of goods that didn't come under any kind of section, such as greeting cards and rolls of material.

As the shelves began to fill, Amber realised that the shop had begun to get a little bit busier as word got out of the revamp.

Belle had popped in for some bread but upon seeing the greeting cards and string, she ended up buying those as well. 'I only came in for a nose around the place,' she said, nodding her approval. 'It's much better. Maybe I'll get Aunty and Uncle in to see what ideas we can steal for redecorating the pub.' Then she laughed. 'I know. Not a chance, I reckon.'

Stanley said that he had been looking for his screwdriver for ages and that the replacement one would work very well.

Another customer had paid for their bread before spotting the rolls of material and had promptly bought the whole roll of flowery cotton to make some cushion covers with.

'Maybe this could work,' said Josh, nodding thoughtfully. 'Everyone can see more of the stock now.'

'Of course it will work,' said Grandma Tilly, who had been coming into the shop on a daily basis. She had said it was to check on progress, but Amber thought that she actually enjoyed sitting on the chair behind the till and chatting to customers.

In fact, Amber was also enjoying talking to everyone who came into the shop. It was still early days for her and she was not used to talking to many strangers, but she was beginning to find a small amount of confidence. In a way, her senses were enlivened as she began to communicate once more with people.

She realised she had almost forgotten how to talk to people in New York. In fact, how to even be with other people. She could slowly feel herself coming back to life again and she felt more connected than she had felt in years.

One afternoon, Amber walked slowly around the shop, wondering what was missing. The trouble was that even when the goods were reorganised, it still felt a little sterile in there.

She stared at the fire burning bright inside the fireplace stove. On yet another dark and wet day, it helped make the place feel much more cosy. But it needed more.

'Hey,' said Josh, coming in through the back room.

He'd been out at the cash and carry and had left Amber at the shop. Not that Amber had wanted to return there. It had been a pretty soulless experience. And that was what Cranbridge Stores was still missing. Soul and heart too, she realised.

And pumpkins, apparently. She watched as Josh placed the three pumpkins he was holding onto the counter.

'Is it Halloween already?' she asked, with a smile.

'Not quite,' he told her. 'But they were on special offer and I figured what the hell. Somebody might ask for them. I've got a small crate full out the back as well.'

She drew her hand down the smooth side of one of the pumpkins, her mind wandering.

'I wonder if I should change the windows to a Halloween display at some point,' she said, nodding thoughtfully.

'If you have the time,' he told her, gesturing at the still empty spaces in quite a few of the shelves. 'There's still a fair bit of restocking to be done.'

'But the place needs something else,' she blurted out.

'Besides the tractor?' said Josh, laughing.

She looked at the top of the shelves and realised there was quite a bit of space on top of each cabinet. And then there was the mantelpiece above the fireplace. An idea began to form in her mind.

'I was just wondering how you felt about a few fairy lights and some autumnal touches inside the shop,' she carried on, feeling brave. 'You know, to match the window.'

'That sounds lovely,' said Grandma Tilly, nodding her approval.

To Amber's relief, Josh shrugged his shoulders. 'Knock yourself out,' he told her. 'As long as you're not planning on redecorating me as well, then go ahead. I trust you.'

His words gave her confidence a mighty boost, she found. And as the afternoon wore on, she began to make similar strings of dried autumnal leaves and fairy lights as she had done for the window displays. Then she draped them along the top of the shelving units and across the mantelpiece, along with some conkers and pine cones that she had sprayed silver. In addition, she grabbed some white candles that they had found in a box and placed them at either end of the mantelpiece in a bunch.

Once she had finished, she nodded her approval to herself.

And she wasn't the only one who liked the autumnal display.

'This is lovely,' said Belle when she came in to buy some tinned tomatoes. 'Really pretty.'

Amber noticed how she warmed her hands up in front of the fire and saw Josh had noticed as well. They locked eyes before he gave her a nod as if to say, yeah, you were right about the fire.

'Don't get too smug,' he muttered as he walked by. But she spotted his wink before he headed out the back.

The doorbell rang out once more and the vicar came in.

'Good morning,' said Glenda, looking amazed at the difference inside the shop. 'Goodness me,' she added. 'I hardly recognise the place.'

'It's really nice, isn't it?' said Belle.

'Absolutely,' said Glenda, looking around and smiling. 'Now, what did I come in for?'

Amber spotted Noah the Labrador tied up outside and wondered if she should place a bowl of water outside for dogs. After all, she had spotted quite a few passing by on their daily walks. Perhaps if the dogs stopped to have a drink, then their owners would be tempted inside.

As the vicar and Belle chatted away, Amber was suddenly struck by how important the shop was to people who lived alone.

Keeping the shop open and in business suddenly wasn't just about profit and loss to Amber. It was about the villagers as well. Somewhere for them to talk and to meet.

With that in mind, she wandered out to see Josh after both the customers had left.

'You know those old benches in the lane out there? I was wondering whether you would mind if we moved them to the front porch,' she asked. 'One on either side.'

He looked surprised. 'Whatever for?'

'It was just an idea I had,' she told him. 'I thought it would frame the windows better. And the new display I've got for the porch.'

'The porch is getting a display now?' He frowned. 'Aren't we going to end up looking like Disneyland?'

She shook her head. 'We're dressing the shop, remember? I think it could work.'

He rolled his eyes. 'OK,' he said, to her relief. 'It's not like they're getting any use stuck out there. But let me check them both first to make sure that they're safe if somebody decides to sit on them. We haven't got the money if we get sued if somebody comes a cropper on them.'

'And the veranda could do with a new lick of paint as well,' said Amber, ducking out of the room before he could protest.

In fact, Josh was kept busy fixing the hole in the roof of the veranda before coating it in wood preservative. It looked much better afterwards, especially when the benches were coated in the same oak colouring.

Once Josh had declared them both safe and dry, he and Amber carried them round to the front porch and placed one underneath each front window.

After Josh had disappeared back inside, Amber stood on the steps and decided that they needed a couple of comfy cushions. Maybe even a rug.

Or a blanket, she realised, making a note to ask Grandma Tilly to knit a couple of autumnal-coloured ones next.

Although with all the rain that was pouring down day after day, maybe life jackets would be a better idea, she thought. And then she realised that they also needed a hat and umbrella stand somewhere. And thought she'd seen one out the back as well.

In fact, the back room was a gold mine of odds and ends that she could reuse. There were a couple of shabby yet perfectly functional hurricane lamps, which just needed a clean before she placed them either side of the front door with fairy lights in them. Then she stole one of Josh's pumpkins and placed that next to one of the lamps. An old wicker basket was quickly filled with logs that she could easily get to in order to keep the fire going.

Last, she made an autumnal wreath for the front door, made out of the berries and leaves that were down by the river.

Feeling nervous, she showed Josh her work.

'Looks good,' said Josh, nodding slowly. 'Looks really good, in fact.'

Filled with enthusiasm, Amber told him some more of her ideas. 'I thought I could cut out some black cats on cardboard for Halloween. As well as lighting some pumpkins that have been carved, of course.'

'Of course,' he repeated, smiling at her excitement.

'Then, in December, we could have a Christmas tree at both ends of the porch,' she carried on. 'As well as one inside.'

'Only if you come back and decorate them,' he said, laughing.

She was bemused. 'Where am I going?' she asked.

'To New Zealand,' he told her. 'Remember?'

That brought Amber up short. She had completely forgotten that she wasn't there for very long.

'Oh. Well, I'm sure even you can decorate a Christmas tree!' she said, fixing a smile on her face to hide her muddled feelings.

'You're kidding,' said Josh, with a grimace. 'Have you seen my artistic skills?'

As he walked away, she realised that deep down it wasn't just the shop that she would be sad to leave behind.

24
———

As Amber walked out onto the porch the following morning, the air was chilly and damp once more. The whole village was encased in low cloud and drizzle.

It was almost the end of October and it certainly felt as if autumn had finally arrived.

She shivered and placed the long cushions onto the benches. She had discovered them in a corner of the back room and figured that nobody would mind if she recovered both cushions with her favourite red and white gingham checked material. She stepped back and ran her critical eye over the two benches. They certainly gave a more welcoming feel to the place, along with the newly placed hurricane lamps and various decorations.

Grandma Tilly was hard at work knitting a couple of blankets. Amber had even dug out an old porcelain bowl and placed a small sign next to it so that any passing dog owners could take advantage of a canine water break.

Her gaze drifted inside to where her decorations were almost finished. The shop was transformed from one week earlier now that it was decorated and sorted. She just had one final finishing touch that she had hoped Josh would approve of. But for now, the tractor remained hidden beneath some tarpaulin.

She was just considering some other decorations when Del's dilapidated coach pulled up in the lane alongside the shop.

She had been expecting it to be empty as it was only just past eleven o'clock in the morning. Upon hearing a clamour inside, however, she watched as a group of people clambered down the steps, all carrying bags and boxes.

'Morning!' said a pretty blonde-haired woman. 'We're the *Cranbridge Times*! We're moving in next door!'

Amber smiled. 'Oh, we heard you were coming. Hi. I'm Amber.'

'I'm Molly,' said the woman, reaching out to wave with one hand whilst clutching on to a box which appeared to be filled with files with the other. 'Gosh! What a lovely setting! Hopefully we won't be too noisy for you.'

She was in her early twenties with a sweet, friendly nature.

'Rubbish,' said a man appearing next to her, who was holding two laptops and a keyboard under his arms. 'We'll bring a bit of life to the place.' He glanced over to The Black Swan. 'Glad to see there's a pub within staggering distance.'

Molly rolled her eyes. 'The idea was that we'll get more work done here in the peaceful countryside, not drink more alcohol.'

'A man can't live on coffee alone,' he drawled, before nodding at Amber. 'Tom Addison, editor and chief of this rabble.'

He was in his late thirties and had an attractive but careworn face with large bags under his eyes.

'I'm Amber,' she replied. 'And Josh, the owner, is inside somewhere.'

'What a pretty-looking place,' said Molly, peering around the veranda. 'Have you just moved in as well?'

Amber shook her head. 'No, but we're in the middle of renovating the place.'

'Excellent,' said Tom, also looking past her and into the shop. 'I hope you've got a coffee machine in there. Our kettle broke. You could make a fortune from us lot.'

'It's yet to be unpacked,' Amber told him, thinking quickly. 'I think it's out the back somewhere.'

'Then I should make that today's priority if I were you,' said Tom, glancing up as Del helped another man carry a desk down the steps of the coach. 'We're going to need caffeine and lots of it. Right, let's get inside. Who's got the front door keys?'

'You have,' called out Molly.

'Have I?' said Tom, walking to the next-door shop and patting the pockets of his jeans. Finally and with a wiggle of the keys and a heavy nudge to the front door with his shoulder, Tom headed inside.

'Where are the bloody lights?' she heard him shout out.

Molly gave Amber a smile. 'He can be a bit sarcastic sometimes, but he only ever means it as a joke. He's really the nicest boss. Ever so kind and such a good writer,' she whispered.

'And you're a journalist too?' asked Amber.

Molly shook her head. 'Oh no! I'm not talented enough for that. I'm the receptionist, telephone operator, bit of everything really. Kate is the real journalist. She's always out and about though. Then there's a couple of part-time staff as well. I'm sure I'll be in often enough for the coffee run, in any case.'

'Talking of which, I'd better see where it is,' said Amber. 'See you soon.'

'Absolutely. We'll be desperate for lunch at some point.' Molly headed out into the rain. 'Ugh. Will it ever stop raining?'

Amber had to agree with Molly. The weather continued to be cold and miserable. The river was certainly looking higher than when she had first arrived. It was almost up to the bank and was flowing faster than she had ever seen it.

Amber headed back indoors, where Josh was just coming out of the back room.

'What's going on out there?' he asked.

'The local newspaper are moving in next door,' she told him. 'They've just turned up in Del's coach.'

Josh nodded thoughtfully. 'I did hear a rumour in the pub that they were moving in soon. Well, hopefully that means a few more customers, eh?'

She hesitated. 'Talking of which, they were asking about a coffee machine.'

He laughed. 'Yeah, we'd all like one of those.'

'So I sort of lied and said we had one.' Seeing his face drop, she quickly added, 'But I was thinking that it might not be a bad idea. Everyone likes a takeaway coffee these days.'

He raised his eyebrows. 'Seriously?'

'I thought that perhaps if we could diversify a bit.'

'We've got a tractor in the shop. How much different do you want it to be?' But his smile softened his words and he blew out a sigh as he thought hard. 'I'm supposed to be buying some more stock.'

'We've got all the stock we need,' she told him. 'We can barely move for it. But perhaps getting them in through the door with the lure of a coffee might get them to start browsing our many varied goods that are already here. And there's a lovely big gap on the table behind the counter where it could go.'

He nodded thoughtfully. 'I'll think about it,' he told her.

'OK, but if they come in and ask for a coffee later today...?' she asked.

'Tell them it's being serviced and to come back tomorrow,' he told her, rolling his eyes. 'I said I'll think about it, OK?'

'Well, maybe not for too long,' she urged him. 'Otherwise they might buy one for themselves.'

'I doubt it,' he said. 'From what I've heard, the newspaper is in as much trouble as our shop is.'

As she went back towards the till, Amber smiled to herself. Josh had said 'our', she realised. Perhaps he was talking about his mum and himself, she reminded herself. But it certainly felt nice to be part of a team for once. She hadn't had that in her jobs before. She had always felt isolated. But then she had always been stuck in the back or front window. Here she was talking to customers and liaising with people. She had thought that she would hate it. But she was finding she actually quite liked it.

'By the way, what's happening with this?'

She spun round to find Josh standing next to the tractor, which was still covered with a heavy cloth.

'It's a surprise,' she told him. She continued to look at him with hope in her eyes.

He sighed at her silent question. 'Fine,' he said eventually. 'Do what you want. At least I don't have to look at it.'

Amber gave a small whoop of joy. She had been desperate to make a display of the tractor and finally he was allowing her to do so. And she knew exactly what colour it was going to be painted in.

'Red!' exclaimed Josh later that day when she opened up the can of paint and showed it to him. 'I didn't realise you were serious when you coloured it bright red on your bit of paper.'

'Isn't it wonderful? Like a real postbox red,' said Amber, beaming.

But Josh was looking even more alarmed than before. 'I thought the idea would be to try and camouflage it, not highlight it.'

'Why would you want to hide it?' she asked. 'It's a display.'

Josh shuddered and quickly walked away. 'I'm not staying around the scene of the crime. I'm off to the pub.'

Amber was quite glad in a way that he was going out again as she wanted to surprise him with the transformation, despite his less than enthusiastic response. With all the metal and leather already buffed and polished, all she had to do was paint the bodywork.

After a couple of hard hours' work, she stepped back and nodded to herself. She knew it had been right to trust her instinct. It looked amazing. Almost like a large toy tractor. She still had the vision of Grandma Tilly's photograph burning in her mind. And she could just see it surrounded by wooden crates full of brightly coloured fruit and vegetables. Maybe even some blackboard signs with prices on.

Clapping her hands in glee, she headed into the back room and had just finished cleaning her hands when Josh came through the door.

'Is it safe to come in?' he asked, peering through a gap in his fingers.

'Let me show you,' she said, leading him into the main shop.

Josh was looking quite relaxed until he saw the bright red tractor and stopped dead in his tracks.

'Well?' she said, watching his reaction. 'What do you think?'

But Josh appeared to be lost for words as he began to move slowly towards the tractor, his eyes wide as he took in the polished metal and bright red colour. He had held out his hand as if to stroke the metal but quickly withdrew it.

'Don't touch the paint,' she warned him. 'It's still not dry.'

He slowly walked the whole way around it as if in a daze until he came to stand next to Amber.

'Well?' she asked again, starting to feel really worried.

She had expected anger or even mockery but what she hadn't expected were the tears that she saw appear in his eyes. He obviously absolutely hated it.

'Oh, Josh!' she whispered. 'I'm so sorry.'

'Why?' he said, his voice hoarse.

'You hate it, don't you?' She was horrified. She had never meant to upset him. That was the last thing she wanted.

But he smiled through his tears and shook his head. 'No. I think I actually love it.'

'You do?' She couldn't believe it.

'I'm staggered. Speechless, in fact.' He looked at her with blazing eyes. 'Mum will love it as well.'

'You really think so?'

He nodded. 'I know so.' He paused. 'And my dad would have loved it as well. I think this was just how he had imagined it could look.' He laughed. 'Except with it working and being outside of course.'

They both looked at the tractor for a moment in silence. Amber hesitated, but seeing that Josh was still upset, she felt compelled to slip her hand into his and give it a small squeeze.

'I think it might be good to have something so special of your dad's inside the shop,' she said, in a soft tone. 'Like a good-luck token or something.'

'I do too.' He nodded and squeezed her hand back. 'Thank you.'

'You're welcome,' she told him.

But as she let go of his hand, Amber had a sudden urge to draw him in closer and give him a hug. But she held back. He was just emotional over losing his dad, that was all. This was absolutely nothing to do with something between them. Because there was nothing between them.

At least, from his point of view.

Hers was more muddled. Because, right there, right at that moment, she desperately wanted to kiss him and hold him. She wanted to take all of his pain away forever.

But she dismissed the notion as a result of the unexpected emotion of the moment. That was all.

Wasn't it?

25

Amber had assumed that Josh had dismissed the coffee machine idea that she had mentioned the previous day as he hadn't brought it up since. But, to her amazement, Belle staggered into the shop the following morning with a massive box in her hands.

'Where do you want it?' said Belle, handing it over to Josh before rubbing her sore arms.

'What on earth is that?' asked Amber, clearing the counter to make space.

'You wanted a coffee machine and your wish is my command,' Josh told her, putting it down onto the counter with a grunt.

'Really?' Amber peered into the top of the open box. 'It's enormous,' she said, looking down at the silver and black machine.

It appeared to have several buttons on the front and a small screen. On top of the machine were various plastic canisters which were discoloured and dusty.

'It's filthy,' he told her, with a grimace, before looking up at Belle.

Belle held up her hands. 'You had the conversation with my uncle about needing a coffee machine. I'm just the delivery girl. Nobody said anything about cleaning the thing.'

'Are there any instructions?' asked Amber.

'In the box,' said Belle. 'It was quite simple, from what I remember. It's just it's barely been used, to be honest. Nobody ever comes into the pub for a coffee.'

Josh brought out his wallet and handed Belle fifty pounds in notes. 'Payment as agreed,' he said.

'Does it work?' asked Amber, looking at the machine once more.

'I'll have my fifty quid back if it doesn't,' said Josh with a pointed look at Belle. 'Anyway, it's all yours,' he told Amber. 'I expect the shop to be full of customers once the aroma of freshly brewed coffee starts drifting out into the lane.'

With the ghost of a wink, he headed out.

Amber giggled to herself before she realised Belle was still standing there watching her. 'You two make a cute couple,' said Belle, looking at her.

'Oh no,' said Amber, violently shaking her head. 'I'm just an old friend of the family.'

'So not cousins or anything?'

'No,' said Amber, tucking her hair behind her ear.

'Excellent. So it's all legal. So what are you waiting for?' asked Belle, giving her a wink before she turned to leave. 'The tractor looks much better, by the way.'

Still blushing, Amber decided to concentrate on getting hold of the instructions for the coffee machine and reading them through. It took her almost the remainder of the morning to clean out the whole machine, especially the empty canisters, which were terribly tarnished. But after some hard scrubbing, the machine was gleaming. She filled up one of the canisters with some filter coffee from a packet in the shop, she plugged it into a socket in the wall and, after sending up a brief prayer as she placed a mug underneath, switched it on.

She went to stand on the other side of the counter whilst it made various dubious noises but soon, to her surprise, it was bubbling away and the aroma of freshly brewed coffee was in the air.

The bell above the door rang as Frank stepped into the shop.

'Good afternoon,' he said, stopping briefly after shutting the door behind him. 'My word!' He stared in amazement at the tractor gleaming red in the middle of the shop.

'What do you think?' asked Amber.

'What a stunning colour,' said Frank, before sniffing the air. 'What's that lovely smell?'

'Hopefully it's coffee rather than paint and fumes,' Amber told him. 'We have a new coffee machine,' she added, pointing at the large silver machine behind the till. 'Just installed and ready for its trial run.'

'Well, that's a welcome sight. How much is a cup of coffee?' he asked.

'One pound,' she told him, off the top of her head. After all, it was only coffee and water.

'Excellent,' he said with a smile. 'I shall have to bring my thermos mug across. I do miss having a decent coffee now that I'm retired.'

'Doesn't mean that you'll get any here though,' said Josh, walking in.

'Nonsense,' said Frank. 'They'll be lining up the street, I'm sure. Especially when I tell my workers next door about it.'

Frank's prediction of how popular the coffee machine would be turned out to be almost true as the staff from the newspaper offices began to head over for a coffee.

'Fill her up,' said Tom, the editor, holding out a large mug. 'I need something to offset that disgusting house wine at the Mucky Duck last night.'

'Mucky Duck?' asked Amber, trying to work out what he meant.

'Let's face it, The Black Swan is far too elegant a name for that place,' said Tom.

'You drank the house wine at the pub?' asked Josh, his eyes raised.

Tom grimaced. 'Never again. Thanks,' he added as Amber handed over the coffee. 'How drunk was I that I don't recall a large red tractor in the middle of this place yesterday?' he carried on, before taking a welcome sip of his drink.

'It was covered up until last night,' said Amber. 'What do you think?'

'It's, er, different,' he said, with a smile.

Josh gave Amber a look but said nothing.

Molly rushed into the shop next. 'Oooh! I heard there was coffee in here!' she said before stopping dead. 'Nice tractor! What a lovely colour!'

'Go on then,' said Tom, with a dramatic sigh. 'This drink's on me.'

'Thanks, boss,' said Molly, smiling, holding out her mug.

Amber filled it up and handed it back to Molly.

'Where are the doughnuts?' asked Tom, looking around. 'Buns? Anything bread-based? I need carbs to mop up my headache.'

Amber shook her head. 'Sorry. No bakery-type things apart from bread. We've got some boxes of biscuits on special offer though.' She pointed to where they had made a display on one of the shelves.

Tom headed over and picked up a box. 'That'll do,' he said.

'Mmm, Jammie Dodgers,' said Molly, looking at the list of biscuits on the box.

'Oi! Get your own,' snapped Tom, before putting down some coins on the counter. But Amber saw him give Molly a friendly nudge with his elbow before he headed out of the shop.

On his way out, Tom passed Belle on the veranda. 'Is the coffee machine working?' she asked, coming inside and closing the door. 'I thought I'd better check that it hadn't blown up or anything.'

'It's brilliant,' Amber told her.

'Great,' said Belle, before looking at Molly. 'My aunt and uncle run the pub and want to throw everyone from the newspaper a party on Friday night to welcome you all to the village.'

'Really?' Molly looked thrilled. 'How lovely.'

'I wouldn't get your hopes up too much,' Belle told her with a grimace. 'And you might want to eat before you get there.'

They watched as Josh staggered into the shop carrying another pile of pumpkins that he had bought and placed them next to the till.

'We can make it a Halloween party!' said Molly, clapping her hands excitedly.

Belle raised her eyebrows. 'To be honest, it would certainly match the whole mood of the pub, so what the hell.'

'We'll have to think about what to wear. I've got some great outfits,' said Molly, looking at Amber. 'What about you?'

Amber shook her head. 'I'm not sure I've got anything suitable,' she muttered, blushing. Parties always made her feel a bit on edge as to the sheer amount of people in them, let alone dressing up in a strange outfit.

'You can borrow something of mine,' Molly told her.

She was ever so young and sweet, thought Amber as she thanked her. But filled with so much more confidence than Amber could ever hope to have.

'Thanks for the coffee,' said Molly. 'See you later.'

She waved goodbye and walked out of the shop with Belle, chatting excitedly as they left.

Amber heard a noise and looked up to see Josh watching her.

She raised her eyebrows in question to him.

'Yeah, yeah,' he drawled. 'You were right about the coffee machine. You have a talent, by the way. For sales, I mean.'

'I don't know about that,' she told him, blushing.

'I do,' said Josh. 'You've already upped our takings today thanks to the coffees and a large box of biscuits as well.'

'I'm not sure it'll make that much of a difference,' she told him.

'Maybe not,' he replied. 'But it's nice to have a tiny bit of positivity around here.'

She nodded, still wondering whether she could bail out at the last minute. 'Will you go to the party? It's fancy dress apparently,' she told him.

'I will if you will,' he said.

Amber was surprised. 'And you're going to dress up?'

'Absolutely,' he told her. 'I'm going as an impoverished shop owner.'

'Humph,' she said. 'Molly was thinking that we could dress up properly.'

'Yeah, you enjoy that. I'll be at the bar with my pint,' he said, nodding at the pumpkins. 'You'd better get carving then.'

'Aren't you going to help?' she asked.

'You're the artistic one,' he told her.

Amber looked around at the whole shop. 'I guess we should decorate the whole place for Halloween as it's the 31st on Saturday,' she said, tapping her chin as she thought of what could be done.

'That's your department,' he told her.

Amber decided to put the problem of what to wear to the fancy dress party to one side whilst she decorated the shop. Carving the pumpkins was quite easy, thanks to a YouTube tutorial. She placed three pumpkins on both sides of the door and on the side of the step, as well as some tiny squashes which she carved and placed in the window display.

'I hope you're going to pay for all that stock,' said Josh.

'You can take it from my marketing budget,' she told him, to which he laughed.

'Here are the blankets,' said Grandma Tilly later that day, carrying in two beautiful orange and red-coloured knitted throws.

She had only just finished the Christmas ones for Amber the previous week so she must have started on the new blankets straight away.

'They're lovely,' Amber gushed, reaching out to stroke one of the little tassels that Grandma Tilly had added. 'Thank you so much.'

'It's nice to feel useful,' Tilly told her. 'If only for a short while.'

'Why don't you stay for a coffee?' asked Amber. 'Or I can do you a hot chocolate?'

Grandma Tilly looked pleased. 'A hot chocolate would be lovely,' she replied, heading over to have a look at the coffee machine.

As the coffee machine gurgled into life, Amber suddenly had an idea. 'Now, how do you feel about knitting us a couple of pumpkins?'

Grandma Tilly looked astonished. 'Pumpkins?'

'Maybe not just pumpkins. A few squashes as well,' said Amber.

'I'm a little muddled,' said Grandma Tilly, looking confused.

'Sorry,' said Amber. 'I should have explained. I was wondering how you felt about knitting me, well, us, a few pumpkins and squashes. To dot around the shop.'

'Have you been at the punch again?' asked Josh, who came over to raise an eyebrow at her.

Amber blushed. 'No. But you're going to sell all the real pumpkins hopefully and they look so pretty in the shop. I thought if Grandma Tilly could knit us a few then they'd be a more permanent feature until we dress the shop for Christmas.'

'Oh! I see!' Grandma Tilly went over to peer inside the box that contained all the balls of wool. 'Well, they're the right colours in any case.' She broke into a winning smile. 'That'll keep me busy for a few days.'

'Do you want me to carry the box home for you?' asked Amber.

But Grandma Tilly shook her head and held up her shopping bag. 'Fill her up, love.'

After she had enjoyed her hot chocolate, Amber and Grandma Tilly watched a tutorial on YouTube about how to knit a pumpkin.

'It should be easy enough,' said Grandma Tilly.

Amber thought that perhaps she had a bit more of a spring in her step as she left.

Later on, Amber cut out bat silhouettes on some black card that she had found hidden in one of the boxes. She then hung them on some black string and lay them across the tops of the windows.

'Nice,' said Josh, nodding his approval.

'I didn't want to go too mad because some older people are a bit funny about Halloween,' she said.

'You've done really well,' he told her.

'Even the tractor?' she asked.

'Don't push it,' he said, grinning.

Amber found she was also smiling as she went to refill the water in the machine, still somewhat amazed that her idea had not only been addressed but had also appeared to work. It had definitely drawn in the newspaper workers next door.

Maybe, just maybe, the plan to redesign their shop would help.

Their shop. She whispered it to herself as if it were a secret that only she knew. But each and every day it felt as if she were becoming a joint owner with Josh. Little by little, their lives were being entwined by the shop and she realised she liked that they were becoming closer day by day.

26

On the day before Halloween, Amber found herself run off her feet with customers dashing in for either pumpkins or sweets. Thankfully, they had plenty of both to keep everyone stocked up ready for the trick or treating the following evening.

Even the pub landlord, Mike, came in, looking for bread rolls.

'I'm doing a BBQ,' he told Amber. 'I've got some meat that needs using up from the freezer that's defrosted.'

She managed to stop herself shuddering just in time.

'See you tonight!' said Mike, giving Josh a wave as he left. 'Don't forget! The burgers will only be two quid!'

'What was that about?' asked Josh.

'Possible food poisoning,' Amber told him. 'He's got some kind of meat he wants to use up for a BBQ.'

Josh grimaced. 'Well, that sounds like a horror story that we don't want to be a part of.'

Amber thought how nice it was to be a 'we'. Even though he was just talking generally, it gave her a warm feeling to be part of something.

'Talking of BBQs, did you see the photo of our mums?' asked Josh.

Amber smiled and nodded. Her mum had sent them a photo of both her and Cathy grinning madly and looking thrilled to be together at last.

'They looked so happy,' she said.

'Not sure how long it'll be until Mum decides to head back,' said Josh, looking at Amber. 'Is that OK with you?'

'It's fine,' she told him, to his obvious relief.

Better than fine, she told herself in secret. She wasn't quite ready to leave Cranbridge yet.

Later on, once the shop was finally closed, she dashed upstairs to try on the black dress that Molly had leant her. Amber had only packed her casual clothes; her smarter dresses were still en route to New Zealand. So she had had to borrow from Molly, who was going to the party dressed as a Hogwarts student as apparently her little brother had plenty of Gryffindor scarves and so on. She had also leant Amber her spare witch's hat. The trouble was that Molly was a lot shorter than Amber and consequently her dress barely reached the middle of her thighs. It was also very clingy.

Amber peered at her reflection in the tiny dressing table mirror, swinging around left and right. 'No visible panty line at least,' she murmured.

And some black tights covered the acreage of bare skin that the dress was revealing.

'Oh well,' she said to her own reflection, popping the witch's hat on top of her long hair, which she was wearing loose. 'At least it's dark outside. It'll just have to do.'

For a second she hesitated. What if people laughed at her? What if they were mean and laughed behind her back? The old feeling of being an outsider came rushing back.

She tried to take some deep breaths, reminding herself that Belle and Molly weren't like that. But she was still feeling sick with nerves as she walked out of her bedroom and down the stairs.

* * *

Josh was waiting in the shop for Amber so that they could walk over to the pub together.

Hearing her come down the stairs in what sounded like heels as opposed to her normal trainers, he began to switch off the lights inside the shop.

He flipped over the sign from Open to Closed and spun around just as he heard Amber come into the shop.

He had been about to say something, but the words and all coherent thoughts flew from his mind instantly.

With the light of the storeroom behind her, Amber was silhouetted in the dark. He found himself staring and couldn't stop. He had a flashback to when she was standing in the middle of the shop in just a towel. Now she was fully dressed, he was even more mesmerised by her long legs. Her body was also looking far curvier than he remembered, with the dress clinging tightly to every inch.

She walked into the shop, every step in her high heels emphasising her outfit.

'So, do I look scary enough?' she asked, fiddling with her witch's hat nervously. Her smile faltered as she looked at his expression.

'Of course!' he told her, quickly. 'You look great.'

'I don't know,' she said, her voice filled with uncertainty. 'Maybe I should get changed.'

'You look fine,' he said, his voice suddenly hoarse. 'Let's go.'

He felt in a daze as they headed outside and hoped the cool night air might bring him to his senses. But as they walked across the bridge, she wobbled in her high heels and he found himself wrapping an arm around her waist so that she didn't fall in the river.

'As long as I don't take you with me as well,' she said, giggling a nervous laugh.

He tried to join in with her soft laughter, but it caught in his throat. All he could think about was the feel of her warm skin through the cotton dress and the curve of her waist as he held her.

Finally after what felt like hours, he let go of her to open the door of the pub.

A series of wolf whistles rang out, at which point Amber bit her lip. Didn't she realise that just made her look even sexier? thought Josh.

'You look amazing,' said Molly, coming up to them and smiling. She was wearing a long Hogwarts cloak and had drawn a lightning bolt on her forehead with eyeliner.

'It's a bit short,' murmured Amber, tugging at the hem of the dress.

'Who cares? You've got the legs for it,' said Molly, putting on a pair of fake glasses. 'Anyway, have some of Mike's special punch and that'll calm your nerves.'

'Special punch?' asked Josh, sensing that everyone's eyes were on them. Or, more specifically, Amber.

'I don't know what's in it,' Molly told them, making a face. 'It's pretty disgusting, but after a couple of glasses you lose all feeling in your tongue so you don't care!'

She giggled and dragged Amber away to a nearby table, where Belle was pouring out drinks from the punch bowl. Belle was also dressed in a black dress and witch's hat, but for some reason, it didn't have quite the same effect on him as Amber's outfit did.

Josh watched them for a second before heading to the bar.

'Pint,' he croaked.

'Wise choice,' said Tom, who was sitting by the pillar. 'That punch could strip paint off the walls. Although the wallpaper in here appears to be doing that all by itself.'

Josh nodded and immediately took a sip of the beer that Mike had just handed over. He turned around to lean his back against the bar and looked over at Amber. He wasn't the only one, he realised. Nearly every red-blooded male in the room was looking at her, Molly and Belle.

Josh glanced over to Tom, who was also looking to where the women stood, nodding thoughtfully to himself.

'Well, you know what they say, it's always the quiet ones,' said Tom, before draining half of his drink in one go.

'What do you mean?' asked Josh.

'Sweet, quiet Amber turning up looking like a supermodel in that dress and living it up.'

Josh grunted. She certainly looked amazing and he couldn't understand why it rattled him so much.

'Chances are she won't stay single for long in that outfit,' carried on Tom. 'Perhaps I should have asked her out after all.'

Josh was horrified. 'No!' he found himself blurting out.

Tom looked at him, amazed.

Josh sighed and cleared his throat. 'Please don't,' he found himself pleading. 'Just don't.'

He didn't know why it felt so necessary that Tom didn't date Amber, but he just couldn't bear the thought.

Tom raised his eyebrows at him in question before understanding crossed his face. 'Ah. I get it.' He nodded. 'Hey, no worries. Anyway, I'm much too cynical and miserable for anyone as sweet as your lovely Amber to be interested in. There's far too much anger and hate in my heart for my ex-wife to fit in someone as nice as Amber.' He took another drink. 'Thankfully the call isn't mine to make as she's far more interested in you instead.'

Josh gave a start. 'How do you make that out?'

'I know people,' said Tom, with a shrug. 'It's my job. And trust me when I tell you that girl likes you.'

Josh turned to look once more at Amber when Tom spoke again.

'A word of advice, friend. Blondes are always the worst heartbreakers. Trust me.'

Josh looked back as Tom twirled his wedding ring round and around on his finger. 'Why do you wear that if your ex-wife caused you so much pain?' he asked.

'To remind me not to be as stupid as to fall for anyone ever again,' said Tom, letting go of his finger to pick up his drink once more and drain his glass. It was obvious that he was getting blind drunk very quickly. From what Josh had heard, this was a daily occurrence where Tom was concerned.

Josh took a gulp of his beer as he digested what Tom had told him. He had tried so long to deny that there was any attraction between him and Amber. Besides, working together would be too hard if they let any chemistry between them get out of hand. It was probably best that he just bury his feelings and hope that she didn't feel the same way about him.

But he couldn't prevent his eyes straying over to where Amber was, whenever he had the chance.

27

A few hours later, Amber was having a lovely time at the party. A very happy, wonderful time with her new friends!

Or it would be if she could just stand up properly.

It must be her high heels, she told herself. Was she so over New York that she could no longer walk in heels?

It didn't matter. She kicked them off and found that she could dance much more easily without them in her bare stockinged feet.

Everything was lovely. Cranbridge was lovely. The shop was lovely. Even the pub was lovely that evening.

Molly giggled as they bumped into each other whilst they danced.

'That punch is so tasty,' said Molly, laughing above the disco music that they had insisted Mike put on the loudspeaker.

'Isn't it?' said Amber, finding her tongue was slightly numb and her words coming out a little thick.

'I told you,' carried on Molly, spinning around on the spot. 'After the first couple of glasses, you don't even taste how disgusting it is.'

Amber giggled, her hair flopping around her face as she carried on moving. It struck her that she was really quite drunk, but it was a party, wasn't it? Everyone was drunk.

Tom certainly was as he had joined them in the middle of the floor a few minutes ago, although when Molly tried to teach him the moves to Beyoncé's 'Single Ladies' he lost his balance and nearly took all three of them out. As it was, Amber managed to land softly somewhere.

It wasn't until she looked around that she realised that it was Josh's lap which had softened the blow.

'Hello,' she said, smiling. She hadn't even realised that he had been sitting near to them until just then. He really was very handsome when you sat this close to him.

'Hello yourself,' he said, smiling.

'You have very nice eyes,' she told him, folding her hands around the back of his neck to stop herself from swaying.

And it was true. His eyes were blue with a tiny fleck of yellow around the outside of the iris, if you peered very closely, which she realised she must be because she could feel his breath on her cheek.

She leaned back and smiled at him again.

'How much of Mike's punch did you drink?' he asked, laughing.

'I'm not sure,' she said, sticking out her tongue and pinching it with her fingers. 'But I can't feel my tongue.'

'Then I would say it's probably time to call it a night,' he said.

'Call what a night?' she asked, frowning.

He gave her a gentle push as he moved and she suddenly found herself standing up. Although she was aware that Josh was holding on to her.

'Why is the room swaying?' she asked. 'Is it an earthquake? Another tractor?'

'Too much punch,' he told her, bending down to pick up something.

Her shoes materialised in front of her face. She looked down at them and then back up at him.

'Don't you think you should put these on?' he asked.

It took Amber a while to put her shoes on as the room spun every time she bent down. In the end, Josh crouched down to slip them onto her feet.

'Cinderella,' she said, giggling.

'As long as I'm not the Ugly Sister,' he told her, straightening up to put an arm around her shoulders. 'Goodnight all,' he called out as they headed out of the door.

She just about heard them all shout goodnight before the door to the pub closed behind them.

'Oh, you're definitely not ugly,' she said, thinking that it was important that he knew this.

He stopped and smiled at her. 'Thank you. Come on, it's cold.'

She had a sudden thought. 'You didn't dance with me.'

'I thought Tom would enjoy it more.'

She frowned up at him. 'I don't like him the way I like you.'

He tugged at her to start moving, but she found she was having trouble walking.

'My feet aren't working properly.'

'I'm not surprised,' he told her, with a sigh.

To her amazement, the next moment she found that she was in his arms as he carried her across the bridge.

'Don't drop me in,' she said, clutching his neck tightly as she glanced down at the water.

'It might sober you up,' she thought she heard him say.

She yawned as he placed her on the veranda next to him whilst he fiddled with the key and let them into the shop.

'In you go,' he said, as he opened the door.

'My feet still don't work,' she told him.

'I thought they wouldn't,' he replied, picking her up once more and carrying her over the threshold.

'Like a bride,' she said. 'Mr and Mrs Kennedy!'

He raised an eyebrow at her as he locked the door behind them. 'I thought that was my parents.'

'If you marry, you'll be Mr and Mrs Kennedy as well.'

'I guess so,' he replied. 'I'd have to find someone to marry me first, of course.'

They slowly went up the stairs, step by step, with Amber still in his arms as he carried her.

'I'd marry you,' she told him, as he put her down next to what appeared to be her bedroom.

He leant against the door frame and swept something off her face. She thought it was a lock of hair. 'You would?' he asked softly.

'Oh yes,' she said, reaching out to stroke his face. His chin was rough where he hadn't shaved since that morning, but it wasn't an unpleasant feeling beneath her fingers. 'You're really very nice.'

His eyes twinkled. 'Gee. Thanks. I'm just nice, am I?'

'No! You're more than that! You're hot!' she laughed before suddenly feeling perfectly miserable. 'Not that you would think the same about me.'

'You obviously didn't look in the mirror before we came out,' he told her.

'I did!' she replied. 'I had to check no VPL.'

He shook his head. 'That wasn't what I meant.'

'Well, you should say what you mean,' she told him, feeling a bit cross-eyed. 'It's very confusing otherwise.'

'And you should go to bed,' he told her. 'You're going to feel ghastly in the morning.'

'But I feel lovely now. Do I get a goodnight's kiss?' she asked, feeling hopeful. After all, it was dark and they were alone.

She felt brave and full of confidence as she looked up at him expectantly.

He stared at her for a very long time as if struggling internally with some monumental decision. Then he bent forward.

Amber found herself holding her breath and opening up her lips slightly.

But at the last second, he moved his face and gave her a gentle kiss on the cheek.

Even in her drunken state, she could feel the disappointment seep through her.

He stepped backwards, his face almost hidden in the dark shadow of the door now.

'Goodnight, Amber,' he said.

'Goodnight,' she replied, hoping her words weren't quite as slurring to his ears as they were to hers.

Then she went into her bedroom, lay down on the bed fully clothed and passed out, still wearing her witch's hat.

28

Josh was not entirely surprised to find that he was alone for the first hour or two in the shop the morning after the Halloween party. But he was feeling cheerful as he reflected back on the previous evening. Whatever truth serum Mike had put in his Halloween punch had certainly brought out a completely different side of Amber. He smiled to himself as he thought about her staggering around on the dance floor before asking him for a kiss when they had returned back to the flat.

Well, at least he knew that she liked him romantically on some level, he thought. Whether she would regret the whole evening remained to be seen.

Although he got the answer to that half an hour later when Amber appeared at the bottom of the stairs at the back of the shop. She was walking extremely slowly, as if she was in danger of falling over.

'Good morning!' he called out, deliberately loudly.

She immediately staggered, clutching her head. 'Not so loud,' she moaned, hanging on to the door frame for support.

She slowly drew up her head and gazed at Josh, who stared at her red-rimmed eyes and pale face.

'Coffee? Paracetamol?' he offered. 'Or do you want to choose a painless death instead?'

'Definitely death,' she groaned, slowly walking over to the counter and feeling her way around until she sank onto the chair behind.

He made her a coffee from the machine, glancing over at her once in a while. She really did look very pale.

'Good morning!'

Amber jumped at the cheery greeting that came from Tom in the doorway and gave a soft cry out in pain.

'Ah, I see Mike's home-made punch has left its mark on you,' he said, grinning. 'At least you made it into work. Molly called in sick!'

'Well, it is Saturday,' groaned Amber. 'Lucky her.'

Josh handed her a cup of coffee which she held between her hands.

'I recommend a plate of bacon sandwiches and an awful lot of water,' said Tom.

Amber shook her head. 'Don't think I could eat anything,' she muttered.

The doorbell rang and Belle walked very slowly into the shop before pausing to lean against the gleaming red tractor.

'Help me,' she whispered.

Amber looked at her. 'You too?' she moaned.

Belle nodded before wincing.

'Listen,' Josh told her. 'Why don't you both take a coffee out into the fresh air? It might help wake you up.'

'What about the shop?' asked Amber, looking at him through blood-shot eyes.

'Yes, you really look as if you'd be up for the job this morning,' Josh told her.

She shuddered, shaking her head. 'Maybe you're right. Are you sure you'll be OK on your own?'

'I'm sure.'

She gave him a small smile and then very slowly rose from her chair and moved back around the counter, still clutching her coffee.

Amber made it as far as the tractor before reaching out to hang on to Belle. Then, clutching onto each other, they slowly made their way outside.

Once they had left, Tom turned around to face him, grinning. 'I must say, it makes a change for someone else to be suffering with a hangover around here. You're OK, I take it?'

Josh nodded. 'I stuck to the beer.'

'Wise move.' Tom glanced at the front veranda where Amber and Belle were now sitting on one of the benches. 'It could work, you know,' he added softly. 'The two of you working and living together.'

'We do that anyway,' Josh told him.

'You know what I meant,' said Tom in a pointed tone. 'She's lovely, single and she's a great partner for you here in the shop.'

But Josh found he was shaking his head. 'She's just passing through. As soon as my mum gets home, Amber will be off to join her parents in New Zealand.'

Tom frowned. 'Has she booked her plane ticket yet?'

Josh shook his head. 'No. I don't think so.'

'You'd think if she really wanted to leave, she'd have booked it by now,' said Tom. 'You know, if she wasn't enjoying her time here? She looked pretty happy last night, don't you think?'

Josh had a brief memory of her asking him to kiss him in the darkness of the flat upstairs. It had taken every bit of his self-control to not take her in his arms. It was the fact that she'd asked for a kiss when she was drunk that was the problem. And he was too much of a gentleman to take advantage of her like that.

'Think about it, yeah?' said Tom, whilst Josh stayed silent. 'Don't become full of bitterness and regrets like me. There's only room in this village for one broken heart at a time.' He picked up his coffee and walked out of the shop, leaving Josh still standing behind the counter.

Was Tom right? Was Amber really delaying booking her ticket because she wanted to stay? Had drunken Amber revealed her innermost feelings by asking him to kiss her? Or was it just the home-made punch putting words in her mouth?

Josh hoped he would find out sooner or later. And that it hadn't just been the punch. Amber had got under his skin. And he found he rather liked it.

29

'Whose stupid idea was it to come outside?' said Belle, closing her eyes to the bright daylight as they sank onto the bench together with a groan.

'Not mine,' muttered Amber, pulling Grandma Tilly's blanket around her shoulders in deference to the cold air. 'What on earth was in that punch?'

'Not my fault,' moaned Belle. 'My relatives can take the full blame for that monstrosity. I don't know what they put in there.'

Amber leant back against the seat and sighed. She didn't want to admit it, but she did feel a little better for being outside. She listened to the birdsong and felt the gentle breeze across her face. The countryside was certainly growing on her.

'Hi.' They both looked up to see Molly hanging onto the handrail of the steps. 'Help me.'

'You look like I feel,' Belle told her, smiling despite her pain.

Molly grimaced. 'I feel so rubbish,' she said, climbing up the steps to lean against the rail in front of them.

'Tom said you called in sick,' said Amber.

'I had to come in,' said Molly, rolling her eyes. 'Kate said she needed some photocopying done and it was urgent.'

'Snotty cow,' muttered Belle.

Amber turned to look at her, surprised. 'Who's Kate?'

'Our senior journalist,' said Molly.

'I don't think she's come into the shop yet,' said Amber.

'Don't expect smiles and compliments. She told me that our pub was a joke,' said Belle. 'I mean, she's got a point, but nobody's ever rude enough to say it out loud.'

'She's not that bad,' said Molly, although she didn't sound as if she meant it. 'And Tom says she's a really good journalist.'

'Well, you should have told her to do her own bloomin' photocopying,' said Belle.

'It doesn't matter anyway,' said Molly, sinking down slowly to sit on the steps of the veranda. 'My flatmate has got her boyfriend around for a sneaky morning in bed. So she told me to hop it.'

'How charming,' drawled Belle. 'You should have told her to get stuffed. It's your flat as well.'

Molly shook her head. 'Oh no! I can't do that. She's been my best friend since we first went to school.'

'But surely your best friend would understand about you feeling hungover?' said Amber.

Molly frowned. 'It's more important that she spends some time with Taylor. That's her boyfriend. They don't get much time together on account of his wife being around so often.'

'Nice girl,' muttered Belle, giving Amber a pointed look.

'My head!' moaned Molly, holding her forehead. 'I don't think I'm going to feel well ever again. What about you?'

'Same,' said Amber. 'I made it downstairs and then Josh sent me outside because I looked so rough.'

'He's quite the he-man, isn't he?' said Molly, in a dreamy voice.

Amber frowned. 'What do you mean?'

'I think the last time I saw you was when he was carrying you across the bridge,' said Molly. 'It was like something from the movies.'

Amber sat bolt upright. 'I'd forgotten all about that!' she gasped, horrified.

'Wish I knew someone who could pick me up like that,' said Belle with a sigh.

'Oh God,' moaned Amber, looking at the two other women in horror. 'I hadn't really remembered leaving the pub. How am I going to look him in the eye after that?'

'It doesn't matter, does it?' said Belle, with a shrug. 'We all made fools of ourselves. I even contemplated kissing Dodgy Del before thankfully my last shred of sanity reminded me that it was the worst idea ever.'

Molly giggled. 'And I danced all the way down the lane before they managed to get me in the back of the taxi to take me back to the flat.'

But Amber was feeling sick to her stomach. 'But now he'll think badly of me. He'll think that I'm an idiot. Which I am, obviously.'

'What are you talking about?' said Belle, shaking her head. 'So you got a bit drunk and he had to carry you home? Most men I've dated would have let me fall into the river and then laugh at me.'

But that wasn't what Amber was thinking. She was now remembering asking him to kiss her. She groaned and sank backwards onto the bench once more.

'Don't worry about it,' urged Molly.

But Amber couldn't do anything but feel anxious and upset about the way she had acted. The fact that Josh had rejected her on top of everything else made her feel like she had made an even bigger fool of herself.

* * *

Despite her hangover, Amber kept busy all day, managing to hide her confused feelings inside.

She would certainly be steering clear of any alcohol from this day forth. Of course, the drink was to blame. When had she ever let go like that? Made a fool of herself? Not for a very long time, she knew.

She wished she could talk to Josh about it but knew that was impossible. He was her friend, that much she hoped after their time together.

But she had crossed a line in asking him to kiss her. She didn't know what the future held, but she was pretty sure that it wouldn't involve the both of them working together in the shop.

She was so cross with herself for ruining what had been a perfectly nice friendship. And for what reason?

Because you wanted to kiss him, said her innermost thoughts. *And you've wanted him to kiss you for a long time.*

She gulped back her feelings, trying to wish them away. But it was no good. She'd have to face him at some point.

Thankfully it was Halloween and they had quite a few people coming into the shop for sweets and pumpkins. Amber found she could keep busy serving them, as well as preparing a tub full of jellied spiders and chocolate frogs to give away to any trick or treaters later that evening.

In fact, she managed to have avoided talking to Josh about anything other than work for the whole day, mainly by way of leaving a room every time he entered it. Once or twice she had caught him looking at her and he even began to make conversation, but she had quickly made the excuse of having to restock some shelves.

It was only once she was standing on the veranda with Josh, saying goodbye to the last of the trick or treaters that they were finally alone.

For a second there was silence and then Amber went to turn around. 'That was fun,' she said, her words coming out in a rush with nerves. 'I think I'll head up and have an early night.'

But he was too fast for her and had already moved to block the doorway into the shop.

'We've hardly spoken all day,' he told her.

'I just feel rubbish, that's all,' she said.

He stared down at her, his eyes boring into the top of her head as she looked anywhere but at him. 'Amber.'

She gave a small start as he took her chin in his fingers and slowly drew up her chin so that her face was close to his.

'I'm sorry,' she said, finally, when she could bear the silence no longer.

'For what?' he asked, smiling.

'Last night. All of it,' she said, closing her eyes in mortification.

'Well, everyone was drunk,' he said softly.

Her eyes flew back open at that. Perhaps she hadn't been the only one to make a complete fool of herself.

'Of course, nobody else asked me for a goodnight kiss,' he added.

She groaned, blushing. 'Oh God, it was the punch. That stuff was lethal.'

He stared down at her for a long time. 'I'm sorry to hear you say that,' he said finally.

'Why?' she whispered.

He smiled. 'Because I was hoping that it wasn't just the punch,' he said softly, his thumb brushing her lower lip.

Then he let go of her and left her even more confused than ever.

30

The following morning, at his usual time of half past nine, Stanley arrived with his travel mug.

'Black, no milk, please,' he said.

Amber was pleased that he was getting into the habit of ordering a coffee along with his daily newspaper. He seemed to be a little lighter in spirits with an excuse to linger in the shop for a while.

After Amber had poured out his drink, Stanley took a sip. 'Oh, that's good,' he told her. 'It's always a luxury to have nice coffee. I used to treat myself to a cup of coffee when I was at the hospital with my late wife. Feels like I'm in an American movie somehow.'

'More like a disaster movie out there with all this rain,' said Josh, who had just arrived back from the cash and carry. 'The roads are getting quite bad.' His hair was glistening wet from the rain and Amber had to turn away in order not to linger on how attractive it made him look.

'The local radio station said that the road to Aldwych is flooded halfway across and that the traffic is terrible,' said Stanley.

Josh nodded. 'It was. I was OK in the van, but if we get this storm later in the week that they're predicting, I reckon it'll be impassable.'

Stanley nodded. 'The fields are saturated. I don't remember the river looking this high for a long time. It used to be so shallow. I even skated on it in the winter when I was younger.'

'How lovely,' said Amber. 'Your very own skating rink.'

She had been to see the Rockefeller Center skating rink when she had been in New York, but she had never skated on there. Filled with couples and families at Christmastime, it had almost seemed to emphasise her loneliness and she had left almost as soon as she had arrived.

In Cranbridge, she realised she didn't feel that way. She knew that living with Josh in the flat meant that she wasn't living alone, but it wasn't just that. It was the interactions with the customers that was helping. As Stanley stayed on to enjoy his coffee, she wondered how many other people in the village could be lonely as well.

Amber wandered over to look at the river through the window. 'Has the river ever flooded Riverside Lane?' she asked. It was nearly level with the bottom of the bank and rushing through at quite a fast current.

'Oh yes,' said Stanley. 'It's been a few good years though since then. At least ten, from what I remember. But it only laps the lane just at the riverbank. Hopefully all those works on the locks lower down the river will help the water flow away.'

Amber looked across at the river once more before turning to look at the shop which they had worked so hard on. Then she mentally crossed her fingers that the river would stay contained.

Because what on earth would happen if it flooded its banks?

* * *

'I can't believe they've named the first big storm of autumn Storm Amber,' said Tom, with a grin the following morning.

Josh watched as Amber's cheeks immediately flooded pink with embarrassment.

'Ha ha,' she said, rolling her eyes as she took his money from him to put into the till. 'Very funny.'

Tom carried on smiling as he picked up his steaming hot coffee. 'No, seriously. Just how dangerous are you?'

'Very dangerous, especially if you're anywhere near open water on a bridge,' said Josh, giving her a knowing look.

'Shut up, both of you,' she told them, blushing and busying herself with going over to put another log into the wood-burning stove.

Josh could smile now in memory of that time a few weeks ago. Was that all it had been? It seemed sometimes as if Amber had been in his life for a lot longer.

As she straightened up, he saw Amber glance out of the window. His gaze followed hers as he saw the branches in the trees outside bend and wave in the stiff breeze, causing a flurry of yellow and russet leaves to be tossed around in the air.

The wind was certainly strengthening, he thought, ducking down to look up at the grey clouds. The rain was continuing to fall, but it was nothing like the monsoon conditions that the weather forecasters were threatening later in the day. They had already had a rush on both candles and matches in case of any power cuts.

'Perhaps they've got it wrong,' said Josh. 'The storm, I mean. It doesn't look that bad.'

'I hope not,' said Tom, as he brought out his phone. 'Misery and chaos make for good headlines.'

Amber spun around and raised her eyebrows at him in surprise.

'Just a little chaos for the headlines,' said Tom, holding up his hand. 'Nothing life-threatening or anything like that.'

Amber continued to look worried as she looked out of the window once more.

'They're saying the worst of it should miss us,' said Josh, joining her by the window.

'Not according to my best source,' said Tom, glancing down at his phone once more. 'Micky Magic is his twitter handle. He's a bloke in a shed somewhere outside of Aldwych. Contrary to what the Met Office, Flood Advisory and all the official chaps are saying, Micky assures me that his barometer never lies and that we'll get hit full in the face here with the heaviest rain.' Tom grimaced. 'So it must be true.'

Amber bit her lip and glanced out at the river once more. It was already lapping against the riverbank.

'We certainly don't need any more rain,' said Josh.

'The whole area is open water at the moment,' said Tom, as he headed out of the shop. 'Hope you guys have some sandbags.'

As Tom walked away, Josh heard him whistling 'Raindrops Keep Falling on My Head'.

'Do we?' asked Amber, turning to look at him. 'Have any sandbags, I mean?'

Josh shook his head. 'Everything but, unfortunately. But we'll be OK. The shop is raised up, remember. We're a foot and a half above the lane.'

'How bad would it have to be?' she asked.

Her brown eyes were filled with worry and he was grateful that she cared so much about the shop. Probably even more than he did, he knew. Although, in truth, he had begun to feel more invested in the shop since the renovations had begun. More so than he had felt in a long time. Since his dad had passed away, in fact.

Josh looked outside once more. 'If it gets as high as the bridge over to the pub, then we'll be in trouble.'

'What do you mean?'

'I mean, it's the same level as the shop,' he told her. 'So if the bridge disappears then it's likely that the shop will flood.'

Amber looked horrified.

'But that would mean it has to become extraordinarily high,' he carried on, trying to reassure her. 'The river's got to come up over the bank and then up the steps and across the veranda to get to the front door.'

Amber nodded. 'OK.'

'Unfortunately, a lot of homes aren't as elevated as us,' he added. It was a grim thought.

'Will Grandma Tilly be OK?' she asked.

He nodded, somewhat relieved. 'Those new bungalows were built on a slight incline. She should be fine.'

'But don't you think she'd better move in here for the next few nights, just in case?' said Amber.

Josh nodded. 'Absolutely.'

'Everyone's worried,' she told him. 'You can sense the fear of everyone who's come in this morning.'

They had had more customers than usual. People who were nervous about driving any great distance in the flooded back lanes would rather come into the shop for their milk and bread. Thankfully he'd picked up more stock than usual, just in case.

The new customers had looked a bit startled at the tractor, but once they had got past the farm machinery in the middle of the shop, they had taken their time to browse for a few different goods. There had been a bit of a run on batteries and wellington boots.

'I had no idea it was this pretty in here,' said one woman.

'We've just renovated,' Amber had told her. 'I'm so glad you like it.'

'I shall come back in here when I've got more time,' the customer had replied.

It was working, Josh had thought. The shop was more attractive and starting to appeal to customers. It was still missing its identity, something that he couldn't place his finger on. But for now, he was just grateful for anyone coming through the front door.

As another gust of wind rattled the veranda outside, he said, 'Let's just hope they're wrong about this Storm Amber.'

'It's not my fault, you know,' she told him with a soft smile.

He smiled back at her; their eyes locked together for a moment. 'I know.'

As wrong as I was about the other Amber, thought Josh as he watched her walk away. He had got used to having her around. Her cheerful smile at the customers. Her companionship. It was nice to have a friend around. He also felt distinctly protective of her. Maybe that's because he knew how little confidence she had in herself. How shy she could be.

He had a sudden flashback to drunken Amber looking up at him in the dark, asking him for a kiss. Thankfully another gust of wind brought him back to his senses as he began to imagine just what would have happened if he had said yes.

31

By the following afternoon, the river was beginning to rise and had almost reached halfway up the grassy riverbank that was on either side. The water had turned a murky brown, full of silt and leaves that were being swept downstream.

And still the rain kept falling.

Amber was spending most of her time in the shop looking nervously out of the window. The rain was becoming heavier with each passing hour, but the actual eye of the storm, bringing high winds and torrential rain, was due to happen around midnight.

It was terribly dark, she thought, grateful for the new overhead lights and the cheery warmth of the wood-burning stove.

Josh had dug out as many batteries, torches and candles as he could find and placed them on the counter next to the till so they were within easy reach. He had also brought in enough logs to keep the stove burning. The air outside was cold and damp, but at least it kept the place cosy inside.

Grandma Tilly was sitting next to the fireplace, keeping warm. She had moved into the flat for the night whilst the worst of the storm swept through. Amber thought she was quite enjoying all the excitement and didn't seem remotely concerned about the flooding or high winds.

'We've survived worse,' she kept saying to them.

Tom rushed in to ask Amber to top up his travel mug with more coffee. 'I'm heading out with Kate to see the state of the roads and grab some photos before the light disappears,' he said. 'Good job she's got an off-roader. Apparently it's starting to get pretty bad out there.'

Outside, the trees were beginning to sway alarmingly in the strong gusts and leaves were being blown all around.

'I'll take a couple of packets of biscuits as well,' said Tom, reaching out to grab some chocolate digestives.

'Your diet is terrible,' said Josh.

'If you had fresh fruit, well, I'd probably not buy it anyway.' He grinned. 'But seeing as there's no choice, I'll have my chocolate biccies. Thankfully man needs sugar not healthy stuff. Right, see you later.'

'Take care out there,' said Amber.

'Cheers,' said Tom, grabbing his coffee and heading out.

Josh was staring at his retreating figure with a questioning look on his face.

'What is it?' asked Amber.

'He has a point. We've not got any fresh fruit or vegetables in here,' said Josh, glancing around the space.

'Is there a market for it?' she wondered out loud.

'I have no idea,' he said.

'I'd love some nice apples,' said Grandma Tilly.

Josh nodded thoughtfully.

But they couldn't continue their conversation as the bell rang out once more as Dodgy Del came into the shop.

'Turned out nice again,' said Del, warming his hands as he stood in front of the fire next to Grandma Tilly's chair.

'You can say that again,' said Josh, who had been restocking the milk in the fridge. 'How are the roads?'

'Almost impassable on the A231 to Aldwych,' said Del. 'I had trouble getting the coach around the floods. I reckon it'll be closed by the morning.'

'How do you get to Aldwych if you don't go via the main roads?' asked Amber.

Del shook his head. 'You don't, unless you want to negotiate the single country lanes. But the chances are that they'll be under water as well as most of them run near the river.' He looked at the batteries on the counter. 'Think I might grab one of those torches as well, Josh. If we lose power, I won't be able to find my pint later.'

'Will the pub stay open?' asked Amber.

Del laughed. 'Are you joking? What will Tom and I do if the place shuts? Nah, I reckon it'll be OK.'

But Del was the only customer who seemed remotely relaxed about the potential flooding. A few more customers than normal had come into the shop, frowning and filling up their baskets.

'The queues into town are terrible,' said one lady, holding on to her milk, bread and beans. 'Thankfully I just needed a few bits. I'm so glad you're open.'

Grandma Tilly smiled and said, 'That's what we're here for.'

The customer nodded. 'Absolutely. I forgot you were here until I saw your new window display. My little one loves seeing the pumpkins. These biscuits will keep us going as well. OK, well, fingers crossed for a dry night for us all.'

'Absolutely,' said Josh, smiling at her as he held the door open.

'Good luck,' called out Amber.

But after the customer had left, Josh's smile immediately dropped. 'The river's almost at the top now,' he told her.

Amber rushed to his side and looked out. It was true. The river was now touching almost the top of the riverbank.

'And it isn't dark yet,' she told him with a worried look. 'What shall we do?'

'I think we stay open as late as we can,' he said. 'Keep the fire burning. Keep warm and dry. Lights on, so people know we're here. Just in case anyone needs anything. Not that we have any boats or anything.'

'I agree,' said Amber. 'Let's just hope we have a quiet night.'

'I'll make some more tea whilst we wait,' said Grandma Tilly.

The winds continued to strengthen as the evening drew in. The wooden veranda moaned and creaked as it swayed from side to side.

Amber brought in the two glass hurricane lamps and other decorative items that she had left outside. She figured they'd be safe inside.

After one particularly strong gust of wind caused one of the benches to move, they also brought both benches inside in case they went through the window or hurt someone. Placing them at the back corner of the shop, it made one side of the shop with the tractor almost impassable.

'But at least we've got somewhere to sit,' said Josh, sitting down gratefully. He looked tired. 'This blanket was a good idea.'

'Made with love, as well,' said Grandma Tilly with a wink.

Amber had brought down some more cushions and blankets from upstairs, thinking that if they were going to be open late at least they'd be comfortable.

There were a few more customers, but nobody was in the mood to stay for too long and chat. They all came in and moaned about the weather. But everyone looked frightened and worried, stressing about whether the river would burst its banks and flood their homes.

'I feel so helpless,' said Amber, as yet another customer rushed out with milk and bread. 'What can we do?'

Josh shrugged his shoulders. 'Exactly what we are doing. Staying open. Being a safe haven.'

Amber nodded. Despite feeling powerless to help, she did at least feel that there was a sense of community that she hadn't felt before in Cranbridge.

Another rattle from the porch made her glance outside once more. But it was dark now and the only way they could gauge the river level was to head out with the torch every half hour.

And still the rain kept coming.

The newspaper office was still open next door, even though they were more vulnerable than the shop as they were at a slightly lower level, nearer to the ground.

'We've got some sandbags though,' Molly told them when she came in later. She stood and warmed her hands by the fire, which was still going strong thanks to Amber's efforts of putting a log on every half hour. 'Don't ask where they got them from.'

Tom came in. 'I'm starving,' he said. 'Have you got anything to eat?'

'Not going to the pub?' asked Josh.

'No time,' said Tom. 'The phone lines are red hot.'

'We could always warm something up in our microwave or oven upstairs,' said Amber.

Tom browsed the shelves. 'Not exactly spoilt for choice, are we?'

He had a point, thought Amber. There were some tins of soup and beans but nothing really in the way of a proper meal. At least they still had a few packets of eggs and bread.

'Why don't I bring the microwave downstairs?' said Josh. 'At least we can warm up some beans or soup.'

'I'd rather have a chicken korma and all the trimmings, but fair enough, thanks,' said Tom with a sigh.

'Shall I make some for everyone?' asked Amber.

Grandma Tilly nodded enthusiastically. 'I can butter some bread.'

'That would be great,' said Tom. 'Most of the team are still out and about. Kate's apparently getting in everyone's way and trying to interview people.'

'I haven't met her yet,' said Amber.

'She's always out,' said Tom, rolling his eyes. 'I've told her that now's not the time to bother people, but she's that ambitious.'

'Everyone who came in has been very worried,' Amber told him.

Tom sighed. 'Nothing we can do but hope for the best.'

Amber knew that it must be serious if Tom wasn't joking any more.

Soon she was handing out beans on toast to Tom.

'Haven't pulled an all-nighter for many a year,' he told them, sitting down on one of the benches. 'Think it might be the time for one though.'

'Us too,' Josh told him. 'We thought we'd better stay open in case anybody needs anything.'

'You don't have any boats back there, do you?' asked Tom, pointing with his fork to the back room. 'You seem to have everything else.'

Josh frowned. 'Do you know what? I've got a feeling I saw one somewhere.'

'Well, I think you'd better dig it out sharpish,' said Tom.

Josh frowned. 'I don't think it'll come to that.'

'Nor do I, mate, but we should probably be prepared,' said Tom between mouthfuls.

After everyone else had left, Amber helped Grandma Tilly upstairs.

'We'll keep the shop open as late as we can,' Amber told her. 'You get some rest.'

'Will do,' said Grandma Tilly, switching on the television once they were upstairs. 'To be honest, I sleep that heavily that I'll probably miss most of the excitement unfortunately.'

'Lucky you,' said Amber.

She was just hoping for absolutely no excitement at all and that the storm would miss Cranbridge completely.

32

After a bit of a rush early in the evening, the shop began to quieten down. In fact, it was too quiet. Without any customers, all that was left was the sound of the storm outside. Every time there was a huge gust of wind, Amber jumped nervously.

'We need a distraction,' said Josh. 'Sitting here fretting isn't helping.'

'What about some music?' Amber suggested. 'I know I've seen a radio somewhere. I'll go and find it. It'll give me something to do.'

After a few moments, she came back in holding what Josh knew to be his dad's old radio. Amber fiddled with the dial until she found a mellow pop music station and left it playing.

Josh stood in shock. How long had it been since there had been music in the shop?

Too long, he knew.

His dad had often sat on the veranda and played his guitar in the afternoons, especially on a hot summer's day. Josh had missed that so much that he ached at the thought of it. How different the whole shop was to when his dad had been there, buying and hoarding who knows what, but it didn't matter. His mother smiled and laughed. His dad sang and hummed wherever he went. There had always been music and laughter in the shop. Now the music had returned and he felt choked with the memories.

'Are you OK?' Amber had come to sit next to him and he hadn't even realised until she spoke.

'The music,' he managed to mumble.

Thankfully, she understood. 'Your dad,' she said softly, placing a hand on his arm.

He nodded.

'He was so full of life,' said Amber. 'That much I remember. He used to sneak me a biscuit when I was hiding in a corner. Try and tempt me out of my shell.'

Josh turned to look at her. 'Why are you so shy?' he asked.

She shrugged her shoulders. 'I don't know. We moved around a lot when I was younger because of my dad's job. It's hard to keep making friends in new places.' She hesitated. 'Girls can be pretty mean when you're growing up,' she told him, staring into the distance in a dream. 'If you're not trendy enough and all that, well, you get picked on.'

He realised now just how badly she had been bullied.

'Well, you showed them,' he told her. 'London and New York designing amazing windows. You've had the glamorous life I bet they would love.'

'It was never like that,' said Amber, letting go of his arm to clasp her hands together as she stared down at them. 'I walked for hours on my own in my free time. I went to all these amazing museums and theatres all alone. I don't know if you have seen the movie *Lost in Translation*, but I felt like one of the characters, just terribly alone in a big city.'

The thought of someone as gentle and kind as Amber being all alone made him feel terribly sad and protective of her.

'You could have maybe joined in with a few things,' said Josh gently.

But Amber shook her head. 'You know me. I can't do that. I'm not brave enough.'

'You've joined in here,' he reminded her, giving her shoulder a nudge with his own.

She smiled up at him. 'I had no choice here. I'm stuck in the shop with the customers!'

'Perhaps it's been good for you,' he told her.

She nodded thoughtfully. 'Perhaps it has.' She stood up suddenly. 'I think I'll put an extra sweatshirt on. It's getting cold. And I'll check on Grandma Tilly as well.'

'I can stay down here by myself if you want to rest,' he told her.

Amber shook her head. 'I won't sleep with this storm going on. Besides, it's not fair to leave you by yourself.'

As she headed upstairs, Josh received a call from his mum.

'Is everything OK?' she asked, sounding concerned. 'Apparently you've got a big storm coming your way.'

'We're fine,' Josh told her, before reassuring her that Grandma Tilly was safe upstairs in the flat and that the river wasn't that bad yet.

He hung up, promising to keep her updated.

The wind had begun to whistle and howl outside. With no more customers, Josh went into the back room, where he managed to pull out the inflatable dingy that they had used on the river when they were younger. Once unpacked, he inflated it with a bicycle pump. Hopefully it wouldn't need to be used, he told himself.

They kept busy through the evening. Amber took down the Halloween decorations and replaced them with the autumnal ones that she had first used. Josh made an inventory of the stock that they had laid out in the shop.

Sometime around eleven o'clock in the evening, Josh made them both a cup of tea.

Amber had pushed the two benches together so that they could move around them. So she sat down on one of them, putting her feet up as Josh did the same on the other bench, facing her.

Amber hugged the hot cup of tea to her chest.

'This is awful,' she said, as the wind continued to blow and gust outside.

'I didn't think my tea was that bad,' he told her.

'You know what I mean,' she said, laughing briefly. 'The waiting.'

'Yeah, I know.'

They drank their tea in silence, all the time hearing the heavy rain hammer onto the roof of the veranda and the side of the building.

Then Josh got up to head outside and look at the river once more.

The beam of light from his torch highlighted how bad things were getting out there.

'I can barely stand up in that wind,' he said, as he came back inside.

Amber shivered at the cold rush of air that had swept in as the door was opened.

'How is it?' she asked.

He hesitated to tell her, but she needed to know how bad it was. 'It's up to the top of the riverbank now.'

Amber's eyes grew wide with alarm. 'But that's level with people's front doors.'

He nodded. 'Yeah.'

'What can we do?'

'Nothing,' he told her. 'We'll stay open with the lights on in case anyone's flooded and needs somewhere to go. It's got another couple of feet to rise to get anywhere near the top of the veranda out there.'

Looking concerned, Amber shrugged on her jacket and went outside to see for herself, so Josh went back outside to join her, the wind and rain immediately swirling around their faces as it swept in under the roof of the veranda.

'Show me,' she said.

He switched on his torch and swung it around. Amber stared in horror at what the beam of light revealed. The river was thick and brown and had completely covered the lane on the other riverbank. It was rushing along, taking wheelie bins and anything not bolted down along with it.

On their side of the river, it was now lapping at the tarmac and slowly creeping inch by inch across.

Down the lane, they could see people waiting anxiously at their front doors watching for any signs that the water would flood their houses.

Josh peered around the corner and saw that the door to the newspaper office had finally been closed. There were a couple of sandbags propped up against the front door to try and protect it.

'They must have gone to the pub,' said Amber. 'Did you want to go over there?'

Josh shook his head. 'I think we should stay here if we can. They say it should peak in the next couple of hours.'

He could see that the river was lapping at the front door to the pub, which thankfully was also up a couple of steps. The door opened slightly as Belle peeked out. She gave them a small wave of solidarity across the darkness and they both waved back.

Amber wrapped her arms around her waist, looking stressed. 'This is awful,' she said.

'We'll be OK,' said Josh, putting an arm around her shoulders.

'Sorry,' she told him. 'You must think I'm ridiculous. It's not even my shop. I should be comforting you.'

He looked down at her and smiled. 'Well, if the flood water suddenly rushes in, we'll climb onto the tractor for safety.'

She smiled at his attempt at humour, but there was no laughter to be found in their dire situation, knowing how devastating flooding could be. He had seen it on the news so often but had never imagined that the village would be surrounded by water like this.

'Come inside,' he told her. 'There's nothing we can do out here.'

But Amber shook her head. 'I think we should wait out here. Otherwise we won't know what's going on.'

'We can't,' he told her. 'The wind's too strong. Come on. I'll sort something out.'

So he moved one of the benches to the front window so that they could still see out onto the lane. Then Josh picked up a couple of the blankets and they sat huddled together under them on the bench.

Josh was trying to remain calm, but he was watching the river with rising panic, although he was trying not to show it to Amber. It was flowing much higher than had been predicted and he wondered whether they would be truly safe, even on their slightly elevated status.

For the first time perhaps ever, he realised that he truly cared about the shop and would be devastated if it became flooded. There were memories here. Happy ones, despite the recent sad times. His parents had danced on the shop floor one Christmas. His grandparents had run the shop when he was little. He and his brother had played on the veranda outside.

If the place filled with water, even the tractor, although not working, would be ruined by the mucky water flooding through the engine.

This was his shop. His home. His dad's legacy. And he wanted to protect it. He understood that now. It was time to step up and defend the Cranbridge Stores.

Because it meant everything to him.

33

Amber found that she was so weary that her eyes kept closing, even though she could hear the wind and rain howling across the veranda outside the window.

She forced her eyes to open once more and looked over to Josh as he stared out at the river. He was handsome, she had to admit. Strong chin. Long eyelashes. A frown creased his forehead with worry, but still it was a good-looking face.

She was more conscious than ever of his thigh pressing up against hers. She had a sudden mad thought that it could be wildly romantic to be sitting under a blanket with him. But it was crazy. There was a storm battering the village all around them. She was just tired and stressed. She just needed to have a little power nap and then she'd be fine. So she closed her eyes once more and this time let her mind drift.

At some point, she awoke with a start. Her eyes flew open and she found Josh staring down as he sat next to her.

'Hey,' he said, softly. 'You awake now?'

His eyes bore into hers and she had trouble speaking. Having been at ease with him for a couple of weeks, she hoped she could just put it down to shyness.

So she nodded. 'What time is it?'

'It's one o'clock,' he told her. 'You dropped off for a while.'

A while? She felt embarrassed that she had fallen asleep on his shoulder for a whole hour.

'What's happening out there?' she asked, peering into the darkness. All she could hear was the wind howling and the sound of rushing water. But she did notice that there were quite a few lights on in the cottages across the river. Nobody was getting much sleep that night.

Josh waved his torch around and she could see that the water was already halfway across the path.

'It's getting closer,' she told him.

'I know. But the Environment Agency say it should have peaked by now.'

Amber blew out a sigh. 'Let's hope they're right.'

The trouble was that the rain was still coming down and the water didn't seem to be receding at all. If anything, it was slowly getting nearer and nearer.

Josh's phone suddenly rang out with a text. In the darkness, his screen shone out as he read the message.

'It's Del,' he told her, getting up. 'Apparently Cherry Tree Lane is under water.'

'Oh my goodness,' said Amber.

'We're getting a group together to check around the village and make sure everyone's OK.'

'We?' asked Amber.

'Del, me, Mike and a few others. I'll text him to say we'll call this headquarters as the shop seems to have survived for now. I'll go grab my wellies and a jumper. I'll check on Grandma Tilly whilst I'm up there.'

He went upstairs, leaving Amber alone in the shop.

She shivered, not wanting to be left alone but knowing that they were relatively safe compared to many others in the village.

Soon enough, a few people began to appear in the darkness, so she opened up the front door.

'Nice night for it,' drawled Del. But even his face appeared more strained than normal.

'How's your house?' asked Amber.

'It's OK for now,' said Del. 'But I got a call from one of my neigh-bours saying that the water was coming in his front door.'

'Oh no,' groaned Amber.

Josh appeared next to them just as Mike appeared.

'I'll text with updates,' he told Amber.

'Me too,' she replied. 'How's Grandma Tilly?'

He smiled. 'Fast asleep,' he told her.

They stared at each other for a beat and she couldn't stop herself from stepping forward to give him a brief hug.

'Take care,' she whispered.

He gave her a nod before he walked down the steps and disappeared around the corner with the other men.

Amber walked up and down the veranda wondering what on earth she could do until she heard her own phone ring out.

It was Belle. 'Hey,' said Belle. 'I can see you pacing over there. You OK?'

Amber peered across the dark river to where the pub was still lit up from within. At one of the upstairs windows was Belle waving.

Amber waved back. 'I'm OK. Josh has gone with the others.'

'It's pretty bad out there, I heard.'

'I don't know what to do,' moaned Amber.

'Keep busy,' Belle told her. 'If it's as bad as we think it might be, then everyone's going to need somewhere warm to dry out. Hopefully the shop is high enough that it'll be out of reach.'

'What about the pub?'

'Aunty Angie thinks the cellar's going to flood, so we're moving as much out of it as we can.'

'Stay safe,' Amber told her.

'You too,' said Belle. 'We'll speak later.'

Amber hung up and they gave each other another small wave. She decided that Belle was right. She needed to keep busy, so she went inside and shut the front door to keep the warmth in. She switched on the coffee machine, making sure that all the coffee and hot chocolate containers were full. Then she put a whole load of more logs next to the wood-burning stove to keep the fire going. She shuffled the bench around so that it faced inwards and then placed a pile of blankets and cushions on the top. Then Amber waited, all the time listening to the rain pouring down outside and hammering against the veranda and upstairs windows.

In the end, she had to switch on the radio so she could block out some of the howling gales outside. Then she sat and began to make yet more string chains of leaves and fairy lights, just doing anything to keep her hands busy.

The door suddenly flew open with a loud jangling of the bell.

She looked up as Josh dashed into the shop. 'There's a whole lane under water,' he told her, breathless. 'About a dozen houses are knee-deep. I'm sending the vulnerable people here because they don't know what else to do and nor do I. The emergency services are getting hammered apparently.'

She nodded. 'It's fine. We're ready.'

And then he was gone again before she had a chance to tell him to stay safe.

Within ten minutes, the first few families had arrived, followed almost immediately by Belle who had seen them out of her window.

One couple with two small children stood shivering in the doorway, wide-eyed and in shock.

'I woke up and there was water everywhere downstairs,' said the man, holding tightly onto his children's hands.

'Sweet tea is what you need,' said Belle in a firm tone.

'The kettle's just boiled,' announced Amber, before she crouched down in front of the kids. 'Let's get you nice and warm, shall we?' She led the family over to the wood-burning stove and dragged the bench over. 'Sit yourselves down here in front of the cosy fire. There's nothing you can do at the moment.'

'We've just had the oak floor fitted,' said the woman, suppressing a sob. She too looked completely stunned.

Amber found herself giving the stranger a hug. 'What's your name?' she asked gently. 'I'm Amber and this is Belle. She lives at The Black Swan.'

'I'm Jane and this is Jeremy,' said the woman.

'Hi, Jane,' said Amber. 'Look, here's a cup of tea. Please sit down. You can stay here as long as you want. It's pitch black out there. We just need to make sure everyone's safe. The clear-up can begin tomorrow.'

'I like the tractor,' said the young boy.

'Do you?' Amber gave him a smile. 'Would you like to sit in the seat whilst I make you a hot chocolate?'

The boy nodded eagerly.

Before long, they were joined by another dozen people, all looking cold and shocked.

'The water's up to our ankles,' said one man. 'They said we could come here.'

'Everyone's welcome,' Amber told them all.

'We've lost everything,' said another. 'The sofa, rugs, dining table. All ruined.'

In the end, the shop became too full to move, so Belle suggested that the families go with her to the pub.

'We've got spare bedrooms upstairs,' she told them. 'It's not The Ritz, but it's warm and dry so your little ones can get some sleep.'

So the pub became the unofficial safe centre for people to sleep in. Meanwhile, the shop was designated flood headquarters for when the sun finally came up.

Just before five o'clock in the morning, when the wind was beginning to calm down and the rain eased, Amber heard voices outside. Then she saw Josh wearily climb the steps and come into the shop.

He smiled at her. 'Hey.' He looked frozen and shattered as he shrugged off his wet coat and wellies.

'Come over to the fire,' she told him, before giving him a gentle nudge onto the bench.

To her surprise, he grabbed her hand and pulled her down with him. It was still piled up with blankets and cushions so made for a soft landing.

'Don't ask me too much,' he told her. 'I can barely speak for being so tired.'

'It's fine,' she said. 'Do you want something to eat? Drink?'

He shook his head. 'No. I just want to hold you.'

Amber blinked, thinking that perhaps she too was so tired that she had misunderstood him. But he was already putting his arm around her and drawing her close into him.

Her body reacted as if it were the most natural thing in the world to move into his arms. Before she could even think straight, his head was dropping down of its own accord and his lips were touching hers.

It was a soft, gentle kiss. The kind of kiss that she had never had before. A kiss that she never wanted to end.

But before it could develop further, they both pulled back slightly. They stared at each other for a moment, both a little breathless and wide-eyed, trying to comprehend what had just happened.

Then he pulled her back in close, this time with her head on his chest. She could feel the rasp of his unshaven chin on her hair. Under her hand, she could feel the beat of his heart as his breathing steadied.

It was just for a few hours, she told herself. He was tired and so was she. It had been an upsetting time and this was solace, that was all.

So she curled up her feet on the bench and finally fell asleep in his arms.

34

Amber woke up later that morning to find that Josh had stretched out at some point during the few hours' sleep that they had managed on the bench and was now almost horizontal as he lay down beside her.

As she tried to stretch her back which was sore from the hard wooden bench beneath them, he too began to wake up.

He slowly lifted his head up, yawning. 'Good morning,' he said.

'Hi,' she replied, tempted to flatten down her hair which was messed up from the wind and the fitful night's sleep. 'What time is it?'

He drew out his mobile from his pocket. 'Seven a.m.,' he told her.

She watched as he looked at her and then his gaze went further to where she lay in his arms. He smiled gently at her.

'People will begin to talk if they find us like this,' he said softly.

'Then we'd better get up,' she told him, blushing.

But as soon as she stood up and out of his arms, she realised that there was nothing she wanted more than to be back in them once more.

The kiss they had shared had been in the aftermath of a harrowing night when the emotions had overcome them. But now it was morning and everything was different.

Josh too stood up and stretched before he went over to the window.

'How's it looking out there?' she asked, before going to join him.

'Well, it stayed dry in here at any rate,' said Josh, opening the front door.

Feeling nervous, they headed outside onto the veranda to survey the damage to the village in the morning light.

'Wow,' said Amber, staring around in horror. 'It's a mess.'

The muddy river water was still three quarters of the way across Riverside Lane but had thankfully not reached either the steps up to the veranda where they stood, nor the front doors of the shops down the lane.

There was a tide of mud, leaves and general debris strewn across the path, but that at least could be swept away relatively easily.

The bank on the other side of the river had not been as lucky, unfortunately. The lane beyond the river was lower and where the river had burst its banks it had spilled across people's front gardens and was lapping against their front doors. Amber could see hardly any sandbags, meaning that everyone's property was almost certainly flooded.

Josh was also looking dismayed at the flooding. 'Think the pub might have just about survived.'

Amber looked across to where the water was splashing against the front steps of the pub. 'Let's hope so,' she said. 'Belle said the cellar was going to flood though.'

'Yeah. I think it probably has.'

She looked back down the lane and saw people were beginning to come out of their houses to survey the damage. Everyone looked a bit shell-shocked from lack of sleep and worry.

'People look shattered,' she said, turning to Josh.

'I know how they feel,' he told her with a weary sigh.

'Those people that were flooded have spent the night in the pub,' she told him. 'They had the spare rooms.'

He nodded. 'That was a good idea. It's going to take a while to get everyone's homes cleaned up.'

'Could we put a sign up on the veranda?' she asked. 'Offering hot drinks. We've got the coffee machine and a kettle. People are going to need some warmth whilst they clear up. It's so cold.'

He looked at her for a long time before nodding. 'You're absolutely right. They might not have electricity with the flooding. And today's not the day to think about profits,' he said.

Amber found herself falling for him just a little bit more at his kindness.

As Josh wrote on a large blackboard offering free hot drinks and snacks to anyone who needed it, she filled up the kettle and coffee machine and brought out some more biscuits. They had left the microwave downstairs, so she headed up to the flat to grab what was the last of their own bacon, ready to make bacon sandwiches for anyone who wanted them.

'Good morning,' said Grandma Tilly, coming out of her bedroom in her dressing gown. 'Everything OK?'

'Not great,' Amber told her. 'The village is quite badly flooded.'

'How awful.' Grandma Tilly turned back around. 'I'll get dressed and head down to give you a hand.'

As it turned out, an awful lot of people needed their help.

'We've had to switch off our power supply,' said Mike, rushing in. 'I couldn't grab a coffee, could I, love?'

'Of course,' said Amber, turning to make his drink. 'How's the pub?'

'Thankfully it's only the cellar which got wet,' said Mike. 'Stuff's ruined down there. My crisps just floated away.'

'Probably because they were a couple of years out of date,' said Tom, coming into the shop. 'As long as the beer barrels are intact.'

Mike nodded. 'They should be.'

'Good,' said Tom. 'The way today's going to pan out, I may need to do a rather large drinking session later.'

'How's the newspaper office?' asked Josh, coming inside to put another log into the wood-burning stove.

'Empty of both water and staff,' Tom told them. 'It came up to the front door and a little inside but no further. I've sent everyone out and about to see what the damage is. Did someone mention something about a bacon sarnie?'

'That sounds good,' added Mike.

'Coming up,' Amber replied, grabbing the second-to-last loaf of bread that they had to start buttering slices.

'At least it's finally stopped raining,' said Mike.

Amber glanced out of the window and saw that the wind had dropped as well.

The shop began to fill quite quickly with customers all sharing their flooding horror stories. Amber worked flat out to make sure everyone had something to eat and, with Grandma Tilly's help, they all had a hot drink as well.

Most of the homeowners had had to switch their electricity off if they were flooded so were also looking to charge their mobiles.

'This is the first time I've felt warm all morning,' said one woman, standing in front of the fire and warming her hands.

A few people were sitting down on the bench as they chatted and drank their hot drinks.

'I'd heard about the tractor, but I thought someone was pulling my leg,' said someone.

Amber and Josh exchanged a small smile before they carried on working.

Some more customers bought a large amount of cleaning supplies and the wellington boots sold out quickly as well.

Josh also made a pile of brooms, rubber gloves and dustbin bags, all of which were soon snapped up.

'Our place got flooded during the night,' said a woman whom Amber didn't recognise. She was looking around the shop and in particular at the tractor in a wild manner. 'I don't know where to start first. We can't have breakfast because the electricity is off.' She glanced down at the two young children she had brought with her.

Amber looked at their pale, tired faces. 'How about a nice hot chocolate and some toast?' she said to the children. 'And let's get mum a coffee, eh?'

The woman sighed with relief. 'Thank you so much. I don't know what to do.'

'Have something to eat and drink and you'll feel better,' Amber told her.

'Who wants to give me a hand with the hot chocolate?' asked Grandma Tilly, leading the children away behind the counter.

'Wow, that smells good,' said another stranger as he came in.

'Bacon buttie and a coffee?' said Amber, with a smile.

'I've not got my wallet on me,' he told her, patting his trousers. 'I'll go back and get it.'

'It doesn't matter,' Josh told him. 'This one's for free today, OK, folks?'

The man smiled gratefully. 'That's great. Thanks so much. My head's all over the place.' He looked around the shop. 'I don't know what I need to start to clear up.'

'We've got loads of rubber gloves,' said Josh, grabbing a nearby box. 'You don't want to be poking around in that filthy water in bare hands. It's not sanitary. Have you taken photos of everything? Marked where the water came up to for the insurance company?'

The man shook his head. 'My phone battery's dead.'

'Bring it in here to charge whilst Amber makes you a bacon sarnie. I've been reading about it online,' said Josh. 'You want to make a note and take photos everywhere.'

'OK,' said the man, nodding. 'Thanks. I'll grab my phone and I'll be back.'

'Did someone say that you're able to charge a phone?' asked a woman who had just come into the shop.

'At the back here,' said Josh, pointing to a socket in the wall. 'I'll grab an extension lead,' he told Amber.

'There's some Post-it notes here,' she said, remembering seeing them under the till at some point. 'I'll write down whose phone is whose.'

'Brilliant,' said Josh, dashing off.

At some point later in the morning, people began to come in for essentials, such as nappies, dustbin bags and cleaning materials, as well as biscuits and any kind of food they could eat whilst they started to clean up.

Amber had barely sat down all morning and could feel herself flagging by lunchtime.

'You OK?' asked Josh, as they briefly stood in the shop alone.

Grandma Tilly had headed upstairs to put her feet up for half an hour, on Josh's insistence as she too was fading.

'I'm fine,' said Amber. 'Just a little weary. But at least we have a warm bed to go to tonight. Some of these people have lost everything.' She frowned, suddenly realising something. 'Have you seen Stanley today?'

Josh shook his head. 'I'm sure he's just busy.'

But Amber was suddenly terribly worried. 'He always comes in here. Always. Dead on half past nine.'

They looked at each other and then at the time. It was almost twelve o'clock.

'You stay here and man the fort,' he told her. 'I'll go round and see if he answers the door.'

'Hey up,' said Dodgy Del, coming through the front door. 'What's this about free bacon butties?'

'That might have to wait. Do you know Stanley?' asked Josh. 'Comes in the pub every Wednesday for his pint?'

'Of course,' said Del. 'He was my old headmaster. Why? What's up?'

'We haven't seen him and he always comes in every day without fail.'

Del frowned. 'He's down Larch Avenue,' he said. 'It's been pretty bad down there, from what I've heard. I'm not sure who checked there last night. Come on.'

Josh slung on his jacket and followed Del out of the shop and down the stairs.

Amber paced back and forth, half-heartedly buttering some more bread and refilling the coffee machine whilst she waited for some news.

Finally, after half an hour of anxious waiting, Del rushed up the steps and flung open the front door.

'We found him,' he said, panting at having run all the way. 'He was trapped upstairs. Place is flooded downstairs. Josh is getting the boat and we'll get him out of there.'

'He's not hurt, is he?' asked Amber.

'Just a bit shaken. Josh wanted you to know,' carried on Del. 'I'd best get back.'

Amber had a little cry of relief after he'd gone, then pulled herself together as the next person came into the shop.

'Hi,' said a woman, coming up to the counter and holding a bag. 'I'm Lesley and I live locally. Look, I've been doing all this baking for a fair that's got cancelled. Anyway, that doesn't matter. I heard that everyone's been coming in here, so I thought you could give them away to some of the families.'

'How kind,' said Amber, looking inside the bag. There were many decorated cupcakes and fruit cakes, all beautifully packaged. 'These look amazing.'

'It's the least I can do.'

As the woman left, Grandma Tilly came back downstairs. 'How's it all going?'

'Look at this,' said Amber, laying out the cakes and telling Grandma Tilly about the stranger's kindness.

'Everyone just wants to help,' said Grandma Tilly.

Amber looked up as Josh came into the shop.

'How is Stanley?' she asked.

Josh sank down onto the crate by the fire. 'Cold. A little bit frightened, I think. He got a bit confused in the dark and couldn't find his phone to call anyone. He's going to stay in the pub until we get his place sorted.'

But as Josh went to stand up, he almost immediately sat back down again, looking pale.

'You look exhausted,' Amber told him.

'Here, have something to eat,' said Grandma Tilly. 'I'll make you a cup of tea.'

He looked down at the sandwich she had just handed him in a sort of daze.

'Eat,' she told him gently. 'You'll feel better for it.'

The sandwich and the tea appeared to bring him back to life a bit.

'Thanks,' he said, once he'd drunk the last drop of tea out of the mug. 'I needed that.'

'I'm sure you did,' she said. 'You must be exhausted.'

In the warm light of the fire, Amber could see he was unshaven and weary.

Josh looked around the shop. 'We seem to have been cleared out of quite a bit of stock.'

Amber nodded. 'They all needed to buy cleaning stuff. And a lot of people were promising to come back in, as well.'

He nodded thoughtfully. 'Well, maybe that will be good. If they come back.' He stood up and stretched whilst he yawned. 'I'd better grab some plywood. Somebody needs their back door boarding up.'

Grandma Tilly took his mug into the storeroom to rinse it out.

As Josh went to head into the back room, he stopped and turned around. 'You did really well today. Amazing, in fact. The coffee and sandwiches was a great idea. It really helped. You're a good person.'

She blushed and looked away. But she found that he suddenly held her chin with his fingers and gently drew it up so she had to look back at him.

'I mean it,' he said, suddenly searching her face more intently. 'You're amazing.'

There was a long silence as they locked eyes. Amber found she couldn't look away and had a sudden urge to kiss him.

Then he gave a little shake of the head as if to wake himself up, before letting go of her chin. With a smile, he left her standing in the shop alone and the moment had passed all too soon.

'Whatever's the matter?' asked Grandma Tilly, as she came back into the shop.

'I'm fine,' said Amber quickly. 'I'm just a bit overwhelmed, I think.'

'You know why?' asked Grandma Tilly, reaching out to squeeze Amber's hand.

Amber shook her head in reply.

'Because you're a villager too now,' she said.

Amber smiled and found herself nodding, knowing it to be true. Perhaps she had finally found a place to call home.

35

Once Stanley had been checked out, Josh left him in the pub to head back to the shop.

'How's Stanley?' asked Amber.

Josh sank down onto the chair by the fire. 'He's OK. More shocked than anything.'

'Poor Stanley,' said Grandma Tilly. 'But that house was getting too much for him. I told him that the bungalow's so much easier. I shall be heading back there myself later.'

'Are you sure?' asked Josh.

Grandma Tilly smiled at him. 'It won't flood now,' she said, reaching out to pat him on the shoulder. 'If anything, I think those stairs have made me realise that my little bungalow is just right for me. I shall go and pack up my bag.'

'I'll walk you home,' said Josh.

But as Grandma Tilly headed upstairs, Josh went to stand up and found that his legs were like jelly.

'You look exhausted,' Amber told him. 'I'll make you another cup of tea. And then I'll walk Grandma Tilly home.'

The tea brought him back to life a bit.

In the warm light of the fire, he could see that she was also looking weary. But he was seriously impressed as to how well she had handled the crisis.

There was a long silence as they locked eyes again.

Josh found he couldn't look away and had a sudden urge to kiss her, just like he had the previous night.

He was just about to lean forward when his phone rang. He brought out his mobile from his pocket and smiled. 'It's Mum,' he told Amber, heading through the shop and outside to get a better mobile reception.

'Hi,' he said, as he went across the veranda and out onto Riverside Lane. 'Sorry, Mum. I meant to call you earlier.'

'That's OK,' she replied. 'Denise heard from Amber, so we know that you're all OK.'

'The village is a mess, Mum.' His voice caught on the words and he realised just how hard he had suppressed his distress until that moment.

'I heard, love.' She sighed heavily down the line. 'Those poor people.'

'We're doing what we can,' he told her, looking around at the mud and debris strewn across the lane.

'Of course you are,' she said. 'You're a good person, Josh. Listen, I've been thinking and worrying about you all day. I'd have hated for anything to happen to you, knowing how unhappy you are.'

'Mum,' he began, but she wasn't listening.

'Look,' she carried on, talking over him. 'It was my parents' shop and then it was ours. But it was never your dream. That was elsewhere.' He heard her take a deep breath. 'Perhaps it's time to let it go. To leave the shop behind, I mean. I promise I won't be upset. I just want you to be happy.'

'OK, but now you need to listen to me,' said Josh. 'I know I've been unhappy and have wanted to leave. But something's changed. I think I could do some good here. Make a life for myself here in Cranbridge.'

As he said the words out loud for the first time, he knew in his heart how much he wanted to stay. He wanted to belong to a community that helped each other out during the worst of times. If any good could have come out of the village being flooded, it was that he liked feeling part of a team. That they were all in this together.

He heard his mum sob down the line. 'I don't want to force you to do something you don't want to do.'

'The thing is, Mum,' he told her, 'I really think that I want to stay. I love the shop. It's my home, and so's the village. I've got friends here.'

There was a pause whilst his mum smothered what he assumed were tears. 'If you're sure,' she finally said, in a shaky voice.

'I am.'

'You can't do it by yourself though,' she said softly. 'You're going to need help.'

He nodded and smiled as he turned to look up at Cranbridge Stores in front of him. 'And I know just the person to ask,' he told her, as he watched Amber through the window.

36

After talking to his mum, Josh felt ready to face the afternoon.

In fact, despite barely having more than a couple of hours' sleep the previous night, he was raring to go. The situation was awful but new and different customers had come into the shop. It had been transformed and, in spite of his reservations about Amber's design, especially the tractor, everyone had been very positive.

He just needed them to keep coming in after life had hopefully resorted back to normal for everyone. But how?

He and Amber stood in the middle of the shop, which was half empty, such had been the high level of customers.

'The first thing we need to do is restock,' he said.

Amber nodded. 'I'm sure more people will need to come in again for more cleaning stuff. Everywhere is such a mess.'

'Good. I mean, not good, obviously,' he said quickly. 'I don't want to capitalise on anyone's misfortune, but if they can buy anything they need from us then perhaps they'll return in the future.'

'Careful,' she told him. 'You're beginning to sound as if you care about the shop after all.'

He looked at her and wondered how she knew him so well after such a short time. He smiled to himself.

'What's so funny?' she asked.

'Me,' he told her. 'All this time I've been telling myself that I can't wait to get out of here. That we all just need to move on. But last night, with the water getting so close, I felt, I don't know, terror at losing it all.'

'But that's good,' said Amber. 'That means you do actually care.'

'I guess so. I'm just a bit surprised, that's all.'

'I'm not,' she said.

His eyebrows shot up as he looked at her.

'This shop is special. I mean, it's actually pretty important to quite a few people, not just your family. People like Stanley. I think we're possibly the only people he talks to some days. And that's the same for a couple of the others as well. I think I've realised that people aren't just lonely in big cities. They can be lonely in villages like Cranbridge as well.'

Josh nodded. 'So we'd better get restocked and fast.'

'I've made some notes as to what we need,' she said, turning around to study the list she had placed on the counter.

As she bent over, her long ponytail moved to one side, revealing the back of her neck. Josh had a sudden urge to press his lips to the pale skin at the bottom of her hairline.

Perhaps it would be better if he kept busy and out of her way for the rest of the day, he thought.

For now, he joined her at the till and looked at the list.

'We've got some more tinned food out the back, as well as cleaning materials. That'll probably clear us out though if the same level of customers come in again this afternoon,' he told her.

'What about milk and bread? We got through nearly all of it.'

Josh frowned. 'The road to the cash and carry is completely blocked. As is the road to Aldwych. I could probably go the long way round, but we're talking twenty odd miles out of the way to get there.'

'If there aren't any trees blocking the other roads,' she said.

Josh nodded, just as the bell rang with another customer.

'Hiya,' said Tom, coming across with his mug. 'It's still crazy busy out there. Plus I didn't even have time for a nightcap last night. I think my body's gone into toxic shock.'

'What's the word on how the area is looking?' asked Josh.

Tom blew out a sigh and shook his head. 'The river's gone down a little. It's terrible downstream. I mean, catastrophic for some poor souls who have lost everything. We're about to head out over that way. If we can get there, of course. So many roads are blocked, I don't know if we can get much further than the next village. Hey, you haven't any of that home-made cake left, have you? Molly brought some in and that's what we had for lunch.'

Amber shook her head. 'Sorry. It was really popular.'

'Not surprised,' said Tom, looking disappointed. 'Nice to have something home-made, you know? Everything I eat these days is either dried or microwaved.'

He and Josh then consulted a map on his phone as they discussed which roads were open.

After Tom had paid for his coffee, he headed out once more.

'We're going to need milk if everyone wants more coffee,' said Amber, holding up a half-empty bottle. 'This is our last one.'

Josh looked at his phone again and zoomed in to look at the number of farms that surrounded the village. 'I wonder...' he said, thinking out loud.

He glanced up to find Amber watching him.

'So the cake was really popular?' he asked.

She nodded. 'Absolutely.'

Josh began to pace up and down the floor as he tried to figure out what was nudging at his brain. 'It was fresh, wasn't it?'

'It looked delicious,' she told him. 'I didn't even get a chance to try it.'

'So people liked it because...?' He stopped, hoping Amber would help him out.

'Because it was tasty?' she suggested. 'Home-made? Made by someone local that they had a connection with?'

'Bingo!' said Josh, nodding. 'That's it!'

'OK,' she said slowly. 'So we need more cake? Is that what you're saying?'

He stopped pacing and took her by the shoulders. 'Why did you hate the cash and carry?'

She blushed. 'Oh, well, it just felt a bit, I dunno, warehouse-like. Not personal.'

'Exactly!' he said, gripping her arms in excitement.

'Er, ow!' she said, wincing.

'Sorry!' he told her, letting go instantly. 'I think we've found our USP.'

Amber rubbed her shoulders. 'You're going to have to break it down for me. I've not had much sleep in the past twenty-four hours.'

'Home-made,' he told her. 'Locally sourced. Not mass-produced. Are you with me?'

'Yes,' she said. But she still wasn't looking convinced.

'What's the matter? Don't you like the idea?' He had thought she'd be thrilled with his plan.

'Of course,' she told him. 'It's just we're surrounded by water. Where are you going to get this kind of thing when everywhere's flooded?'

He brought out his mobile and pointed at the map. 'Look at the number of farms around here. There's a mix of dairy and vegetable farms. How about we source some fresh stuff from them for today and worry about the home-made stuff later on.'

'I can ask any customers that come in if they know of anyone local as well,' she told him.

'Excellent!' Josh could feel the excitement surge through him. 'This is it. I can feel it!'

She laughed. 'What are you talking about?'

'Saving the shop!' he said. 'I think we can do it.'

Amber bit her lip. 'You mean, despite the tractor in the middle of the floor?'

'I love the tractor!' he told her, picking her up and twirling around. 'The tractor stays! Are you with me?'

He put her back down and she was looking up at him amazed, but her brown eyes were shining bright. 'I think so,' she said.

'Excellent! Right. You restock where you can and I'll get out and see what I can find.' He stopped suddenly and smiled at her. 'I knew the tractor was a good idea!'

He ducked out the back of the shop just in time as a bale of kitchen rolls whizzed past his head.

37

Despite living in the area on and off for the past twenty years, it was the first time that Josh had actually driven to any of the local farms. But he was quite enjoying himself, he found, as he hummed along to the radio. He had a good feeling about what he planned to do next, even though there were a number of trees down, including one on the road to Tully's farm, the first one he had on his list to visit.

But he didn't even need to get as far as the farmhouse as he came across Joe Tully using his tractor to move a giant tree trunk which had fallen across the lane.

'Afternoon,' said Josh, getting out of his van.

'Hi,' said Joe.

They had a met a couple of times in the pub and chatted about football and the weather. But they had never talked too much about work.

'Need a hand?' asked Josh.

'All done thanks,' said Joe. 'How's the village looking?'

'It survived,' Josh told him. 'Some homes were flooded. The pub cellar was under water. Thankfully, it didn't get as high as the shop.'

'At least that's something,' said Joe. 'What can I do for you?'

'Well, the road to Aldwych is still blocked,' said Josh. 'Going to take a couple of days for the water to go back down, they reckon.'

'Aye,' nodded Joe. 'It normally does. Haven't seen floods like this for a long time.' He looked out to the fields beyond. 'It's a mess out there. We've had to bring the cattle in because there's no grass for them to feed on, only mud.'

Josh nodded and looked around them. All the grass in the fields was under a layer of mud.

'It's such a tough time for everyone,' he said. 'And we're running low on everything. It's pretty bad in the village, as you can imagine. Trouble is, the locals need supplies. Milk especially. They cleared us out this morning. So I was wondering whether you had any we could take off your hands.'

Joe looked surprised but pleased. 'As it happens, one of our deliveries couldn't get out, so I've got some milk going spare.'

'Anything you want to give us would be great,' said Josh, smiling.

So they headed up to one of the converted barns, where Joe showed him the refrigerated bottles of milk.

'Look, if these go well, I was wondering whether you'd like to make it a permanent arrangement,' said Josh. 'I want to use more local produce and we can't get more local than your farm.'

Joe beamed. 'Sounds like a good plan,' he said and glanced to a nearby fridge. 'Tell you what, I've been dabbling with making cheese. Only Cheddar, nothing fancy, but we're trying to diversify, make a few extra quid on the side. You know how tight things are these days.'

'Any cheese would be great as well,' said Josh.

'You can taste some, if you'd like.'

Seeing how keen Joe was, Josh took the sliver of cheese that he was offered and tasted it.

'That's beautiful,' he said. 'Strong but smooth.' He had been prepared to lie a little bit in case it was bland, but it tasted amazing.

'We've started to sell it online, but it's early days yet,' said Joe.

'I'll take a box full, if you can spare it,' Josh offered.

Joe's face lit up into a smile. 'Of course.'

So he waited whilst Joe cut and wrapped up differing sizes of the Cheddar.

'You know,' said Joe, as he helped pack Josh's van up with the goods.

'If you're thinking about using more local farms, Mark Tonks over on Cedar Lane has also been looking at selling online. His beef is the best that I've had. Might be worth a visit.'

'That sounds great,' said Josh, shaking his hand. 'Thanks for the tip. I'll be in touch.'

In fact, Joe's advice paid off. Mark the beef farmer had a number of steaks and packets of mince that he could give Josh.

'This is great,' said Josh, as he packed some boxes into the back of his van. 'I'll let you know how I get on.'

Everyone was going to get paid after the products were sold. Josh was amazed, but the trust between the local people was astounding. And there was a feeling of everyone in it together as Mark then tipped off Josh about the pig farmer in the next village who not only had bacon but also handmade sausages.

Consequently, Josh's van was loaded once he finally arrived back at the shop late afternoon.

'What's all this?' asked Amber, as he carried in various crates.

'Fresh, local milk, cheese, bacon, sausages and beef,' he said, putting a box down on the counter between them.

'Wow,' said Amber, peering through the packets.

And she wasn't the only one showing interest. A couple of customers who had been merely browsing immediately bought some milk and meat. By early evening, Josh had to bring out more supplies of the local food, such was the level of demand.

The rush continued all evening until nightfall, when finally the shop became quiet once more.

'What a day,' he declared, sinking down onto a box next to the fire.

'You won't believe how much we've taken,' Amber told him, smiling down at him as she stood nearby.

He couldn't remember seeing the till that full for a long time, if ever. Thank goodness he'd started the contactless payment system only a few days previously. Now more than before, they needed customers to have a choice on how to pay.

'Everyone loves the local produce,' carried on Amber. 'We've had great feedback. All positive. Oh and a couple of people were asking about potatoes and fruit. Nobody can make it out of the village and I think they're running a bit low.'

'I had an idea to source some fruit and vegetable farmers tomorrow,' he told her.

'Good,' she said, sounding pleased. 'And I had a little idea as well.'

'Oh yes?' He raised his eyebrows at her in question.

'Do you remember my original design for the shop? With the tractor?'

He laughed. 'How can I ever forget?'

'Shut up,' she muttered.

He really did love to make her blush, he thought.

'Well, you probably don't recall,' she told him. 'But in my design I had a number of crates placed around the tractor.'

'What for?' he asked.

'Fruit and vegetables,' she said, smiling.

Even though he was tired, he made the effort to stare over to where the red tractor was and tried to envisage how it could look.

'I think it could really work,' she carried on. 'They don't need to be in the refrigerator and I found a whole load of blackboard signs and paint out the back. We could write the prices on those. A touch of gingham cloth. Maybe some pumpkins. Rustic but still in keeping, if that's OK? It would almost be like our very own market stall.'

She was looking at him warily as if waiting for him to flat out refuse the idea. Instead, he nodded. 'I like the sound of that. Should I start wearing a cowboy hat?'

'Well, it would match that old leather jacket of yours,' she told him.

'I'll have you know this was my dad's,' he replied, tugging at the zip. 'It's a classic.'

'Like the tractor?' she said.

'You're the boss. Sort of.' Josh found he was smiling as he leant back against the chimney breast and closed his eyes.

'What do you think?' he heard her ask.

'Sounds grand. Carry on, ma'am,' he told her, keeping his eyes closed and giving her a mock salute.

He sat and rested whilst he heard Amber moving around the shop.

He knew her so well that he knew that she was already beginning to sort out the crates. But he didn't mind. He trusted her taste and design.

She had finally begun to have a little confidence in herself and it was lovely to see her blossom, he thought.

He opened his eyes briefly and watched as she gave a little skip of joy as she rushed into the back room to pick up more decorations.

Josh closed his eyes once more, smiling to himself.

38

The following morning dawned bright and sunny, which, Amber observed, seemed to lift everyone's spirits.

'Aren't people kind?' said Glenda, the vicar, as she swept into the shop. 'We asked for donations for those poor people who have lost so much in the floods and we've been inundated!'

'All thanks to your very own *Cranbridge Times*,' said Tom, who had come in for his third coffee of the day. 'And Molly rang the local radio to put the word out as well.'

'That's great,' said Amber, bending down to give Noah the Labrador a stroke as he sat down in front of the till counter.

'What kind of things do you need?' asked Josh.

'Oh! Anything that can be spared,' said Glenda. 'Nappies, toothpaste, dog food, such random things you've never seen, but it all helps!'

'I'll drop a couple of boxes into the church later,' Josh told her.

'Thank you so much,' said Glenda, suddenly doing a double take at the crates that now surrounded the tractor. 'Is that new? I don't remember all of this before.'

'The tractor's old,' said Josh, giving Amber a wink. 'But the produce is new and local. Very local. All within ten miles of our village.'

Josh had rushed out first thing that morning and had come back with a van full of fresh fruit and vegetables from the local farms. Potatoes, carrots and parsnips jostled for space alongside the apples and pears that Amber had filled into each separate crate. She had to admit to herself that it looked absolutely perfect.

'Excellent!' said Glenda, grabbing one of the paper bags to fill with apples. 'I see I shall have to come in here more often!'

She wasn't the only enthusiastic customer saying that they would be returning. As more villagers came in for hot drinks and yet more bin bags and everything else needed for the big clean-up, they too were noticing the new range of meat and vegetables.

Amber wasn't at all surprised that the local produce was a huge hit with everyone who came into the shop. Each customer seemed to be running low and, being unable to get to the huge supermarket still cut off with the floods, everyone was rushing into the shop to try and restock their own cupboards.

Consequently, Josh had to head out for more stock from all the local farms.

He certainly appeared to be a lot happier, she thought, watching him restock the fridge and whistling to himself. It was like a completely different man. She wasn't sure what had changed, but he seemed so much more relaxed for the past couple of days.

She was also secretly thrilled that her design idea for the fruit and vegetables had worked. She had arranged all the wooden crates around the tractor at varying heights. Where the crates were broken or looking a bit grubby, she covered them in the gingham cloth that she had found. Once covered, she built up the crates on top, artfully arranging the vegetables inside and then attaching a small blackboard showing the price. The final touch was some more dried leaves and fairy lights, as well as a few pumpkins for good measure, across the top of the tractor.

'No plastic packaging either,' said one customer, nodding her approval. 'It's so important for the carbon footprint.'

Amber nodded as if that was what she had intended all along. But, yes, she supposed it did also reduce the waste. Especially as the majority of customers brought their own bags with them anyway. Those that hadn't, she'd had the inspired idea to use up the brown paper bags that

Josh had found. He had seemed particularly thrilled with the fact that they could use them.

She had also made sure that the word 'local' was used as often as possible so that everyone understood where their food was coming from.

She was particularly pleased to see Stanley come into the shop at his usual time.

'You're back,' said Amber, hesitating as to whether to give him a hug or not. In the end, she thought what the hell and gave him a brief hug. 'How are you?'

'All the better for seeing you, my dear,' he told her, staring around the shop with wide eyes. 'Well, you have been busy whilst I've been otherwise engaged.'

'Do you like it?' asked Amber.

Stanley nodded. 'Some lovely-looking apples, I see.'

'All local,' Josh told him, looking proud of himself.

'And there's local meat and dairy products too,' added Amber. 'Take a seat and I'll make you a coffee, if you'd like.'

'Thank you, my dear.'

Whilst he drank his coffee, they updated Stanley on all the recovery efforts after the flooding.

'I hear you're moving into one of the bungalows?' asked Josh.

'Unbelievable stroke of good fortune,' Stanley said. 'By the end of next week apparently. I shall miss my old home, but I shan't miss the stairs, I must confess. Although Belle is doing a marvellous job of looking after me at the pub in the meantime.' He looked a little teary as he looked at Josh. 'And I must thank you for coming and finding me.'

'That's what neighbours are for,' said Josh.

'Good neighbours,' said Stanley, in a firm tone of voice. 'I am most grateful for your kindness. I hope you'll let me buy you a drink at some point in the near future.'

'Of course.'

After Stanley had finished his coffee, he put on his hat and scarf ready to leave. However, the front doorbell rang as the next customer came in. It was Frank, the newspaper owner.

'Stanley! How are you?' said Frank. 'Heard you had to be rescued.'

'Oh, it was nothing,' said Stanley. 'Just a little bit of excitement in my advancing years. Nice to run into you like this. I haven't seen you for weeks.'

'Ships that pass in the night,' Frank told him.

'A little rusty round the edges after all this rain,' Stanley replied.

'Are you in a rush?' asked Frank. 'Thought I'd treat myself to one of the coffees that everyone's talking about.'

'I'll take a cup of tea,' said Stanley. 'We can take it outside where Amber's put some lovely comfortable cushions on the benches and catch up.'

'OK, I'll get these,' said Frank. 'But if Arsenal beats Chelsea tonight, you can buy them tomorrow.'

'You're on,' Stanley smiled.

A few minutes later, the elderly gentlemen were sitting on the bench outside, putting the world to rights and drinking their hot drinks.

'I have a feeling they might never leave,' said Josh.

'Does it matter? Look how much happier they are. Besides, aren't they a walking advert for our takeaway drinks?' she told him, smiling.

Josh laughed and wandered away.

Amber realised that she felt so much stronger than she had ever felt before. Despite the awfulness of people being flooded out, she had handled it all and they had made it through. She had had to introduce herself to new people when they had been flooded out as well as speak to them. After all, their problems were far worse than hers. She was growing more confident. And she liked feeling that way at last.

'Hiya,' said Molly, coming into the shop. 'Have you got any more biscuits or something to help Tom's hangover?'

'We probably should think about some pastries or something like that at some point,' said Amber to Josh.

He nodded. 'Need to find a baker somewhere. I'll have a think. Anyway, I'm just going to drop this box into the church for the donations fund.'

As he wandered off, Molly grabbed one of the last packets of Jammie

Dodgers. 'That'll have to do,' she said, putting it on the counter. 'He's been like a bear with a sore head this morning.'

'So why does he drink so heavily?' asked Amber.

Molly glanced over her shoulder, but the shop was empty, apart from Josh who was in the far corner. 'His wife left him about six months ago,' she said in a whisper. 'He's heartbroken. He's OK when he's busy, but I think he struggles when everyone goes home. So I'm not sure him living over the pub is going to work out so well.'

'Definitely not for his liver,' said Amber, nodding.

The bell signalled the arrival of another customer just as Molly had finished paying and was turning to leave.

'Hiya,' Molly said brightly to the woman who had walked towards her. 'I didn't realise you came in here?'

'First time for everything,' snapped the dark-haired woman.

'Then let me introduce Amber,' said Molly, turning to her and smiling. 'This is Kate Hooper, one of our journalists.'

'Senior journalist,' said the woman, fixing on a smile.

Amber's smile froze on her face as she registered the woman's name. Kate Hooper? As in Catherine Hooper?

As she stared into the stranger's face she realised that her suspicion was right. It was the worst of her school bullies.

39

Kate Hooper stared at Amber critically, her head on one side.

'Have we met? I recognise the name,' she said, prowling up to the counter.

'I-I...' stammered Amber. She was completely stunned. All those years of comments and snide laughter were now fresh in her ears once more. The mocking and cruel jibes. It all came rushing back to her and she felt so anxious, she thought she might vomit.

Kate turned to Molly. 'Is she a mute? I don't do sign language.'

'No,' said Molly, turning to look at Amber in concern. 'Are you OK? You've gone ever so pale. It must be lack of sleep. We've all been on the go for the last few days.'

But Amber could still feel Kate's eyes burning into her. She gulped away her nausea and stared at the floor as she finally found the words. 'St Winifred's,' she muttered. 'Mrs Cole's class.'

Kate peered at her for a moment. 'Oh! School! I'd forgotten all about that place, to be honest. Of course, I left the area as soon as I could. This is only a temporary relocation.'

Molly frowned. 'Actually, I think Tom's quite set on staying here. He likes the village.'

'He's the only one who does,' said Kate, with a sniff. She turned to look at Amber once more. 'You were one of the quiet ones, yeah? I think I remember. Always had your head in a book.'

Amber nodded, still unable to speak any further for fear of retching.

'Well, I'd have thought you were more suited to a library, but this is quite sweet, I suppose.' She looked around the shop, her eyes scrutinising everything. 'So you're a shopkeeper now.'

Amber shook her head. 'It's not mine,' she muttered.

'Oh, so you're just staff? How nice,' said Kate, in a patronising tone. 'I suppose you must be pleased to have some kind of career in any case. After all, you did always struggle so much at school, didn't you?'

Amber felt a flare of anger at that point. It was on the tip of her tongue to tell Kate how she'd worked in London and New York, but then Josh came over and the words failed her.

'Hello!' said Kate, suddenly breaking into a hundred-watt smile. 'Are you just browsing as well or did you have something more sophisticated in mind?'

Josh gave a little start in surprise at her flirty nature but merely smiled. 'If there's a lack of sophistication in this place, you can blame me, seeing as I own it.'

'Do you?' Kate was all smiles and sweetness. 'I was just saying how lovely it is.'

As she continued to flirt and laugh extravagantly at another of Josh's quips, Molly leaned in to whisper to Amber. 'Are you sure you're OK?'

Amber shook her head in response, not being able to find the words.

'I'm just going to take Amber outside for a second,' Molly said. 'I need to ask her advice about something. Back soon!'

Then she grabbed Amber's hand and dragged her past where Josh and Kate were still chatting and out onto the veranda. Molly kept walking quickly down the steps and along Riverside Lane to one of the benches by the river. Then she sat down and pulled Amber onto the bench as well.

'What's going on?' asked Molly, looking closely at her face. 'What's wrong?'

Amber was blinking away the tears that had suddenly formed in her eyes. She didn't even realise that she was wringing her hands together over and over until Molly's own hand came down on top of hers.

'Steady,' she told her, in a calm tone. 'Take some deep breaths.'

'Hiya. Is everything OK?' said Belle, who was walking across the pedestrian bridge towards them. 'I saw you both rush out of the shop. Is Amber ill?'

'I don't think so,' said Molly, still looking concerned.

They both looked at Amber once more, but she stayed quiet. It had always been her default mode of defence. To withdraw almost immediately upon any kind of criticism or bullying. Like a snail being poked with a stick, she would retreat under her shell and stay there until it was deemed safe.

Belle crouched down in front of her. 'What is it?' she said. 'Tell me what happened.'

'We were chatting and everything was fine,' Molly explained. 'Then Kate, you know, our journalist, she came into the shop and suddenly Amber looked ill.'

'Don't tell me,' said Belle, with a groan. 'She made some bitchy comment and upset her.'

Molly nodded. 'Well, you know what she's like. But, hang on, I think they went to school together. Is that right?'

Amber nodded, feeling Belle's eyes boring into the top of her head as she stared down at the grassy bank beneath her trainers.

There was a short silence until Belle spoke, this time more softly than she had ever done before. 'Was it bad? At school, I mean?'

Amber nodded again.

'Oh no!' Molly squeezed her hand as she continued to hold Amber's with her own. 'Girls are so awful sometimes,' she said. 'I always had my best friend to look out for me. She's always been the mouthy one, so I hide behind her. Even now.'

'And you can imagine what a name like Belle's like at school,' said Belle, rolling her eyes.

'I loved *Beauty and the Beast*!' said Molly, smiling.

'Yeah except my happy ever after is more a screaming nightmare,' said Belle.

'Why?' asked Molly.

'That's a tale for another time when we have lots of gin to drink,' said Belle, briskly.

There was a sadness about her, thought Amber. Belle was a closed book but very friendly as well. Amber wondered how lonely Belle really was behind the strong, cynical façade.

'So how are we going to deal with this Kate?' asked Molly, whispering once more. 'Could you tell her how you feel?'

Amber shook her head almost violently. 'I can't,' she whispered. 'I can't face her. Not even after all this time. I know it's not a big deal in the scheme of things. So many people have lost all their possessions in the floods. It's just when I saw her, I felt about thirteen years old all over again.'

And all the pain and misery had returned as well, she thought.

'We moved around a lot when I was young,' Amber added. 'Lots of different schools. It was hard, not having friends.'

'Kids can be tough,' said Belle.

Amber's smile was tight as she nodded in agreement. 'Then after I lost my job in New York, my parents suddenly retired early to New Zealand and I'm still looking for somewhere to call home.'

'This is as good a place as any,' said Belle, nodding thoughtfully. 'Now, about the other problem. That bitchy Kate. There's only two options as far as I can tell. One, I push her in the river.'

Molly giggled and even Amber managed to smile in response.

'Or two, we can poison her with Aunty Angie's cooking, which, let's be honest, isn't exactly unimaginable.' Belle gave them both a winning smile.

Amber managed a small laugh and the release of emotion caused the tears to finally flow.

'You're OK,' said Molly, giving her a hug and holding her tight. 'We've got your back.'

'And your front too,' said Belle, squeezing her knee.

'Thanks,' said Amber, when she could finally speak again.

'That's what friends are for,' Molly told her.

'And I know I could do with a couple around here,' said Belle. 'You two are about the only women I know in my age group.'

'Me too,' said Amber.

'Me three,' added Molly, giving her another squeeze.

And so, for the first time in her life, Amber found that she had friends. And she found herself feeling a little stronger because of it.

* * *

The rest of the afternoon passed in a blur of activity, for which Amber was grateful. But every time the shop bell rang out again, she gave a start. She found she was always glancing up nervously towards the front door, mainly in fear that Kate would return.

'You OK?' asked Josh later that day, looking at her. 'You've been a bit quiet these last hours.'

It was true, she realised. The ease between them had been shattered once Kate had returned into her life. It was as if all her confidence had been eradicated in that one instance and she was back to the shy girl hiding behind the book once more.

'I'm just tired,' she told him, forcing a smile on her face.

'I'm not surprised,' he said. 'It's been a crazy time. Maybe you should take a day off.'

'It's fine,' she said. 'I'll just have an early night tonight and get some sleep.'

He nodded thoughtfully. 'Good,' he said.

But it wasn't good, she knew. She missed their easy chats, the stolen moments.

Perhaps it was for the best, she told herself. Perhaps when she left it would hurt a little less if she kept her distance from now on.

The trouble was that she knew that she had fallen in love with Josh. But he hadn't made a move since the night of the flood when they had kissed. Perhaps he regretted that too.

She had probably made a fool of herself, despite what Molly and Belle had said. Cranbridge wasn't her home. And the shop wasn't really hers, after all. It was time to leave. She would wait until Cathy returned and then she would fly, as she had originally planned, to stay with her parents in New Zealand.

She was trying to stay strong. But she knew deep down that leaving Josh and the village of Cranbridge in the next couple of weeks was going to be the hardest thing of all that she would have to face.

40

The river slowly receded back into its normal path. However, it was still running high and they all had one eye on the weather forecast at all times. Josh was out a lot of the time, helping with the big clean-up operation. The roads needed to be swept and hosed down. Trees needed to be cut and removed from lanes and roads. Fences had to be put back up. But with everyone pulling together, the work soon progressed.

Finally, the electricity was deemed safe enough to be returned to the flooded properties and the families moved out of the pub and back into their houses. They had all lost so much, but, thanks to everyone's donations, which had taken over almost all of the floor space of the tiny church, at least they had the basics to take home with them and start again.

Josh had begun to venture further to other farms which stocked local meat and vegetables. Local eggs were now displayed at the shop, along with the local cheese and milk.

'This is wonderful,' said one customer as she handed over the payment for her purchases to Josh. 'So nice to have all this on our doorstep. I had no idea.'

'Thanks,' he told her. 'That's good to know. Everyone seems very keen on the new layout of the shop.'

'The food is great too,' she told him, as she packed away her goods into the bags she had bought with her. 'To know it's local makes such a difference.'

'It's not hard when we're surrounded by such great farms,' he replied.

'Well, I shall be doing all my Christmas food shopping in here. And passing off some of it as my own as well,' she told him with a wink.

'I won't tell a soul,' he replied.

As she left, his smile faded a little as he remained deep in thought. It was almost the middle of November. Christmas was just around the corner and he needed to plan for what he hoped would be bumper sales.

'I thought you'd be expensive,' said another customer.

Josh shook his head. 'Just the market value for good, local produce.'

The customer nodded. 'Good idea. I hope you continue to flourish.'

'So do I,' said Josh with a sigh, after the customer had left the shop. 'I've just heard they've reopened the road into Aldwych at last.'

Amber looked up at the concern in his voice. 'I'm sure it'll be OK,' she told him.

Josh wasn't so sure.

Despite the recent jump in sales, he felt miserable. Amber was subdued as well, he found. She kept telling him she was just tired, but perhaps he'd gone too far in getting so close to her. They had kissed the night of the flood. Maybe he'd pushed her too much when he should have left her alone. For that reason, he felt guilty, especially when it was because of her that they had achieved so much in the shop. But most of all, he missed her company. Their little chats and her soft laughter.

Kate, the journalist, had asked him out for a drink. But despite her best flirty efforts, it was no use. Despite Kate's obvious charms, there was only room for one woman in his life. Amber had snuck into his heart when he had been least expecting it. And he had no idea what to do about it, especially as she had tentatively mentioned only the previous day about booking her onward flight. She was just waiting for confirmation from his mum as to when she was returning.

He wanted nothing more than to kiss her again. But it wasn't fair on either of them. She would move on, leave the country and go and live with her parents in New Zealand. He would stay, and then what?

The thought of running the shop without Amber by his side brought him no joy. How would he decorate the seasons? He certainly didn't have her eye for detail nor her talent for design. He could continue with all their tentative plans, but it all seemed quite pointless. Especially because, despite the increase in local customers, they were still running at a loss.

'The trouble is that the customers have dropped away a little now that the road to Aldwych is open again,' he said, that night in the pub. 'I mean, the locals have been great, but it's only a small village.'

'I know what you mean,' said Mike, leaning on the other side of the bar and staring around the empty pub.

'Do you think if you became one of those artisan pubs it might help?' asked Tom, picking up a chip and showing them just how soggy it looked.

'We've tried,' said Mike. 'The missus just won't have it. She says good home cooking is what's important.'

'I agree,' said Tom, putting his fork down with a look of disgust on his face as he stared at his half-eaten food. 'Let me know where I can find some and I'll be right there.'

'I suppose we could always buy some ready meals and just nuke them in the microwave,' said Mike.

'Sounds delicious,' drawled Tom, rolling his eyes. 'And there was me thinking that home-made should be just that.'

Josh listened into the conversation, barely taking it in, but he did wonder whether it was worth pursuing some more ready meals in the shop. Amber had mentioned tired commuters a while ago. Was there a market there? But the trouble was that it might not make any difference anyway.

'You OK?' asked Tom, looking across at him.

Josh sighed. 'Decent food or not, it still doesn't get the punters past the door.'

'And they're all heading the other way now that the road to town is open again,' said Tom, guessing the truth.

Josh nodded. 'Exactly. Everybody will head back to the supermarket and that's that. And there's no chance of passing trade where we are.'

Tom nodded thoughtfully but remained silent.

On the next bar stool along, Dodgy Del gave a start. 'You know what, there might be something in that. Leave it with me.'

Josh and Tom looked at each other before exchanging a shrug of shoulders. Josh had no idea what Del was talking about, but it was unlikely to make a difference.

He said as much on the phone to his brother when they spoke later in the week.

'Look, you've done your best,' said Pete. 'You've taken care of Mum and the shop for the last couple of years. But isn't it time to take care of you now?'

'Have you been reading Mum's *Cosmopolitan* again?' drawled Josh.

'Ha ha. Very funny,' said his brother. 'Look, Mum was talking when she was over here. She's quite happy to let the shop go now.'

Josh gulped. 'She is?'

'I think you'll be surprised when she comes back from New Zealand. She doesn't want to be tied to it any more. It was a big thing for her to come abroad and the break has done her good. She's got plans for the future and they don't include running the shop any more.'

'But it was always Dad's dream too,' Josh told him.

'Yeah. Exactly,' said Pete. 'Dad's dream, not yours, mine or Mum's.' He paused. 'Look, think about it. You could get a visa and come out to join me. You'll get a job with no problems. Especially with your sales skills. You can stay with me for a while until you get on your feet.'

Josh frowned. 'Sounds as if you've thought it all through.'

'I've talked about it with Mum, like I said. She knows you haven't been that happy either. There's no shame in saying that it didn't work. Dad wouldn't want you to waste your life in Cranbridge.'

But as he got off the phone to his brother, Josh was filled with doubt. No, he was certain his dad wouldn't want him to be unhappy. But he wasn't as miserable as he used to be. He was beginning to feel at home in the village with his friends. The shop was struggling financially, but there was hope these days that perhaps their fortunes were changing.

The shop looked great. He had finally found his foothold as to what type of business he wanted to run.

And then there was Amber.

But she was thinking of leaving soon. So, maybe he should do the same.

41

One morning, Amber had just placed the latest delivery of potatoes into the appropriate crate next to the tractor, when the bell above the door rang.

She looked up as a lady came in with a large box. 'Hello,' she said to Amber. 'I'm not sure if you remember me.'

'You're Lesley,' said Amber, thinking fast. 'You donated all those lovely cakes just after the storm.'

'That's right,' said Lesley, smiling. 'What a good memory! Look, I hope you don't think this is cheeky, but I've made some more. They were supposed to be for a massive party that's been called off and now I'm stuck with them all. There's lemon drizzle, Victoria sponge and cherry cake. All home-made. I'd hate to see them go to waste, so I wondered if you wanted to try and sell them in your shop? With a cut of the profit for you, of course.'

Amber looked across to Josh, who came over and carried on the conversation with Lesley. They agreed the commission on each cake whilst Amber displayed them by the counter. Then they priced each cake up accordingly and waited to see if they would sell.

It didn't take long. People were still desperate for a treat after the misery of the floods and soon Amber overheard Josh calling Lesley and asking if she wanted to make it a more regular occurrence.

It turned out that Lesley had a friend who made pastries and so a daily delivery of fresh croissants and Danish pastries was soon filling the shop with a tempting aroma along with Lesley's home-made cakes.

Then someone else had made bramble jelly, which was beautifully wrapped in jars with ribbons around the side. All the ingredients were also listed on a small cardboard tag.

Day by day, the shop was slowly restocked with home-made goods.

Stanley filled up his shopping bag each day almost to the brim. 'This is wonderful,' he said. 'I wanted to cancel my weekly delivery from the supermarket anyway and this is the perfect excuse. You have everything I need.'

He then set his shopping down behind the counter whilst he waited for Frank to join him for their morning coffee. People were beginning to view the shop as a meeting hub and Amber was often updating everyone with the news regarding the roads reopening and even the weather.

It was mid-morning later in the week when Amber heard a commotion outside the shop. She went to the window and peered out, somewhat amazed to see at least twenty elderly ladies standing in a group and looking around.

She went outside, wondering if they were lost and needed help.

'Ah! There she is!' called out Del, whom she hadn't spotted just around the corner having a cigarette as he looked into the coach engine. 'Our saviour!'

'Hi,' said Amber, a little self-consciously. 'What's going on?'

'The coach broke down,' he shouted out to her. 'We've only been going for around twenty minutes, haven't we, ladies?'

They all nodded, looking thoroughly miserable and shivering.

'Come inside,' urged Amber. 'It's warm in there whilst you wait.'

So the shop quickly filled up with the coach passengers and Amber offered them all a free cup of tea and coffee whilst they waited for Del to fix his coach.

'Looks like it may take some time,' said Josh, weaving his way through the crowded shop. 'He's still got the bonnet up.'

'Perhaps I could try one of these cupcakes whilst we wait,' said one of the ladies. 'How much are they?'

'Only £2,' Amber told her. 'They're handmade by a lady in the village.'

'How marvellous,' said another lady. 'Did you hear that?'

'It's wonderful,' said the lady who had bought the cake and already had her mouth full.

'And that's from the Chairwoman of the Women's Institute!' said the particularly glamorous lady in front of her. 'Shall we all partake, ladies? I don't know about you, but I need the energy.'

'That's because of your boyfriend wearing you out, Rose,' said Grandma Tilly, who had just come through the front door.

The glamorous lady in front of her gave a throaty, somewhat naughty laugh before giving Amber a wink. 'Tilly Kennedy! You'll make me blush in front of this nice lady.'

'You've never blushed in your life, Rose Harris,' said Grandma Tilly, with a knowing smile.

'The upper classes never do, dear,' said Rose imperiously.

Amber immediately wondered who she was but was too shy to ask. Thankfully Grandma Tilly did the introductions.

'This is Rose Harris. She's the sister of the Earl of Cranley. They live in Willow Tree Hall, a few miles down the road.'

Amber nodded, having heard somebody mention the stately home before. 'I'm Amber,' she said, shyly.

'I think I met a Sam Harris recently,' said Josh from nearby.

'My grandson,' Rose told him in a proud tone.

Josh nodded. 'Nice guy. We were thinking about stocking some of your Willow Tree Hall cider here in the shop.'

'How splendid,' said Rose, looking around. 'It's doing ever so well sales wise. And it would fit right in.' She looked around the shop. 'Such a pretty place. I shall tell all my family and friends about it. And you're only just down the road from us!'

'Well, we need all the customers we can get,' said Josh with a smile, before he headed outside to see Del.

'What a handsome one,' said Rose, giving Amber another wink. 'I do like a man in a leather jacket.'

Amber blushed and turned around to refill the coffee machine.

Whilst the ladies browsed the shelves inside the shop, she went outside to find out how long they might have to wait.

'What do you think is the matter?' Josh was asking Del, who was now sitting on the bottom step of the coach.

'Couple of missing fuses,' Del told him.

Josh looked surprised. 'Missing? Do you think they fell out on the road here?'

'Nah, mate,' whispered Del. 'They're in my pocket!'

Josh stared down at his friend, who was now grinning at him.

'Well, you said you needed the customers,' said Del. 'If I can drag it out for long enough, I'll get them in the pub next for a drink before we get back on board. They'll still have time to wander around their National Trust garden later.'

Josh was speechless for a moment as he stared up at Amber in amazement. 'I don't believe it.'

'You've broken down on purpose?' she whispered.

'A couple of bottles of that local cider wouldn't go amiss,' said Del, with a wink.

'You're on if we make a profit,' said Josh, laughing.

'Great,' said Del, springing up. 'I'll try and break down later on this week as well. Got to give the place a fighting chance, eh?'

As he walked away, Amber found that both she and Josh were laughing. For once, Dodgy Del's nickname was working in the shop's favour.

42

Back in the shop, Josh told the ladies that the problem with the coach engine should be fixed in a short while.

'Such a shame to have to leave,' said Rose, who appeared to be the leader of the group. 'But we shall return. It's been years since I've been to Cranbridge. Do you remember the Christmas fair they used to hold here?'

'You're going back a few years now,' said Grandma Tilly, nodding thoughtfully. 'You were only on your second husband then.'

Josh screwed his face up as he tried to think back in time. 'I remember the lane outside being packed with stalls and people,' he said.

'That's right,' said Rose, nodding. 'It was always very pretty. Seemed to herald the start of Christmas, from what I remember.'

'We're going to hold one again this year,' said Grandma Tilly.

Josh turned to look at his grandmother somewhat incredulously with raised eyebrows but said nothing.

'With all the stalls along the riverbank?' asked another lady.

Grandma Tilly nodded. 'Absolutely,' she said. 'Lots of home-made goods.'

'Really? How marvellous,' said Rose. 'When's it being held?'

Grandma Tilly looked across at Josh, obviously realising that she hadn't quite worked out all the details of her lie.

Oh, what the hell, he said to himself.

'Saturday, fourth December,' said Josh, with a smile as he plucked a date out of thin air. 'Two weeks from today. All afternoon and into the evening. We'll be trying to raise funds for the recent flood victims.'

Grandma Tilly nodded in agreement. 'That's right.'

'We'll be there, won't we, ladies?' announced Rose. 'We must support our local villages.'

There was a general chorus of approval.

'Your carriage awaits, ladies!' announced Del, who had just opened up the front door.

With lots of waves and goodbyes and taking their many purchases with them, Josh was left behind in the shop with Amber and Grandma Tilly.

'A Christmas fair?' he said, laughing as soon as they were alone and looking at his grandmother.

'It used to be marvellous,' said Grandma Tilly.

'It's a great idea,' said Amber.

'I'm glad you agree,' said Grandma Tilly, picking up her handbag. 'You'll have great fun organising it.'

'Me?' said Amber, wide-eyed with disbelief.

'I'm too old to cope with all that, dear,' said Grandma Tilly. 'Right, I'm off to look at my afternoon soap.'

She left the shop more quickly than Josh had ever seen her move.

'What are we going to do?' said Amber, looking at Josh.

'I'm sure it'll be fine,' he told her.

She looked relieved. 'You're right. I'm sure you'll be able to sort something really good out for the fair.'

He took a step forward. 'Oh no,' he replied, shaking his head. 'This is all on you, Miss Green.'

'Me?' she told him, aghast. 'I can't organise anything like that!'

He smiled. 'Of course you can,' he told her. 'In fact, you're going to have to, because I sure won't have the time!'

Amber was still looking horrified. 'But...' she began, her voice trailing off.

'Why does Saturday, fourth December ring a bell anyway?' said Josh out loud.

'It was the date that your mum's flying home,' Amber told him.

'That's right,' he said. 'Well, she'll love a Christmas fair being held in Riverside Lane.'

Amber was looking deep in thought. 'I suppose I'll have to stay until the fair and then I could always leave the day after.'

Josh felt as if someone had punched him in the stomach.

He reached out and lifted her chin so that she had to look into his face. 'You're really leaving?' he said, searching her eyes for the truth.

'I was always going to leave,' she told him softly. 'This was just a stop-off on the way through to my parents, remember?'

He abruptly let go of her chin and stared down at her.

'I thought you liked it here,' he said.

'I do,' she replied in a small voice.

'I thought that you and I were a good team,' he told her.

'We are.'

He ran a hand through his hair as he tried to make sense of it all.

'But your mum's coming back, so you don't need me any more,' she said.

Josh found he couldn't breathe. The thought of Amber actually leaving had been an idea that he'd been trying to bury away.

'Well, I'm sure Mum will want to see you before you leave,' he said, thinking quickly. 'Especially with all the changes to the shop.'

Amber nodded. 'Of course. OK. Well, I'll book the flight for the Sunday.'

'Right,' said Josh, his mind reeling.

'Well, I'd better get organising,' said Amber, with a soft smile. 'There's a Christmas fair to organise in less than two weeks.'

After she had wandered away, Josh remained standing in the middle of the shop, trying to work through his feelings. The shop was rejuvenated. The floods had receded. Even the Christmas fair would help. It felt as if Cranbridge was getting a fresh start, that there was hope at last. So why did he feel as if his own life was just ending?

43

Amber reached up to cut down another branch of holly from a nearby tree before dropping it into the large pile next to her.

'The holly and the ivy indeed,' said a voice next to her.

She spun around to find Stanley standing next to her, all wrapped up in his heavy coat, scarf, hat and gloves.

'Glad somebody's dressed appropriately,' she told him, with a shiver. 'It's freezing! I didn't bring my coat out with me as it's been so mild lately.'

'At least you're wearing a jumper,' he said.

She looked down to where her jumper had snagged many times on the sharp pointy ends of the holly leaves. 'Good job it's not my favourite,' she replied, with a smile. 'Are you out for your morning walk?'

'Actually, Frank and I are catching the bus into Aldwych together. Just a little shopping.'

'And you didn't come to us? I'm hurt. Really hurt.' She gave him a wink to show that she was joking.

Stanley appeared to be much happier these days, she thought. Despite having to move out of his home and into a bungalow, he was much busier going on various days out with Frank.

'My dear, if I could get everything in your wonderful shop, I would.'

She gave him a very gentle nudge with her elbow. 'You're allowed to go into town. Besides, I think it's nice that the two of you are going together.'

'We figure safety in numbers if it's a little busy,' said Stanley. 'And we're going to treat ourselves to a little lunch as well.'

'Well, enjoy yourselves,' she said.

He said goodbye and walked slowly around the corner towards the bus stop. Amber watched him until he was out of view before bending down to pick up an armful of branches that she had cut.

'I hope you left some berries for the birds,' called out Frank as he headed past with a wave.

'Of course,' she told him. 'Stanley's just headed up there. Enjoy your day out.'

'Will do,' he replied. 'Thank you!'

It was certainly a beautiful day to be outside, she thought. She placed the holly onto the veranda and looked back at the view. Under the low winter sun, the grass was sparkling and silver from the early frost. The river had finally lost its muddy colour and was crystal clear once more as it ran slowly through the centre of the village.

Did she miss the bright lights of Christmas in New York? Not especially, she found. She had realised that getting to know everyone personally was far nicer than the faceless neighbourhood in which she'd been living and working for so many years.

A couple of neighbours waved as they walked down the other side of the river. People were out and about more these days than she had ever seen before. Life was beginning to return to the narrow lanes of Cranbridge. More people stopped and chatted to each other. Friendships were being formed. And hopefully just a little bit of the loneliness that had seeped into the village was now ebbing away as well.

And if she needed bright lights, then the sheer amount of fairy lights that was placed around the village would almost certainly outshine Manhattan. Everything on Riverside Lane was all set for the Christmas fair that weekend.

In the shop, everything was twinkling and festive as well. There was a decorated Christmas tree in each window, as well as a new wreath on the front door. A couple of small Christmas trees flanked the front door outside. Even the tractor had some holly and a couple of poinsettias on its seat. Christmas music played on the radio and the air was filled with the scent of oranges, cloves and cinnamon, thanks to some home-made pomades that she had made and placed along the mantelpiece above the fire.

The shelves were looking ready for Christmas as well. Mince pies jostled for space next to Christmas cakes and decorated cookies. In the crates surrounding the tractor, seasonal vegetables were ready to be bought, alongside an order form for local turkeys reared on one of the nearby farms that could be collected on Christmas Eve.

Amber caught her breath at the thought of not being in Cranbridge for Christmas. She took a deep breath and suppressed her tears. For now, she would just have to make do with the festive decorations.

She had just finished putting the finishing touches to the holly along the tops of the shelves, entwined with fairy lights, when Josh came in through the door.

'Wow,' he said, stopping short as he stared around.

'What do you think?' she asked, as she came back down the small stepladder.

'I think it's beginning to look a lot like Christmas,' he told her, smiling.

For a second their gazes locked and she held her breath. Then he turned away.

Amber sighed, the misery eating away at her inside. The Christmas fair was only three days away. But that also meant that her flight to New Zealand was a mere four days away. She couldn't believe that she was leaving so soon.

Thankfully the Christmas fair was keeping her busy. The idea for the fair had gone down very well with all of the villagers and everyone was very excited about the upcoming weekend.

'We're up to twelve stalls already,' Amber told Grandma Tilly, who was sitting on a chair next to the fire. She often came in for the company as she knitted. 'And I'm going to wrap each of your blankets with a ribbon and place them in a large basket in the corner ready to be sold.'

'I've been knitting as fast as I can,' said Tilly, her fingers flying as she knitted the red wool bales in her lap. 'Three blankets are done already.'

'They're so pretty,' said Amber, looking down at the red Scandi design that Tilly had chosen. 'I'm sure they'll sell really quickly. The pub is going to serve drinks outside. There are a lot of food stalls as well. Then there's a whole range of others, like Christmas wreaths and even home-made decorations.'

'It's going to be wonderful,' said Grandma Tilly.

Amber nodded in agreement.

It would indeed be wonderful, if only her heart wasn't breaking, she told herself.

All the time, she was aware that the countdown was on. Time was running out.

Cathy was flying home that weekend so at least Amber would get to see her one more time before she left. Apparently, Cathy had a big surprise for them both. Amber had no idea what it was, but it was wonderful to hear Cathy sounding so happy on the phone.

Amber also thought that saying goodbye to Josh might perhaps be easier with Cathy around. Because it was going to be the hardest thing she had ever done.

She swayed between cancelling the flight and staying, almost on a daily basis. She loved Josh. She knew that now. But he had never told her how he felt. Perhaps it wasn't the same for him. Perhaps it never would be.

But she hadn't told him how she felt either. She wasn't brave enough to face the fact that he might not feel the same way. Anyway, it was too late now.

She looked up at the front door as yet another large group of visitors arrived. In fact, since Dodgy Del's deliberate breakdown, there appeared to be a number of problems with quite a few of the local coach firms now. They were breaking down just by the shop on an almost daily basis.

'It'll cost us any profit in Willow Tree Hall cider if we're going to have to pay off all the drivers,' said Josh in a low voice to Amber as they watched yet another coach party make their way up the steps to the front door.

'Won't someone guess?' asked Amber.

'They haven't so far,' said Josh, before laughing. 'Well, you've got to hand it to Del.'

'Only if there's beer in it,' said Amber, turning back to her list for the Christmas fair.

There was so much to think about. She had drawn up posters that were now in most people's front windows and all along the front of the veranda. Tables and chairs were going to be borrowed from the back room of the pub. Gazebos and umbrellas were going to have to be begged, borrowed or stolen from anyone that had one. Amber was just praying that it would stay dry and that they wouldn't need them. But rain wasn't the main concern. It was actually the threat of snow, which might or might not appear.

'I don't see snow being a problem,' Grandma Tilly had said at the time. 'It'll be far prettier than all that mud anyway.'

Amber had privately agreed with her. She just hoped that it wouldn't be so cold as to prevent anyone coming to the fair.

Then there was the decoration. Her idea to wind fairy lights around the trees along the riverbank sounded great, but the reality of watching Josh, Tom and Del up a ladder had made her fear that they would end up in the water again.

She smiled to herself whenever she thought about when she had first seen Josh all those weeks ago, dripping wet in the middle of the river. He had been so angry, so unhappy. And now? Well, the shop was slowly becoming more profitable. They had more customers than ever before. He was obviously pleased that the business had turned around. She was so pleased for him. The family deserved some happiness. She just wished she could be there to share it with them.

At total odds with the pain in her heart, she had begun to feel confident in herself. For the first time that she could remember, she could face strangers with a smile. She trusted her abilities. She was finally living the full life that she had so longed for. She could face anything, except losing Josh. But it would have to be done.

Once the Christmas fair was over, she would move on. It would be time to look forward to the future.

It wasn't just Josh she would miss, though. Molly and Belle had taken her out for a couple of drinks the previous night, where there had been much sniffling and tears. They had begun to be close over the past few weeks. Amber would miss her new friends terribly. And the other villagers too. Grandma Tilly, of course. Stanley and Frank were like the grandfathers she never knew she needed. Tom was funny. Even Mike and Angie in the pub and their many arguments had grown on her. The villagers of Cranbridge had stolen her heart. And though she knew their lives would carry on as before after she'd left, she just wasn't sure where hers was going to take her without Josh.

* * *

Despite feeling utterly miserable about Amber leaving, Josh was actually pretty positive about the business. The shop seemed to have turned a corner profit-wise, in large part thanks to the frequent coach parties that were now a daily occurrence. The Christmas fair organisation was going well and bringing in even more new suppliers. Even his mum had called to say that she was coming home with a surprise. She had been disappointed about the news that Amber was leaving but perhaps not as upset as he thought she would have been.

They hadn't dwelt on it too much in their phone call. He didn't want to ruin the last few days of her holiday with her best friend. Anyway, she had some kind of exciting plans for the future now apparently. They didn't involve him, she assured him.

And so life would move on. He would have to move on. He just wasn't convinced how he was going to do that.

Keeping busy helped. Along with all the coachloads of customers arriving, there had been a surge in other visitors into the shop. Mainly thanks to Tom placing a large editorial about the importance of local business in his newspaper. Cranbridge Stores had featured heavily with regard to the community spirit they invoked during and after the storm.

Amber had even shed a tear or two when she had read it. 'Seasonal food,' she'd read aloud. 'No big corporations. Local people for local customers. All that and a tractor as well! Oh! This is so great, Tom,' she had said, leaning over to give him a peck on the cheek. 'I must go and show Grandma Tilly.'

Once she had left, Tom had turned to look at Josh, who was frowning at him. 'Relax,' he'd said. 'It's just my magnetic personality with the ladies. Nothing more, I promise.'

Josh knew deep down that he trusted Tom. He trusted Amber. He just didn't like the idea of her kissing anyone who wasn't him.

Sometimes he regretted making that first move. He had kissed her and at the time it had felt like the right thing to do. The only thing that he had ever wanted to do. He ached inside for her, but their time together was about to come to an end. And he had no way of stopping her from leaving.

44

The day of the Christmas fair dawned bright and cold. A hard frost covered the ground and made the trees glisten and sparkle. The predicted snow had stayed away despite the somewhat overcast sky.

As the low winter sun began to sink in the sky, Amber weaved her way through Riverside Lane. Normally so quiet, it was now bustling with people. Trestle tables were covered with piles of goodies to be bought.

The first stall she could see was piled high with beautiful gift boxes of home-made chocolate. The next had decorated advent candles. She could also see festive Christmas wreaths made from holly and spruce, lots of decorated fruit cakes and pretty bottles of home-made gin.

The stallholders were milling around, drinking their hot drinks and taking a peek at what everyone else was selling.

Amber realised that she'd better head back to the shop to help Josh and began to weave her way through the hundreds of people packing out the lane. She had never seen it so busy. It was even more packed than she had imagined and the fair had only just begun. She would have loved to have done a little shopping herself, but she couldn't even get near any of the stalls, such were the customers crowding around each one.

'Hi,' said Molly, appearing in front of her. 'Wow! This is amazing!'

'I know, it's great,' Amber told her. 'It's such a success.'

'You will come for that farewell drink with me and Belle later,' said Molly.

'I promise,' said Amber, reaching out to give her arm a squeeze. 'I've got to get back to the shop. I'll see you tonight.'

Amber gave her a smile, despite her heartbreak at leaving the following day. And there were still so many goodbyes to be said, she reminded herself. One in particular that she was trying not to think about.

As she drew near to Cranbridge Stores, she looked over the bridge to where Mike and Angie had set up a couple of tables outside the pub to serve drinks. Even they appeared to be laughing and getting into the festive spirit with no sign of any arguments yet.

Amber headed up the stairs and into the shop. It too was packed with customers, not only with villagers but people from the surrounding area as well.

Everyone who came in expressed their delight at the pretty layout and home-made goods. There were a few surprised looks at the tractor as well, but everyone was positive.

With the music playing softly in the background, conversations and laughter flowed all around. Life had returned to Cranbridge Stores. Hopefully it wasn't temporary, thought Amber.

Later in the afternoon, Josh appeared by her side. 'I've got to head over to see Mike,' he told her. 'There's a problem with one of the beer pumps, apparently.'

'OK. See you in a while,' she said.

She watched him leave. It seemed as if they were destined to spend their last full day apart. But perhaps that would make it easier for her when she eventually had to say goodbye to Josh.

'This is wonderful,' said a customer, coming up to the counter with a full basket of goods to purchase. 'I hate the shops at this time of year. But this is bliss. I feel I've got Christmas spirit again, as opposed to being ready to kill and with hatred filling my heart.'

'I know how you feel,' said the woman next to her, picking up a large slab of gingerbread cake and placing it in her basket. 'This is such a nicer way to shop.'

Somewhere in the throng, Grandma Tilly was giving out baskets and helping people find what they needed. When there finally came a lull and the shop was empty for a moment, Amber encouraged her to head outside to see the stalls for herself.

'I won't be long,' said Grandma Tilly. 'And I'll keep an eye out for Cathy as well. She landed over three hours ago.'

'She's probably stuck in the crowd out in the lane,' said Amber. 'Keep your mobile on you and I'll call if she arrives here first.'

Once alone, she quickly rushed around the shop tidying up the depleted stacks of produce. Then, when the bell rang once more, she straightened up. It was Brenda, one of the villagers whose home had been flooded.

'Hi,' said Amber. 'How are you?'

'This is wonderful,' said Brenda, smiling. 'Well done for organising it all.'

'Thanks,' Amber told her.

But her good mood disappeared instantly as Kate stalked into the shop. 'Is Josh here?' she snapped, by way of greeting.

Amber shook her head. 'No.' She found herself automatically blushing.

She had seen Kate in the distance a few times around the village but had always managed to avoid speaking to her until now. That all too familiar sick feeling instantly returned to her stomach.

'Pity,' said Kate, picking up a jar of home-made pickles before putting it down again with disdain.

Amber decided to just take a deep breath and try to ignore her. 'How's the clean-up going?' she asked Brenda.

Brenda rolled her eyes. 'It's just taking so long to sort out the insurance. Hopefully then we can order the new carpets.'

'Oh! Were you one of the people that were flooded last month?' asked Kate, getting out her phone and sticking it right in the woman's face. 'Do you mind if I ask you a few questions.'

'Well...' said Brenda, looking uneasy.

~ 'Great,' carried on Kate. 'So you were devastated I should think by the level of destruction in your home?'

'Actually, we were one of the lucky ones,' Brenda told her. 'It was only ankle-deep in our home. Next door had it far worse.'

'And who do you think should take the blame?' asked Kate. 'The council for not providing more flood defences? The farmers for ripping up their hedges?'

'It was just one of those things,' said Brenda, glancing around her as if looking for an escape. 'I really must go.'

'And what are the chances of your property flooding again?' carried on Kate. 'Will you ever be able to get insurance again? And what about if you ever want to sell it?'

Brenda looked upset. 'I hadn't really thought about it.'

'I read that property prices can plummet once you've been flooded,' Kate told her. 'Do you think you're in negative equity now? And have the bank been kind or unhelpful, would you say?'

Brenda cleared her throat. 'Plummet?' she repeated.

'Oh yes, by at least half, they say,' said Kate. 'Had you plans to move? Would you say that your life will never be the same?'

Amber watched as Brenda's eyes filled with tears and was so angry that she finally found her voice.

'That's enough!' said Amber. 'Can't you see you're upsetting her?'

'I'm a journalist,' said Kate, giving her a sneering once-over. 'I have to ask the difficult questions.'

'Not in my shop, you don't,' Amber told her. 'I think you should leave.'

Kate looked surprised. '*Your* shop?' she said.

'I'm standing behind the till, aren't I?' Amber replied, filled with anger. 'So I get to choose who stays and who gets thrown out of here. You do not get to upset anyone in here. And by the way, you can drop the sneering attitude about me working here. Because I've decided that I'm good at designing. That's why I was headhunted for in New York. And, yes, I might only work in this shop, but I like it. In fact, I love it. I love Cranbridge. And I love Josh too!'

There was a sudden silence filled only with Amber's deep breaths as she struggled to keep control.

She flinched as Kate suddenly laughed and opened her mouth to speak. Amber prepared herself for the mocking cruelty that she had been so used to.

But it never came.

Kate gave a start as her arm was suddenly held by Tom, who had appeared nearby.

'I heard everything,' he said, his voice for once cold and hard. 'Including your harassment of these nice ladies. Go back to the office, pack up your things and don't come back. You're sacked.'

Kate snatched her arm away from his hold. 'I've had a job offer anyway,' she told him. 'London. Far away from this grotty little village and your miserable little paper.'

Then she swept out of the door without looking back.

'I didn't mean to cause any trouble,' said Brenda, who had remained silent throughout the whole confrontation.

'You didn't,' Tom said, anxious to reassure her. 'I'm sorry if she upset you.'

'Thank you,' said Brenda, turning to giving Amber a watery smile as well. 'And thanks to you too. There's so much that I can't face at the moment.'

'That's OK,' said Amber. 'Please don't be upset. Enjoy the fair.'

'Thanks. I will.'

After Brenda had left, Amber was finally able to let her smile slip. She sank shakily down onto the stool behind the counter.

Well, she had actually done it. She had faced up to Kate at last. She wouldn't allow herself to be bullied any more. She was a strong, independent woman. Just look at what she and Josh had managed to achieve together. And that was what it was all about, she realised. Being together.

She suddenly stood up and looked at Tom in shock.

'Go,' said Tom softly.

Amber nodded at him and rushed towards the front door, where she nearly ran down Belle who was about to come in.

'I hope you're still on for that drink tonight,' said Belle.

'I need you to keep an eye on the shop!' said Amber, brushing past her.

'Hey! What's going on?' asked Belle.

'I need to see a man about a tractor!' shouted Amber over her shoulder as she hurtled down the steps and out onto the lane.

45

Amber's immediate problem with trying to find Josh was that Riverside Lane was packed with people.

She looked across the crowd but couldn't see him at all.

But she did suddenly see Cathy, looking suntanned and smiling as she walked up to Amber with Grandma Tilly alongside.

'Hello!' she said, sweeping Amber into one of her bear hugs.

Amber was momentarily caught off guard as she let herself be enveloped into her godmother's warm embrace.

'Hello,' she managed to croak back, suddenly finding the emotion of the past couple of weeks catching up with her.

Cathy finally stepped back and held her at arm's-length. 'Hey! Whatever's the matter?'

'Nothing,' said Amber, brushing away a tear as she smiled at her. 'I'm just pleased to see you.'

'Well, if you're pleased to see me, then I can't imagine what your next reaction will be,' said Cathy, pointing over her shoulder.

Amber spun around and was amazed to discover her parents standing directly behind her.

'Mum!' she cried out in shock. 'Dad! What are you doing here?'

'Darling, we've missed you so much,' said her mum, rushing forward to hug her.

Amber stood in shock as they both embraced her.

'But I'm flying out to join you tomorrow,' Amber told them, once she had recovered her voice.

'I know,' said her dad, looking guilty. 'I did tell your mother that we ought to have warned you.'

'We just thought it would be a nice surprise,' said her mum.

'I don't understand,' said Amber, feeling very confused. Surprise was an understatement, she thought.

'Our little adventure didn't quite work out for us,' said her dad.

'Why am I not surprised?' murmured Amber.

Her mum sighed. 'The truth is, darling, that we missed our home too much. It turns out that whilst New Zealand is a lovely, wonderful country, it's just not here. Your father missed his garden. I missed my Cathy. Once she arrived to stay with us, we realised all that we'd given up.'

Amber tried to take it all in. 'So you're moving back to England?'

'That's the surprise,' Cathy told her. 'They're moving to the village to live.'

'Sometimes dreams aren't quite what you imagine, are they?' said her dad.

'No,' said Amber. 'They're really not.'

'Isn't it marvellous?' said Cathy. 'We haven't told Josh yet. Do you know where he is? I'd love to see him.'

Amber stared back at Cathy. Perhaps there might just be a different way for her now. As her dad had said, dreams weren't always the way you imagine.

'Wait right there!' she told them all, before stepping forward to give both her parents, Grandma Tilly and Cathy a kiss on the cheek. 'I'll go and find him!'

She had faced down her bully. Now she needed to be brave once more.

She knew what needed to be said. She just hoped Josh wanted to hear it.

* * *

Josh checked his phone again. It was very strange that he had yet to hear from his mum when she had landed a few hours ago. He hoped she hadn't had an accident on the way home.

He was just about to dial her number when he saw Amber rushing towards him across the pedestrian bridge. She looked very worried and serious, which made him even more concerned.

He told Mike that he would be back in a while and left the pub to meet Amber on the bridge.

She had a strange look on her face as they drew near to each other and he became even more worried.

'Have you heard from Mum?' he asked.

Amber nodded. 'She's just arrived,' she told him. 'She's fine.'

Josh relaxed again. 'Good. I was starting to worry.'

'I need to talk to you,' said Amber, glancing around them.

Josh too looked around and found that both sides of the river were absolutely packed with crowds of people.

'Come with me back to the shop,' said Amber, abruptly turning around.

But she seemed to slip on the frozen paving stone of the bridge as she spun around. Josh automatically grabbed her arm to steady her, but it was too late.

As if in slow motion, they both fell into the river – again.

46

The shock of falling into the river almost made Amber lose her train of thought as she sat in the freezing cold water.

'That's so cold!' she cried out.

'I don't believe this!' said Josh, sitting next to her as the water spilled around them. 'We're in the river again!'

Amber began to laugh at the ridiculousness of them ending up in the river once more. And this time they had an audience, as the crowds on both sides of the bridge were now watching them.

Josh swore and stood up, the water rushing from his clothes and body. He turned and held out a hand to help her up as well. And that was what he did, she realised. He helped her out whenever she needed it. And there was no way she was going to let him go.

Her heart was thumping. Humiliation was no doubt just round the corner waiting for her if he turned her down, but she didn't care any more. She loved him too much to worry about pride. Besides, they'd just fallen into the river. What could be more humiliating than that?

She let him pull her up and then looked at him.

Josh turned to begin to lead her out of the water, but she stood still.

'What's the matter?' he asked, turning back to her when she didn't move. 'Are you hurt?'

She shook her head, staring up into his handsome face. 'No.'

She took a deep breath to speak before she looked around. Everyone on the riverbanks was still watching on. So she had to do this with an audience? So be it, she thought.

So she took a step forward, grabbed him by the collar and leaned in to kiss him. This wasn't a gentle, brief kiss on the lips. This was pure passion and love, everything she felt for him.

With a start, he drew his head back from hers.

'What are you doing?' he whispered, glancing over her shoulder at the crowd behind her on the lane.

She too looked up and saw that whilst everyone was looking somewhat amazed, a few were also nodding their approval.

'I'm kissing you,' she told him. 'Because I wanted to and because I love you.'

'You do?' Josh looked utterly amazed.

'Yes,' she said, sounding more confident than she felt.

She then held her breath, hoping beyond everything that she hadn't got this completely wrong.

'I, er...' He blew out a long sigh as he glanced over her shoulder at the waiting crowd. 'Look, can we talk about this somewhere else?'

She shook her head. 'Absolutely not. I want to say this right here, right now. I love you. I love him!' she added, shouting as loudly as she could.

There were a few giggles and mutterings from the onlookers at her announcement.

'I said I love him!' she shouted out again, finding that she was smiling broadly now.

'We heard you!' called out Tom from the riverbank. 'We're just waiting for his reply.'

She turned to look at Josh, smiling at his confusion and, yes, embarrassment. 'Well?' she asked softly. 'Do you have a reply for me?'

'What's happened to you?' asked Josh, dragging a hand through his hair. 'You're not ever like this. Have you been at Mike's punch again?'

She shook her head. 'Nope. It's still me. You just helped me change, that's all. You've made me stronger, proud of my work. And I'm able to believe in myself, finally. I've made friends, good friends here in this village.' She reached out to stroke his cheek. 'But that's nothing if you're not here. Because I don't want to leave Cranbridge.'

'We don't want you to leave either!' she heard Molly call out from the bridge behind them.

Amber turned to give her a knowing wink before she looked back at Josh. 'So, if you'd like me to stay here and run the shop with you, then that would be great. Better than great. Perfect, in fact.' She paused. 'If you love me, that is.'

She held her breath again.

People shuffled from foot to foot in the cold as everyone waited for Josh's reply.

He looked at everyone staring at them before gazing down at her.

'Of course I love you,' he murmured.

'Speak up, lad!' cried out Stanley. 'Some of us can't hear so well.'

'I love her, OK?' shouted Josh, rolling his eyes before he looked at her once more. 'Despite the fact that you keep trying to drown me in the river. And that you've turned my life upside down. And the tractor is now in the shop.' He took a step forward and brought her close to him, wrapping his arms around her. 'I love you,' he told her once more.

The crowd erupted into loud cheering upon hearing this.

And then Josh kissed her with so much passion that the final tiny bit of doubt Amber had held on to was gone forever.

Once they finally drew apart, Amber was aware of the continued whooping and cheering from all around them. Suddenly embarrassed at what she had done, she tried to hide in his coat.

'Oh no!' he told her, taking her chin out of his chest and holding her at arm's-length. 'This is all on you. You can't hide now.'

She giggled, blushing furiously. But for once she didn't mind. After all, she had Josh by her side, the man she loved and who loved her in return. Nothing else mattered.

Josh held her around the waist and as they waded back across to the riverbank, Amber glanced up to see Cathy, Grandma Tilly and her parents nearby. They were all clapping and nodding their approval.

'Wait a minute!' said Josh, as he helped her out of the river. 'Is that your parents next to my mum?'

'Yes,' Amber told him. 'That was their big surprise.'

'Life's full of them at the moment,' said Josh, taking her hand in his as they walked towards their families.

Amber's mum and Cathy were looking a little teary as they stepped forward to embrace them although at arm's-length in deference to their wet clothes.

'How wonderful,' said Cathy, reaching out to squeeze Josh's arm. 'I knew this would all work out.'

'What are you talking about?' said Josh, leaning down so that Grandma Tilly could kiss him on the cheek.

'Our little plan, of course,' said Amber's mum.

'To get you two together,' added Cathy.

Amber looked at Josh in amazement before they turned back to their parents. 'Are you saying this was a set-up?' she asked.

'Well, we hoped things might work out between the two of you, of course,' said Cathy, smiling. 'But this is even better than we had imagined. Do you mind?'

Amber looked at Josh once more as he burst out laughing.

'Not particularly, Mum,' he said. Then he reached out to take Amber's hand in his. 'But please leave me in control of my love life from now on.'

'So, is anyone going to show me around my shop?' asked Cathy.

Josh raised his eyebrows.

Cathy laughed. 'OK. *Your* shop.'

'I'll let Grandma Tilly do that,' said Josh, glancing down at his wet clothes. 'We need to get changed.'

'Isn't it marvellous what they've achieved?' said Amber's mum, looking around at the crowds milling around in Riverside Lane.

'It feels like a village again,' said Grandma Tilly.

As Josh led Amber away, he told her, 'They're right. It feels like home again. And it's all down to you.'

She squeezed his hand as they walked up the steps and into the shop. 'I seem to remember that you were right beside me the whole time, so you can take some of the blame as well.'

He stopped to draw her into his arms. 'Mostly I was unpacking boxes,' he said, smiling down at her.

'Or sitting in the middle of the river,' she said as his head dropped down to hers.

'That too,' he murmured, as their lips met.

And as they kissed once more, outside on Riverside Lane, the snow finally began to fall.

47

It was the last weekend before Christmas and the shop was all ready for the last-minute rush.

'It looks great,' Josh told Amber as he looked around.

She followed his gaze and had to agree with him. All the shelves were packed with daily necessities, as well as a wide range of home-made goods ready for the festive celebrations. Boxes of chocolates and Christmas cakes jostled for space alongside wrapping paper and Christmas cards. A row of ruby red poinsettias were lined up on the bonnet of the tractor. Below, in the various crates, potatoes, Brussel sprouts, carrots and parsnips were piled high waiting to be peeled for Christmas dinner.

The Christmas music played on the radio and the fairy lights twinkled on the oak beams that crossed the ceiling.

'Do you think we've forgotten anything?' she asked.

Josh shook his head. 'You're joking,' he told her. 'There's no room for anything else in here.'

Thankfully the shop was no longer the chaotic mess it had been when she had first arrived. Everything was organised and in place despite the shelves bursting with goods.

'Yep. I think we've covered every shopping requirement,' she said, smiling.

'Absolutely,' he said, laughing. 'Cranbridge Stores. Everything you never knew that you needed!'

'Oh! I like that!' she told him, her eyes gleaming. 'We should put that on a sign outside!'

'I was joking,' he said, stepping forward to draw her into his arms.

'I'm not,' she said, looking up at him. For a second, she couldn't breathe, such was the love she felt for him. He continued to have that effect on her, each and every day.

A smile played on his lips as he leaned forward, a gleam in his eyes that was full of intention.

The bell rang out over the front door and he reluctantly let go of her. Josh rolled his eyes before walking away.

'Good morning,' said Tom, heading through the shop.

'Good morning,' said Amber, smiling. 'Coffee?'

'Yes, please,' he told her, reaching out to a nearby basket full of decorated cookies. 'I am also going to buy this snowman biscuit, but on the absolute assurance of secrecy. Otherwise it'll ruin my reputation as a hard businessman.'

'Of course,' Amber told him, handing over his full flask of coffee.

'I'll have that robin cookie as well,' he told her, slipping both into his pocket. 'For Molly, that is.'

'I understand,' said Amber, grinning.

'Shut up,' muttered Tom. 'I don't know why I ever liked you.'

He gave her a wink as he paid for his purchases before heading out of the shop.

Amber enjoyed the banter and conversation that she had with the customers. Working in the shop had given her a sense of belonging she hadn't had before. Now that she had a daily connection with other people, she never felt lonely any more.

It was incredible how the small daily interactions made all the difference to her self-confidence as well. Small acts of kindness went a long way too. She felt happier, more connected and ultimately healthier for it too.

Of course, the love of a good man helped as well. Josh told her how much he loved her each and every day. The thought of spending the rest of her life with him brought her a sense of peace and happiness she never knew possible. She couldn't imagine being anywhere else but Cranbridge.

As she headed over to the window, she glanced at the fireplace, where, with one last design flourish, she had placed a couple of framed photographs. There was one of the shop as it had looked in the 1900s, as well as Todd next to the tractor and playing his guitar on the veranda. She felt sure that Josh's dad would have approved of the changes that they had made to the shop. Certainly, Grandma Tilly and Cathy had voiced their admiration for all that they had achieved.

Todd would definitely have adored the fact that the tractor was now a much-loved feature of the shop. In fact, as word of the new and improved Cranbridge Stores had gone beyond the village, many new visitors were asking to have their photographs taken next to it. Josh was even talking of incorporating a tractor into a new sign outside the shop.

Amber glanced out of the huge bay window. It was a beautiful frosty morning on Riverside Lane. The snow had melted, but the cold temperatures had remained. The ground outside was glistening white and the blue sky reflected in the steady flow of the river, shallow once more.

More importantly, the lanes and avenues of Cranbridge had begun to come back to life and people were out and about. Everyone was starting to connect once more. They used the benches outside the shop to sit and chat. Neighbours would wave and chat with each other. Mums would come in for a coffee and a gossip. It was becoming a community again.

The Christmas fair had been a huge success and had brought more customers than ever before into the shop. Yes, things were still tight, but they were scraping by. After all, they had a reason to keep fighting to keep it open. Because Cranbridge Stores meant something to the village and to the family as well.

It wasn't a big glamorous department store in London or New York but in a way, Amber was glad. Cranbridge Stores was so much more special and here she was appreciated and valued.

Of course, her plans for the shop weren't finished yet. Her trusty drawing pad was always under the counter and full of brand-new designs that she found herself sketching out throughout the day. She was bursting with so many ideas for the coming months and years and couldn't wait to see them come to fruition.

Josh too had fresh ideas for keeping the business more sustainable. They were trying to avoid all plastic packaging where they could and were pleased that the milk that they were now buying from local farms was being delivered in glass bottles. They still had some way to go but he was very pleased with the feedback they were receiving from all their customers.

Even the Christmas trees that they were selling at the front of the store were potted with roots, ready for replanting. Christmas had almost arrived and Amber couldn't wait to celebrate it with Josh and their families. Cathy and her parents had rented a house in the village temporarily until they decided on their next big adventure. Josh and Amber had invited Cathy to stay in the flat with them but Cathy was keen to give them both their own space. In addition, Cathy seemed keen to start her next journey in life and Amber's parents were more than happy to help, having missed their friend so much in recent times. So it seemed to be the perfect solution for them all.

As she straightened up the boxes of shortbread on the windowsill, Amber heard Josh murmur behind her, 'Finally, we're alone.'

She felt his lips on her neck and leaned back, thinking of nothing else but the joy of being in his arms.

But almost instantly the shop bell rang as someone came through the front door and they sprang apart.

Amber turned to smile at the woman who had just come in. 'Good morning,' she said.

'Good morning,' replied the customer, who turned away to browse the shelves.

Amber spun around and found Josh still standing next to her.

'One of these days, I'm going to take that bell and throw it in the river,' he told her, under his breath so that only she could hear his words.

'You wouldn't dare,' she whispered, laughing softly.

Then he bent his head quickly once more. A kiss so light and swift brushed her lips before he walked away.

Amber smiled to herself. She was confident in her feelings as well as her own skills these days. And she was happy. Beyond happy. She had a man who she loved and who she looked forward to building a future with in Cranbridge. Storms would always come and go, but together she and Josh could face anything whilst waiting for the sun to come out again. And it always did.

ACKNOWLEDGMENTS

A huge thank you to my lovely editor Caroline Ridding for taking me under her wing once more and for being so generous and encouraging. As always, it's been an absolute pleasure working with you.

Thank you to everyone at Boldwood Books for making me feel so welcome and for all their hard work on this book, especially Jade Craddock for her wonderful work yet again on the copy edits and Nia Beynon for being a marketing superstar.

Thank you to all the readers and bloggers for their enthusiasm and reviews which keep me going on the days when the coffee fails to hit the spot.

Thank you to all my friends, especially to Jo Botelle and the lovely DWLC ladies, Kerry, Claire, Adrienne and Kendra, for their endless support and encouragement.

Huge thanks to my wonderful family for all their continued support, especially Gill, Simon, Louise, Ross, Lee, Cara and Sian.

Finally, thanks once more to my husband Dave for listening and helping with my imaginary world problems. As always, I could never have written this book without your love and support.

MORE FROM ALISON SHERLOCK

We hope you enjoyed reading *The Village Shop for Lonely Hearts*. If you did, please leave a review.

If you'd like to gift a copy, this book is also available as an ebook, digital audio download and audiobook CD.

Sign up to Alison Sherlock's mailing list for news, competitions and updates on future books.

https://bit.ly/AlisonSherlockNewsletter

ABOUT THE AUTHOR

Alison Sherlock is the author of the bestselling *Willow Tree Hall* books. Alison enjoyed reading and writing stories from an early age and gave up office life to follow her dream.

Follow Alison on social media:

f facebook.com/alison.sherlock.73
🐦 twitter.com/AlisonSherlock
BB bookbub.com/authors/alison-sherlock

ABOUT BOLDWOOD BOOKS

Boldwood Books is a fiction publishing company seeking out the best stories from around the world.

Find out more at www.boldwoodbooks.com

Sign up to the Book and Tonic newsletter for news, offers and competitions from Boldwood Books!

http://www.bit.ly/bookandtonic

We'd love to hear from you, follow us on social media:

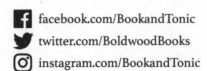

facebook.com/BookandTonic
twitter.com/BoldwoodBooks
instagram.com/BookandTonic

Lightning Source UK Ltd.
Milton Keynes UK
UKHW042027080223
416606UK00002B/114